DEMOCRACY, THEATRE AND PERFORMANCE

Democracy, argues David Wiles, is actually a form of theatre. In making his case, the author deftly investigates orators at the foundational moments of ancient and modern democracy, demonstrating how their performative skills were used to try to create a better world. People often complain about demagogues, or wish that politicians might be more sincere. But to do good, politicians (paradoxically) must be hypocrites – or actors. Moving from Athens to Indian independence via three great revolutions – in puritan England, republican France and liberal America – the book opens up larger questions about the nature of democracy. When in the classical past Plato condemned rhetoric, the only alternative he could offer was authoritarianism. Wiles' bold historical study has profound implications for our present: calls for personal authenticity, he suggests, are not an effective way to counter the rise of populism.

DAVID WILES is Emeritus Professor of Drama at the University of Exeter. He has written and edited many books, including *Greek Theatre Performance* (2000), *Theatre and Citizenship* (2011), *The Players' Advice to Hamlet* (2020) and *The Cambridge Companion to Theatre History* (2013), all published by Cambridge University Press.

DEMOCRACY, THEATRE AND PERFORMANCE

From the Greeks to Gandhi

DAVID WILES
University of Exeter

CAMBRIDGE
UNIVERSITY PRESS

Shaftesbury Road, Cambridge CB2 8EA, United Kingdom

One Liberty Plaza, 20th Floor, New York, NY 10006, USA

477 Williamstown Road, Port Melbourne, VIC 3207, Australia

314–321, 3rd Floor, Plot 3, Splendor Forum, Jasola District Centre, New Delhi – 110025, India

103 Penang Road, #05-06/07, Visioncrest Commercial, Singapore 238467

Cambridge University Press is part of Cambridge University Press & Assessment, a department of the University of Cambridge.

We share the University's mission to contribute to society through the pursuit of education, learning and research at the highest international levels of excellence.

www.cambridge.org
Information on this title: www.cambridge.org/9781009167994

DOI: 10.1017/9781009167970

© David Wiles 2024

This publication is in copyright. Subject to statutory exception and to the provisions of relevant collective licensing agreements, no reproduction of any part may take place without the written permission of Cambridge University Press & Assessment.

First published 2024

Printed in the United Kingdom by CPI Group Ltd, Croydon CR0 4YY

A catalogue record for this publication is available from the British Library

Library of Congress Cataloging-in-Publication Data
Names: Wiles, David, author.
TITLE: Democracy, theatre and performance : from the Greeks to Gandhi / David Wiles.
DESCRIPTION: Cambridge, United Kingdom : Cambridge University Press, 2024. | Includes bibliographical references and index.
IDENTIFIERS: LCCN 2023042151 (print) | LCCN 2023042152 (ebook) | ISBN 9781009167994 (hardback) | ISBN 9781009167987 (paperback) | ISBN 9781009167970 (epub)
SUBJECTS: LCSH: Democracy. | Democracy–History. | Theater–Political aspects. | Rhetoric–Political aspects. | Oratory–Political aspects.
CLASSIFICATION: LCC JC423 .W4756 2024 (print) | LCC JC423 (ebook) | DDC 321.8/09–dc23/eng/20231208
LC record available at https://lccn.loc.gov/2023042151
LC ebook record available at https://lccn.loc.gov/2023042152

ISBN 978-1-009-16799-4 Hardback

Cambridge University Press & Assessment has no responsibility for the persistence or accuracy of URLs for external or third-party internet websites referred to in this publication and does not guarantee that any content on such websites is, or will remain, accurate or appropriate.

Contents

List of Figures	*page* vi
Acknowledgements	vii
Introduction: Democracy as Performance	1
1 Rhetoric in Athens	19
2 Acting versus Sincerity: Aeschines versus Demosthenes	39
3 Puritan Democracy: The English Revolution	63
4 Oratory in the French Revolution	90
5 American Democracy: From the Founders to Feminism	117
6 Democracy as a Universal Good: Gandhi, Tagore and the New India	145
7 Theatre and Theatrocracy in Democratic Athens	169
Notes	184
References	207
Index	236

Figures

0.1 Unmasking the hypocrite. In Molière's *Tartuffe* (1664/1669), Orgon discovers that Tartuffe has been trying to seduce his wife. *page* 15
2.1 Aeschines (a) and Demosthenes (b): Roman copies of Greek bronze originals. 40
3.1 A meeting of the General Council of the Army, with Thomas Fairfax presiding. 80
4.1 The Fountain of Regeneration: Hérault de Séchelles receives water from the statue of Nature. 99
4.2 A meeting of the National Assembly in 1793, with an artistic representation of the way all eyes are focused on the speaker. 104
4.3 Parodic representation of a meeting of the Jacobin Club in 1792. 110
5.1 Outside the Astor Place Opera House, the National Guard fire at the crowd. 127
5.2 Edwin Forrest as Macbeth. 130
5.3 Frederick Douglass speaking from a London stage: "The man who wields the blood-clotted cow's-hide during the week fills the pulpit on Sunday." 134
6.1 Muhammad Ali Jinnah and Mohandas Gandhi photographed in 1944. 161

Acknowledgements

I realised in 2019 that because of the times this was the book I had to write, the question I had to solve. There are often institutional pressures not to straddle disciplines. When I chose to stray beyond the formal boundaries of my parent discipline, Theatre Studies, and the normal territory of its promiscuous offspring 'Performance Studies', in order to enter into dialogue with Political Science, I knew that I would have few fellow travellers on my journey. Writing proved an unusually lonely process because of Covid lockdown, and I discovered just how much library work can be done remotely. I build, nevertheless, on a multitude of conversations, academic and non-academic. I'm especially grateful to Jim Davis for helping me convene an occasional reading group, where participants offered me valuable pointers and objections. In this context I thank Michael Bachmann, Tracy Davis, James Harriman-Smith, Fiona Macintosh, Elaine McGirr, Willmar Sauter, Pat Smyth and Anne Varty. I received further helpful feedback when I spoke at Wolfson College Oxford, at the International Federation for Theatre Research (IFTR) in Shanghai and Reykjavík, and as a visiting professor at the University of Malta. I'm grateful to Edward Davenport, Stephe Harrop, Emma Van Imwegen and Ellen Wiles for their scrutiny of short sections, which helped me pitch my prose. During Covid I engaged in practice-based research via local environmental activism, which reinforced my understanding that, left to its own devices, the conviction of being right proves deeply unpersuasive.

All translations are my own unless otherwise noted.

Introduction
Democracy as Performance

In place of aristocracy there arose a vile theatrocracy.[1]

(Plato)

What happens once democracy has been used up? When it has been hollowed out and emptied of meaning? ... What we need today, for the sake of the survival of this planet, is long-term vision ... Could it be that democracy, the sacred answer to our short-term hopes and prayers, the protector of our individual freedoms and nurturer of our avaricious dreams, will turn out to be the endgame for the human race? Could it be that democracy is such a hit with modern humans precisely because it mirrors our greatest folly – our nearsightedness?[2]

(Arundhati Roy)

Democracy tends to favour short-term decisions and put local before global interests. Perhaps, therefore, it is not the best way for our species to organise a world that is sliding rapidly from the Holocene into the Anthropocene. And maybe in retrospect democracy will one day be dismissed as a human folly. In this book I shall counter the characteristic human problem of 'nearsightedness' by taking the long view of the historian. When Roy suggests that democracy has been 'used up' or 'hollowed out', are we hearing a time-honoured complaint because people have always dreamt of a golden age when democratic politics once supposedly worked? Or has the democratic project lost conviction more recently because of the form democracy takes in the age of corporate capitalism? When today's politicians pander to the 'avaricious dreams' of the supposedly free individual, it is easy to blame them for their personal weakness and failure to tell us the truth about a degraded planet. Perhaps, however, democracy has always required politicians to be actors, speaking the lines the audience wants to hear as their only means to stay in power. If so, is democracy inherently a form of theatre? And was Plato right to relabel democracy as 'theatrocracy'?

I take up in this book the problem of political honesty. When the pre-democratic Greek reformer Solon went to watch a performance by the first tragedian, Thespis, he complained that he witnessed a form of lying. When Thespis responded that tragedy was merely a kind of 'play', Solon lamented that this theatrical *pseudologia* or 'false speech' would soon spread to things that mattered, that is, become the norm in politics.[3] Unlike Solon, Athenian theatre audiences evidently valued *pseudologia* as a means of telling truth about the world. The problem is, there are different kinds of truth. Boris Johnson, when campaigning to become British prime minister in 2019, famously waved in the air a kipper sealed in ice and plastic, proclaiming that this wrapping was an imposition by the European Union. On one level this was a flat lie, and the relevant regulations were British. On another level, the ploy won emotional recognition from many who felt that they had lost control of their lives, and that their political selves had lost touch with their own biological selves subject to touch, taste and smell. Johnson's political instincts led him to an image traditionally associated with the King of Carnival, whose enemy was the Lenten herring.[4] In the *Washington Post* the distinguished political commentator Ann Applebaum pronounced that a doomed Conservative party was allowing Johnson to entertain them while their ship was sinking, but in the event Johnson won a triumphant victory in the next election.[5] If Johnson's stunt was an insult to the intelligence, then there were many British electors happy to see the intelligentsia being insulted, possessing enough emotional intelligence to distinguish categories of truth.[6]

In this book I shall look at democracy through the eyes of a theatre historian, seeking to develop the conversation between Solon and Thespis. I will argue that democracy always was and always will be an art of performance. Ever since Aristotle first formulated his theory of catharsis or 'purgation',[7] it has been understood that theatre works not on the intellect but on the emotions. That is why theatrical scholarship has something unique to offer political science.

In the case of Johnson's kipper there was a clash between factual truth and theatrical or emotional truth. Political persuasion always operates on the level of feeling rather than disembodied reason because reason can never resolve the question of values, of what constitutes the well-lived life. As the philosopher David Hume put it, a factual 'is' can never translate into a moral 'ought'.[8] Jonathan Haidt sums up the findings of modern cognitive and social science when he describes 'reasons' as 'the tail wagged by the intuitive dog',[9] and in another helpful metaphor he suggests that the 'mind is divided into parts, like a rider (controlled processes) upon an elephant (automatic processes).' Since the rider, in this case, evolved to serve the elephant, it follows that 'if you want to change someone's mind about a moral or political issue, *talk to the elephant first*.'[10] Analytic intelligence is a mixed blessing when most choices are made on the basis of unconscious emotions, rationalised only in retrospect. As the neuroscientist Tali Sharot explains, 'The greater your cognitive capacity, the greater your ability to rationalise and interpret information at will, and creatively twist data to fit your opinions.'[11] The cognitive scientist George Lakoff claims that most of 'what we understand in public discourse is not in the words themselves, but in the unconscious understanding that we bring to the words', putting a figure of 98% onto the contribution of the 'cognitive unconscious', and he regrets that today politicians on the left generally have a poorer grasp of this principle than politicians on the right.[12] While science has, paradoxically, embraced human irrationality, popular sentiment clings to the idea that we make rational choices on the basis of individual free will.

This book was written in the shadow of Brexit (Britain's vote to leave the European Union), and the presidency of Donald Trump which culminated in an attack on the US Capitol. The UK referendum was a shock to me because I live in Oxford where there was no 'leave' poster to be seen on the streets. I move in social circles where there was no debate, and the vote left me feeling that part of my identity had been stripped away since I could no longer call myself a 'European'. The immediate narratives around me were vehement: this vote was the product of 'populism', not 'democracy', because it was founded upon lies. And as the narrative built up it often took the form of: 'How could these (uneducated) people be so stupid?', 'How could they vote against their own economic self-interest?' In other social settings, a different story was told: here at last the 'people' had succeeded in asserting their will over the elite. In the USA a similar question was being posed: 'How could so many people vote for an incompetent, narcissistic liar?' And the counter-narrative went unheard: 'Here at last was a man who voiced my anger'. The failure of democracy lay not in these competing narratives, but in the lack of any arena for mutual listening.

From my perspective as a theatre scholar, it was clear that there had been a failure on the level of performance. Johnson and Trump are accomplished performers with the skill of making the spectator in the back row feel that they are being personally and intimately addressed. Rational argument was powerless against men who knew how to play on the emotions of their audience, and the rationalists achieved nothing by unmasking the lies of people who made no pretence to be truthful. Conversely Johnson and Trump succeeded in unmasking the essential hypocrisy of the rationalists, who pretended they were not themselves driven by a complex of emotions, with outrage at human suffering tangled up with personal benefits derived from globalisation. In these political battles, two levels of *pseudologia* were at play.

Critiques of populism run into the problem that democracy means by definition rule by the people or populace, and one person's populism is another person's authentic democracy, so I prefer to see Johnson and Trump not as sources of the trouble but as symptoms. For chapter and verse on the 'crisis of democracy', we might turn to a report published in 2020 by the Centre for the Future of Democracy in Cambridge which concluded: 'Across the globe, democracy is in a state of malaise. In the mid-1990s, a majority of citizens ... were satisfied with the performance of their democracies' – but not so any longer'.[13] Dissatisfaction was particularly marked in the UK and USA, with higher satisfaction reported in regimes condemned by liberals as 'populist', particularly among the young. Meanwhile, a survey of 2350 British adults aged 18–34 in 2022 found that 61% agreed with the proposition that 'having a strong leader who does not have to bother with parliament and elections would be a good way of governing this country'.[14]

The existence of this democratic malaise seems obvious enough without such surveys, and explanations are not hard to find: democratically elected representatives powerless to resist corporate lobbying or halt the rising inequality of wealth; social media killing investigative journalism, while dividing society into tribes with no common language; the internet deluging us with facts but little fact-based argument; China's demonstration that democracy is not the only way to deliver material prosperity. The term 'democracy' has ceased to resonate with people who have no living memory of fascism, Stalinism or imperial rule, though it has a much more positive ring for the educated young in places like Hong Kong, Iran and Saudi Arabia.

The first problem is to know what the word means. "Democracy!" has always been a convenient rallying cry to shout at your opponent, whoever they may be. When Winston Churchill observed in 1947 that 'democracy is the worst form of Government except for all those other forms that have been tried from time to time', he spoke as an orator using a familiar ploy to claim that he himself embodied the democratic voice of the people while the ruling Labour Party was a 'dictatorship'.[15] 'Democracy' has been an unstable term since its first emergence in Athens because the word *demos* refers ambiguously both to the *common* people – those who distinguish themselves from the few, the rich, the noble – and to the *entire* people, and populists have been adept at conflating these two definitions, bracketing themselves with the 'people' against an elite or supposed elite.[16] In a sense, the vitality of democracy lies in the battle to define yourself as a democrat, and today there seems less interest in that battle.

In a recent essay entitled 'Why feelings trump facts' inspired by his participation in a parliamentary enquiry into 'citizenship and civic engagement', the political scientist Matthew Flinders observes that 'citizenship' means little to younger British people who have a new focus on 'belonging'. Quoting multiple international surveys that identify a growing gap between governors and governed, he laments the methodological failure of the social and political sciences to address the problem of 'feelings'.[17] Flinders points us towards a wider social transformation, where, within the context of what has come to be called 'identity politics', a new sense of self yields a changed attitude to democratic debate.

In her 2022 BBC Reith lecture, the Nigerian novelist Chimamanda Ngozi Adichie argued for the importance of disagreement and commented on the moment when she first came as a student to the USA more than two decades earlier: 'I quickly realised that in public conversations about America's difficult problems – like income inequality and race – the goal was not truth, the goal was to keep everyone comfortable. And so, people pretended not to see what they saw, things were left unsaid, questions unasked and ignorance festered. This unwillingness to accept the discomfort that honesty can bring is in its own way a suppression of speech.'[18] The word 'honesty' can all too easily be used as a cover for conscious or unconscious hate speech, and in this book I shall scrutinise these troublesome categories of 'honesty' and 'sincerity'. Adichie points us towards a marked swing of the pendulum in determining how freedom of speech must be balanced against the wish not to hurt others.

An extreme case arose as I worked on this book when Kathleen Stock, a Professor of Philosophy at the University of Sussex, awarded an OBE for services to education, was driven from her post by charges of hatred for transsexuals. Her brand of feminism which only a few years earlier looked radical and progressive was viewed by many in 2021 as reactionary. My concern is not with the rights and wrongs of the charge against Stock, but with a cultural context where democratic debate became impossible. In Stock's angry words, the students and more importantly colleagues who condemned her en masse had learned to 'mark disagreement as an instant sign of bad and corrupt character. "Of course someone like HER shouldn't have a platform", they say. "She is a bad person". Case closed. It's a remarkably handy and self-serving worldview...'[19] Adichie expressed herself no less bluntly: 'There is something honest about an authoritarianism that recognises itself to be what it is. Such a system is easier to challenge because the battle lines are clear. But this new social censure demands consensus while being wilfully blind to its own tyranny.'[20] These are controversial positions, but they point to a problem of the moment. Democracy is a culture of disagreement, allowing differences to be resolved through words rather than violence, and when words are understood as a form of violence and moral categories are not open to challenge, then democratic debate is constrained, for better or worse.[21] Democracy is manifestly under challenge from the far right, while on the left it has slipped down in the order of priorities, and perhaps the concept has just become too difficult.

The disengagement of the young from citizenship and democracy has complex causes, but a new sense of 'who I am' and 'my right to be who I want to be' looms large, along with a new sense of my ethical obligation to others. Scepticism about democracy is not linked to any diminished passion for social justice, rather the opposite, and the problem is that democracy seems an ever less plausible route to achieve social justice. Universities have done little to create a culture of democratic debate, with the transformation of collegiate structures into managerial structures, consumer satisfaction the mark of good teaching, and grant income the measure of professional success. It is not my intention in this book to wade any further into the muddy waters of contemporary public argument, but rather to step back from the contentions of the present in order to establish a context for these arguments. It is all too easy to imagine that a golden age of democracy has vanished, but historical scrutiny reveals that at any given moment in the past democracy was riddled with contradictions and cruelties. It has always been a quest rather than a state of being, and I continue to value the quest for 'true' democracy. As Sophia Rosenfeld argues, 'truth, like democracy, isn't something that simply exists in the world. It is, rather, something that we must always consciously and collectively forge.'[22] If this is to be achieved, a shared understanding of what has gone before is indispensable.

Theatre-makers understand that their job turns upon moving the emotions of others, not upon being themselves. Novelists have the same need, and when Adichie argues for 'honesty', she writes not as a philosopher but as a writer and teacher of writing concerned with censorship of the imagination, an inevitable consequence if her private self is going to be identified with the characters she imagines. Politicians are trapped in the same bind, playing roles that they think will secure instinctive identification or approval, constantly attacked when a gap appears between the role and its creator. Through his historical work on the 'fall of public man', Richard Sennett has done much to inform my perspective on Western democracy. Sennett drew on the metaphor and institutional realities of eighteenth-century theatre in order to argue that before the age of Romanticism someone (normally male, to be sure) could enter the public sphere without feeling that a vulnerable private self was invested in every civic action.[23] In a useful essay on 'performance and democracy', the British theatre scholar Nicholas Ridout takes his cue from Sennett when describing his own experience of trotting out 'ready-mades' in political conversation, prompting him to conclude that becoming 'other than oneself ... is a precondition of democratic politics'.[24] The problem of role-playing is a perennial one. Theatrical communication is both complex and reciprocal, which is why, given the disciplinary lacuna which Flinders identifies in the realm of feeling, political science has much to glean from theatrical scholarship. Feelings have a history, and the search in modern political life for revelations of an authentic 'I am' is historically produced.[25]

Hannah Arendt's experience as a stateless Jewish refugee helped her see a gap between democracy as defined by the Athenians and the later ideal of democracy as an electoral system intertwined with a sense of universal human rights: 'We are not born equal', Arendt argued, in defiance of the preamble to the US Declaration of Independence, 'we become equal as members of a group on the strength of our decision to guarantee ourselves mutually equal rights.'[26] Though Francis Fukuyama proclaimed notoriously after the collapse of the Soviet Union that Western liberal democracy had become a universal ideal which marked 'the end of history', from Arendt's perspective 'liberal democracy' is a flat contradiction since of its nature the democratic state creates inequity through exclusion.[27] Her Jewish background alerted her to the role of Protestant Christianity in defining freedom as a function of the individual will rather than public life, and she turned to Athens for an alternative model. The democratic Greek *polis*, claimed Arendt, 'provided men with a space of appearances where they could act, with a kind of theater where freedom could appear.'[28] Democracy and theatre emerged in Greece at the same historical moment, in a symbiosis that broke down when democracy became a matter of individual rights.

Arendt blamed the atrocities of the French Revolution on a romantic quest for personal authenticity, and argued that politicians who follow their convictions and aspire to truth and sincerity are doomed to fail because the dark 'life of the heart' is always distorted and transformed by the 'light of the world'.[29] If feelings are transformed through the process of their public representation, then liberal politicians seeking to persuade the public of their sincerity and personal authenticity are forced to choose between self-deception and hypocrisy. Nowadays only 'deception', Arendt argues, 'is likely to create a semblance of truthfulness',[30] whereas in antiquity, where truth was a philosophical not a political virtue, what mattered was the character of the speaker as defined by his actions.[31] Arendt drew inspiration from Aristotle's argument that in the theatre what counts is not character but 'action', and applied this principle to democratic politics.[32] From her perspective, the modern problem of democracy is one of performance. Over the centuries Christianity, which draws much of its thinking from Plato and from Judaism, has created a cultural mistrust of appearances, denouncing the inherent immorality of actors and of theatre. Recognising this cultural legacy, Arendt insisted that no amount of *honesty* will of itself stir a crowd of individuals into collective action because emotions respond to *appearances* rather than realities.

Chantal Mouffe is a Belgian political philosopher who owes much to Arendt when she pulls apart two strands shaping modern political life. 'On one side we have the liberal tradition constituted by the rule of law, the defence of human rights and the respect of individual liberty; on the other the democratic tradition whose main ideas are those of equality, identity between governing and governed and popular sovereignty.'[33] Because there is no rational way to synthesise these two ideals of liberty and equality, Mouffe urges that democratic politics should be 'agonistic', but not 'antagonistic'.[34] Seeing no end to the process of trying to reconcile these opposites, Mouffe adopts the Greek term *agon* to capture the positive ideal of a structured and performative contest. A theatre performance in Athens was termed an *agon*, part of a public competition, and Greek tragedies and comedies feature a further *agon*, a set-piece verbal contest between two dramatic characters.[35] Liberalism prioritises the rights and freedoms of the individual over those of the community, and because the Athenians for better or worse, in what was never an easy human process, tried to put community first, they help us set liberalism in perspective.[36] I have not couched this book as an assault on liberalism, but rather as an attempt to understand the limitations of a tradition that has made me the kind of person I feel myself to be.

The most important theoretician whom I will draw upon in this book is Plato. Plato describes a recurrent process whereby democratic anarchy spawns demagogues ('leaders of the *demos*' or what we would today call 'populists'), and a demagogue quickly morphs into a dictator or 'tyrant'.

Introduction: Democracy as Performance

According to Plato, tragedians in the theatre praise tyrants, likening them to gods, and for this reason he bars them from his idealised Republic, leaving them to 'circulate round other cities, attracting crowds and hiring men with fine, loud persuasive voices to drag the citizens towards tyranny and democracy'.[37] Democracy and tyranny sit next to each other on Plato's spectrum of constitutions, and he saw theatre as a device for securing the tyranny of demagogic rule. The persuasive or convincing voice of the tragic actor merges in his analysis with the voice of the demagogue to build the same collective surrender of rationality and admiration for a factitious hero. Plato's description of Greek tragedy seems counter-intuitive until we recall that in Greek city states most so-called tyrants were populist orators who won the support of the *demos* by suppressing aristocrats. In Athens it was the populist tyrant Peisistratos who first established the festival where tragedies were performed,[38] the playwright Aeschylus had a close relationship with Hieron the 'tyrant' of Syracuse, while Euripides wrote not only for Athens but also for the Macedonian 'tyrant' Archelaus.[39] For Plato, who believed in rule by a deserving elite, the thread that binds the actor and the demagogue is rhetoric, the power of a public speaker to command the emotions of a crowd and subject them to his will.

Aristotle was more sympathetic than Plato to the democratic ideal, and looked for a middle course. Unlike Plato, he recognised that the only alternative to rule by violence was rule by public persuasion, and this meant giving a central place to the art of rhetoric. He knew that mass juries and political assemblies would never be composed of philosophy students, and that collective decisions would always turn upon emotion rather than logical argument. He grasped also that emotion cannot be separated from cognition. 'The emotions', Aristotle wrote, 'are those things that bring about change to make people alter their decisions.'[40] Although his influential *Art of Rhetoric* analysed the psychology of emotion, he steered clear of addressing the problematic art of the performer. Writing a generation after the death of the great playwrights Sophocles and Euripides, he lamented that nowadays tragedies win the prize in dramatic competitions thanks not to playwrights but to actors, 'and the same thing happens in political contests because of the decay of polities'.[41] Put another way, it wasn't what you said that counted in the democratic Athens he knew, but how you performed those words. Aristotle's phrase 'decay of polities' refers to precipitate edicts passed in defiance of the constitution, and he goes on to complain that 'where the laws are not supreme, demagogues arise. Merged into a single entity, the *demos* turns into a king'. Like toadies paying court to a monarch, demagogues 'get their power because the *demos* controls everything, and *they* control the thinking of the *demos*.'[42]

Today Western liberals are caught in an intellectual trap. They complain about spin, mendacity and emotional manipulation, but lack any positive ideal of rhetoric of the kind that Aristotle and later Cicero in republican Rome tried to elaborate. How in practice can a politician be both honest and a consummate performer? If we seek a politician whom we judge to be 'honest' rather than 'eloquent', it is likely we shall be drawn to some individual whom we trust because they resemble ourselves, and this individual meanwhile will fail to win trust from people unlike ourselves. The human tendency to identify provides the entrée to leaders like Trump and Johnson, adept in the role of a flawed, rebellious human being who speaks as he thinks, and both are probably honest liars in the sense that they know how to bring themselves to believe what they say in the brief moment of saying it. Cicero established a principle that countless later orators have echoed. In Churchill's phrasing of the mantra, for example, the orator who wants to convince the multitude 'must himself believe. He may be often inconsistent. He is never consciously insincere.'[43] Gorgias, a flamboyant Greek rhetorician, set out the paradox of theatricality in these terms: 'The deceiver is more honest than the non-deceiver, and the deceived is wiser than the undeceived.'[44] Many who vote for populists like Trump and Johnson are plainly not naïve but share this view.

When democracy was reinvented in the eighteenth century, it was tied to procedures of *representation* via a system of elections. This was different from the participatory Greek system based on mass meetings and lotteries for the random selection of officers. The cultural climate of the Enlightenment put a premium on rationality and amongst the educated classes it was taken for granted that elected representatives would be more capable of reasoned deliberation than the common people, often demeaned as 'the mob'. Our modern thing called democracy was inspired not by quarrelsome Athens but by the Roman Republic, and this Rome was seen to be governed by free citizens, men with a decent level of education and property, capable of engaging in deliberation that was emotional but also reasoned. When the republican ideal slowly yielded to the modern democratic ideal of full adult suffrage, the educated and property-owning classes did not instantly relinquish their grip on power – and perhaps they never did. Greece was not the cradle of modern democracy, but it remains a revealing social experiment showing how a shared understanding of agonistic performance allowed power to shift with a minimum of internal violence.

An important distinction needs to be established between rhetoric and deliberation.[45] For Plato deliberation meant 'dialectic', the conversational to-and-fro undertaken by his students in the corridors of Academe.[46] In Athens, fifty citizens chosen by lot gathered in the Council Chamber to deliberate the agenda, but the Assembly where decisions were made was a space for rhetoric because 6000 people cannot in any meaningful sense 'deliberate' together. The essential difference is performative. In deliberation all are equals, typically seated, while rhetoric makes a clear distinction between the performer, normally standing on a podium, and his or her audience. Proponents of 'deliberative democracy', an ideal often associated with Habermas' response to the rhetoric of fascism, point to all that can be achieved by a diverse group of randomly selected citizens sitting down together to work through disagreements, but there is a snag: few have been willing to grant binding legitimacy to decisions so reached.[47] As John Parkinson puts it, small groups may deliberate, but it is the harsh reality of large-scale democracies that the majority must take 'a seat in the stalls, while the few occupy centre stage.'[48] Mouffe's critique is more trenchant, arguing that conflict needs public enactment because conflict is part of being human.[49]

Alan Finlayson is a British political theorist who champions rhetoric over deliberation. Building on Aristotle's claims that the human being is in the first instance a 'political', that is, social animal rather than an individual, Finlayson follows Aristotle to define rhetoric as 'the ability to identify in any particular situation the available means of persuasion', the only way to put political judgements before the people en masse.[50] For Finlayson modern 'post-democracy' has suppressed collective decision-making in favour of aggregated individual preferences, and neoliberalism will always seek to denigrate and destroy rhetoric.[51] An important strand of mainstream political science is based upon 'rational choice theory' which assumes that voting reflects the calculations of individual 'actors' about personal benefit.[52] This theory, which seeks to equate the individualistic logic of the marketplace with the logic of the ballot box, receives little support from the analysis of actual voting behaviour.[53] People are, as Jonathan Haidt puts it, inherently 'groupish'.[54]

Back in 1897 Churchill rejected complaints that rhetoric had been killed off by newspapers and public sophistication,[55] and although the same claim about the demise of rhetoric is often repeated in the context of digital media and a culture of the soundbite, we should recall how Boris Johnson wrote a eulogistic biography of Churchill, the most celebrated British orator of the twentieth century, and as Prime Minister kept on his desk a statue of the great Athenian orator Pericles.[56] There is no escaping rhetoric, broadly defined, because history offers few compelling examples of collective leadership, and in practice a single leader needs to win over the many. The skill of engaging a crowd changes in a recording studio, where there is always anxiety that recorded words will be taken out of context, but the art of talking to persuade in the heat of the moment remains for better or worse central to democratic life. Philip Collins, once a speechwriter for the British Prime Minister Tony Blair, claimed in 2018 that '[r]hetoric and democracy are twinned; their histories run together.' Setting up Pericles' 'funeral speech' pronounced over the Athenian dead as a foundational moment, Collins argues for 'better' rhetoric as the key to defending liberal democracy from populism.[57] Political speech writers are a group who normally seek to keep themselves invisible, because no politician will let it be seen that they are actors voicing words written for them by others.[58]

Collins' introduction to political rhetoric focuses on the written word, with nothing on body language or the art of adjusting the written word to a specific performer, and Finlayson has the same textual orientation, influenced by Aristotle's sense of priorities.[59] Performance is harder to analyse than a written text because the traces it leaves are elusive. A speech on television or circulating on social media responds to the public mood of the moment, and the single lens of a camera offers a poor impression of the exchange that takes place between speaker and listener. My undertaking in this book will be a delicate one as I try to catch key features of past performances, accessible only through inferences built on the material traces which those performances have left. For all its difficulties, the attempt is worth making because democracy is and always has been a mode of performance. For theatre historians, unlike political scientists, the challenge of recovering lost performances is a familiar part of their trade.

In my last book I examined the rhetorical tradition which was the foundation of European stage acting from the Renaissance until the nineteenth century, and which assumed that the skills of preacher, politician and actor were essentially the same because they used public speech to move an audience.[60] In mainstream twentieth-century stage acting, the emphasis shifted, and acting became less the art of moving the emotions of an audience than of expressing something hidden inside the actor. The name of Stanislavski came to be associated with words like truth, belief and motivation, and the private psychological processes of the actor were the new focus of Western actor training.[61] In the same era it grew harder for politicians to frame democratic arguments about issues as they faced a similar audience demand for inner truth. The new focus upon who I am made it harder for politicians to concentrate on the problem of what makes an audience change its mind.

Alongside 'rhetoric', the other key term which has always tied democracy to theatre is 'representation'. Plato opposed tragedy more vigorously than any other form of representational art because here, confusingly, humans represent other humans. As an aristocrat who considered his mentor Socrates a martyr and victim of democracy, Plato yearned for a society without social mobility where there would be no gap between a person's nature and their social role. In the Christian era Pope Innocent III was another notable authoritarian who hated representation. Innocent loved to wield his authentic relic of Christ's cross, and laid down the doctrine that in the Mass the bread does not *represent* the body of Christ but changes its substance to *become* that body. This proposition was tied to a political claim that, as Pope, Innocent was not God's representative but his actual voice with authority over secular monarchs and the right to launch a Crusade against Moslems.[62] In the Enlightenment era Jean-Jacques Rousseau was an enthusiastic reader of Plato who shared his hostility to representation. Having made his name as a playwright, Rousseau published a manifesto condemning theatre, and this anti-theatricalism chimed with his political argument that the state should be governed by a homogeneous 'General Will' without any elected representatives.[63] Modernist theatre renewed Rousseau's assault on the falsity of representation, and in avant-garde aesthetics the emphasis shifted from 'representing' a character towards ideas like 'presence', 'enactment' and 'embodiment'.[64] In this book, avoiding looser notions of 'the performative', I shall keep my sights fixed on theatre as a historically defined practice of representation, and for this reason a paradigm to understand the historical phenomenon we call democracy.[65]

Arguing that the concept of political representation derives from the arts, the political theorist Frank Ankersmit distinguishes a 'resemblance theory' from a 'substitution theory',[66] and as an example of 'resemblance' cites an American Federalist who championed bottom-up localism in 1787: 'The very term, representative, implies, that the person or body chosen for this purpose, should resemble those who appoint them – a representation of the people of America, if it be a true one, must be like the people'. The Federalist emphasises that those 'who are placed instead of the people, should possess their sentiments and feelings'.[67] For the opposite view, Ankersmit turns to Edmund Burke, who argued that it was not his job to represent the views of his local electors in Bristol because his duty in Parliament was to follow his conscience and judge on behalf of the nation. To put the representational dilemma another way: if we think of democratic politicians as performers on the political stage, then they may either play their script in the character allocated to them by their electorate, or they may hold onto a clutch of masks and improvise in response to the moment. As in art, so in politics representation entails choice in how to play one's role.[68]

The revolutionary activist Thomas Paine understood that American Independence produced 'representation engrafted upon Democracy'.[69] For Paine, pure democracy without representation could be no more than an abstract theoretical construct. Barely two years after Paine's *Rights of Man* fired up the American public, Robespierre in France, with the moral authority of Rousseau behind him, jettisoned representation on the basis that he himself embodied the General Will. Arendt argues that Robespierre's private virtues and motivations might have been genuine and heartfelt, but in the public arena they 'degenerated into mere appearances and had become part of the show in which Tartuffe was bound to play the principal part.'[70] Tartuffe is the calculating religious hypocrite in a play by Molière that provoked public outrage in Louis XIV's Paris (Figure 0.1). Molière took for himself the complex role of the patriarch Orgon whose devotion to Tartuffe renders him an unconscious hypocrite blind to his own domestic tyranny, and the cruelty of Orgon presages for Arendt the blind cruelty of Robespierre's Committee for Public Safety.

While Arendt was a communitarian who believed that human fulfilment lay in active political citizenship, Judith Shklar, another escapee from the Holocaust, embraced the individualistic ideals of American liberal democracy, arguing that personal cruelty is the worst of all human evils. While Arendt's imagination was fired by the heroes of Sophocles who held the fate of the city in their hands, Shklar in *Ordinary Vices* (1984) found inspiration in Molière's three archetypes of hypocrisy: Tartuffe who knowingly dons a mask of Christian self-righteousness, M. Jourdain the social snob, and Alceste the misanthropist who trumpets his moral honesty. What Shklar witnessed in post-war America was a world more concerned with unmasking hypocrisy than with cruelty, and she argued for a reversal of priorities. Reading *Tartuffe* as a political parable about a 'Puritan culture of fear', she concludes that 'liberal democracy cannot afford public sincerity', because hypocrisy is 'a very necessary pretense, a witness to our moral efforts no less than to our failures'.[71]

In *Political Hypocrisy: The Mask of Power, from Hobbes to Orwell and Beyond* (2008) the English political philosopher David Runciman notes

Introduction: Democracy as Performance 15

Figure 0.1   Unmasking the hypocrite. In Molière's *Tartuffe* (1664/1669), Orgon discovers that Tartuffe has been trying to seduce his wife.
Source: Frontispiece to *Tartuffe* in the first edition of the *Oeuvres complètes de Monsieur de Molière*. Bibliothèque nationale, Paris, 1682. Engraving by Pierre Brissart.

the origin of the word 'hypocrisy' in *hypokrites*, the Greek term for a stage actor, and makes much of Hobbes' argument that every ruler or ruling body has to don a *persona* or 'theatrical mask'.[72] Hobbes underpins his argument that '[t]o over-personalise politics, to collapse the distinction between the mask and the person behind the mask, is either culpable hypocrisy, or self-delusion'.[73] He builds on Shklar in order to argue for the necessity of hypocrisy in the liberal political tradition because all politicians need to separate their public and private selves. In an afterword published in 2018, Runciman comments on the success of Bill Clinton and Tony Blair who, as 'sincere liars', managed to wear their masks without seeming effort, and he explains the rise of Donald Trump on the grounds that most people prefer overt liars to hypocrites.[74]

The danger of proving oneself a Tartuffe haunted alike the puritans of the English revolution and the rationalistic protestants who drove the American revolution and 'enlightened' French revolutionaries. Rousseau, a product of puritan Geneva and a fierce advocate of personal and public sincerity, admired Molière as a writer but complained of the playwright's moral compromises, which he blamed on the demands of a public audience.[75] Molière was a brilliant unmasker of hypocrisy because he was himself a 'hypocrite' in the form of a stage actor, a profession vilified by the puritans upon whom Tartuffe was modelled. He was an actor who happened to write and not, as viewed by Rousseau and most modern scholarship, a writer who happened to act. I will show in this book how the practical workings of the stage shine a light on the paradoxes that Shklar and Runciman begin to unpick when they explore that other form of stage acting, democratic politics.

In Chapter 1, I will examine the interplay of theatricality and political persuasion in fifth-century Athens. Here there was no civil society distinct from political society, so comedy and tragedy were inextricably part of the political process. Because the heady ideals formulated in Pericles' funeral speech, the nearest we have to a democratic manifesto, proved unworkable, the contradictions of democratic life led Plato to attack political rhetoric as the enemy of truth. The relationship of rhetoric to truth will be a thread guiding my path. Chapter 2 is devoted to a single case study: a rhetorical duel between Aeschines, a trained stage actor, and Demosthenes, who tried to demonstrate personal sincerity by making it clear he was no such actor. The first set himself up as a champion of democracy, the second as a champion of nation, which leads me to the central difficulty identified by Arendt: democracy is posited on a bounded nation and on an artificial entity taken to constitute the *demos* or 'people'.

Post-classical democracy, particularly in the USA, owes a huge debt to the Protestant assumption that every individual should be true to his or her private conscience. Chapter 3 is therefore devoted to the English puritan revolution, and it centres on two stories. I begin with the puritan lawyer William Prynne, who lambasted theatre as part of a broader attack on the trappings of aristocracy and monarchy, while his own techniques of persuasion were in practice deeply theatrical. From Prynne's dogmatic conviction, I turn to Putney where soldiers and officers in Cromwell's army debated as equals, and in an extraordinary democratic enterprise tried to demonstrate that they all spoke with open hearts, which is to say without hypocrisy or theatricality. In chapter 4, I turn to France, a Catholic culture which broadly embraced rhetoric and theatre, but was profoundly influenced by a citizen of Protestant Geneva, Rousseau. I trace how six different orators approached the task of persuading the *demos* of France to build a more honest and more democratic world.

In chapter 5, I pass to the USA, founded on an uneasy compromise between secular rationalism and a puritan tradition that was not granted any formal place in the Constitution. Sennett's bourgeois 'public man', epitomised by President John Adams, lost his claim to moral authority when working-class Irishmen, liberated slaves and finally women found their voices and demanded an equal place at the democratic table. Only one idea could unite these disparate groups, a shared insistence that people are not in the first instance social beings and performers of social roles but are unique and inimitable individuals. Chapter 6 takes me to twentieth-century India as it threw off the shackles of empire, and a new question arises: does the postcolonial condition mean that democracy must be discarded as unwanted Western baggage, a belief system incompatible with Indian tradition, or does it mean that India should partake of democracy as the thing it was too long denied? I pit Gandhi, a man who laid claim to total sincerity, against Rabindranath Tagore, a man of the theatre who believed that truth lay in metaphor, both men sharing much the same unease when faced with the Western democratic model.

Rather than bring my story up to the present, where perspective becomes ever harder to achieve, I have couched my concluding chapter as an epilogue. I turn back to Athens, and instead of looking at democracy as a form of theatre I place theatre within democracy. If democracy cannot liberate itself from rhetoric, then it must embrace rhetoric, and to that end it needs audiences attuned to the pleasures, tricks and techniques of rhetoric. In Athens, I argue, theatre was the pre-eminent place where democratic citizens were formed. I write as a historian, but plainly there are implications for modern education.

The democratic revolutions of England, France and America have left their residue, creating patterns of behaviour that continue to distinguish these cultures in the present. Historical distance, like geographical distance, reveals the contingency of much that we take for common sense. Globalisation has in practice made it harder to think historically because the diversity of the present is overwhelming. Why think back, it is common to ask, when there is so much to discover about the present? Why attend to older political experiments when recent years have witnessed such profound transformation? Two answers. First, the past shapes the present in unsuspected ways, and it is only through recognising cultural patterns that we can free ourselves from being trapped by them. Second, behind the facade of diversity constructed by globalisation and consumerism lie constants that stem from technology, the marketplace and the dominance of the English language. The past introduces us to a cultural other who may have bracingly different assumptions about the performances people give in order to function as social and political beings.

Presentists throw up another challenge to theatre historians: Why attend to live theatre in a world that now belongs to cinema, digitization and multimedia spectacle? If theatre has become, as some would see it, an exercise in cultural nostalgia, then in the same vein we have to ask, is democracy also something we should feel nostalgic for, a cultural practice of yesterday which a technological revolution has rendered at best unappealing, at worst unworkable? It is a question that I leave open, confining myself to the simple overarching argument that democracy is and has to be a form of theatre. Despite gloomy prognostications, theatre has always had a knack of reinventing itself, and democracy may or may not prove to have the same resilience.

CHAPTER I

Rhetoric in Athens

The Greek experiment has inspired most of those who dream of a more complete, participatory and emotionally satisfying form of democracy, and Athens was a success story insofar as its democracy proved robust enough to survive for nearly two centuries. Any moral evaluation of Athens must of course be heavily qualified. In the debit column sit three major negatives, and these can either be seen as fundamental flaws that invalidate the whole Greek project, or as mere historical anomalies: slavery, women, and war. Athens relied upon slave labour, but citizens often worked alongside slaves,[1] slaves could acquire personal wealth, and an early critic of democracy complained that Athenian slaves could not be told apart from poor citizens,[2] while in modern European democracies it can be argued that slave conditions have been exported to overseas sweatshops, factories and plantations. Women in Athens lacked voting and property rights, but they were more than receptacles for authentic citizen seed, and whether they were free enough to attend the theatre and contribute to public opinion is a matter of continuing controversy.[3] Max Weber described Athens as a 'warrior guild',[4] and rowing warships or fighting side-by-side was a bonding activity that made democracy possible, with colonisation imposed by force of arms the consequence of an empowered *demos* hungry for land. These are the standard reservations, while on the credit side of the balance sheet sit economic prosperity, stability and cultural value. Democracy appears to have rewarded innovation, fostering trade and initiative. Rich and poor achieved a *modus vivendi* which, however troubled, fractured only briefly at the end of the Peloponnesian War, and spared Athenian democracy over the two centuries of its existence from vicious civil wars of the kind that Thucydides describes elsewhere in the Greek world.[5] Painting, sculpture and theatre are symptomatic of the individual agency and group energy that shine through the pages of Thucydides, the great historian of the war against Sparta. Since the value of art to human beings can never be quantified, we return to the basic conundrum of democracy:

no amount of rational discussion will ever resolve the problem of what constitutes a well-lived life.

Pericles' Funeral Speech

Perhaps 'democracy' is such a murky concept today because antiquity never bequeathed us any canonical manifesto setting out a 'classical' vision of what democracy is or ought to be. The great orator Demosthenes, often held up as an icon of democratic commitment, left us the texts of many speeches but no extended statement of principle. Pericles' speech commemorating the dead at the start of the war against Sparta is the nearest thing we have to a statement of principle, and we possess it in words summarised or reinvented by the historian Thucydides. Nicole Loraux explains that this is all we have because democracy was rooted in orality and resisted the fixity implied by written documents.[6] Thucydides' unfinished *History of the Peloponnesian War* resembles a tragic drama, with the people of Athens its flawed collective hero treading the path to ruin. The Athenians are pictured by Thucydides as men who 'analyse or mull over their decisions, and who consider that actions fail not through talking, but through failure to talk and learn before embarking on the right course of action',[7] and as plays are punctuated by choruses so his *History* is punctuated by orations.[8] Pericles' 'funeral speech' wraps up Act I of Thucydides' drama, defining a high point of collective idealism in response to mass casualties after the first year of war.

In this speech, which aims to instil in mourners a martial spirit and collective self-belief, Pericles articulates a core value: 'We bear the name of a democracy because we live not for the few but for the majority.' Though he insists that Athens is not ruled by the few, or in other words is not an oligarchy, Pericles veers away from any direct assertion that this means direct rule by the masses, claiming rather that the poor have equality of opportunity within a kind of meritocracy, and he emphasises the rule of law, laws being both written and unwritten. Although Pericles sounds like a modern liberal when insisting that freedom means tolerance of the diverse ways in which citizens choose to live their private lives, his voice seems very different when he condemns as useless anyone who opts out of political life.[9] The American Declaration of Independence holds that 'all men are created equal' but that they are also 'endowed by their Creator with certain inalienable Rights, that among these are Life, Liberty and the pursuit of Happiness'. In Pericles' formulation 'happiness equates with liberty, and liberty with courage', so liberty is a positive not a negative condition, and happiness, as a public not a private state of being, may entail surrendering one's individual life for the public good.[10] For Pericles morality is group-oriented, far removed from the Enlightenment conception that individuals are possessed of 'Rights'.[11] Although Pericles makes no direct mention of theatre, beyond referring to *agon*s and sacrifices that bring repose to the mind, tragedy played its part in defining the unwritten laws that bind society together, and the Athenian invention of tragedy as a dialogical genre underlies Pericles' claim that Athens needed no triumphal poetry from the likes of Homer.[12]

Pericles' funeral oration is not a timeless manifesto but the record of a performance at a moment in time. Delivered from a temporary platform in the public cemetery, his speech greeted the arrival of a cortege of wagons belonging to the ten artificial tribes into which Athens was divided, and these wagons carried the corpses or skeletons of tribal members ready to be interred in a collective grave as citizens rather than individuals. The funeral speech was institutionalised in order to suppress female keening over family members, using the male genre of public speech to weld the diverse Athenian public into a single body. In his preamble, Pericles refers to the trust placed in him to speak well, and the difficulty of finding measured words when each listener has personal opinions. Whether Pericles' ability to transform these private opinions into collective opinion should be admired as the work of a 'leader' or condemned as 'demagoguery' is a matter of historical judgement for the historian, and Thucydides chose to construct Pericles as the former for purposes of his narrative, conjuring up an image of the quintessential democratic leader acceptable to rich and educated Athenians.[13] Plutarch was not alone in challenging this interpretation.[14]

Thucydides' Pericles turns the ritual act of praising the dead into a political argument for continuing the war, and in the historian's spare prose we miss the raw emotionalism suggested by a metaphor which Aristotle preserved from some alternative version of the speech: 'for the city to lose its youth is like a year deprived of spring'.[15] We also lose from the written text the attributes of performance evoked in Plutarch's biography of Pericles: a tongue like a thunderbolt, the benefit of coaching by a musicologist comparable to the training of an athlete, and 'an aura of grandeur and more weight of purpose than any demagogue'. In addition to his command of language, we learn that Pericles had 'a composed face never distorted by laughter, a serene gait and subdued dress never disturbed by emotion, a tone of voice that was never uncontrolled, and many other striking features.'[16] Monumentalised by later historians as a timeless statement, Pericles' speech was a performance designed to meet the needs of the moment and negotiate a power relationship. Thucydides explains that Pericles was a man able to 'lead the masses rather than be led by them', a speaker who could

> depress rashness into caution or raise men back from irrational fear to valour. In name a democracy, this was in reality rule by the top man. His successors, with less to distinguish between them, each struggled to be top, and abandoned statesmanship as they turned to pleasing the *demos*.[17]

It is not a big step from Thucydides to Plato and the charge that democracy must inevitably lead to demagoguery. To look at the funeral speech carefully is to see that there was never a perfect moment of Athenian democracy, a harmonious point of balance comparable to Pericles' Parthenon. Democracy was always a species of performance, provisional and subject to renegotiation. Just as the word 'drama' in its Greek root refers to 'something done', so 'democracy' was and is something done, a physical exertion of power.

Oratory in the Athenian Democratic System

When we take a long view of history, Greek democracy and Greek theatre seem to be convergent phenomena. An aristocrat named Cleisthenes in 508 BCE organised Athens into a network of local communities or 'demes' to ensure that no single part of the city-state (*polis*) could dominate the rest, with all citizens feeling interconnected through cross-community 'tribes', and this seems to be the decisive change in the story of democracy's emergence.[18] Greek tragedy appeared during the same period, but we have no evidence for a precise chronology, nor secure data about Thespis, the shadowy figure first said to have superimposed speech on choral dance.[19] The key artistic innovation came when one singer stepped out of the chorus to engage in dialogue with it, replicating the dynamic that underpins democracy where speech is deployed in order to act upon a group, within a relationship characterised by balance and interaction rather than authority. In oligarchic Sparta there was a rich choral culture, but no comparable mixing of choral dance with the art of the speaking voice.[20] Dancing in unison bred discipline and social integration, and these qualities were necessary but not sufficient conditions of democracy. Tragedy was an Athenian innovation that spread rapidly across the Greek world, and enough data has now emerged to show that in the late 400s and 300s BCE tragedy was broadly fostered by democracies and populist dictatorships but shunned by aristocratic oligarchies. Eric Csapo and Peter Wilson instance the 'striking examples of cities like Rhodes, Thebes and the cities of Arcadia that embraced theatre as soon as they threw off the oligarchic yoke and became democracies'.[21]

The three sites in Athens for deploying the democratic language of persuasion were law-courts, assemblies and theatres. A panel of 6000 jurors supplied juries for the courts where no less than 201 men and sometimes thousands sat in judgement. A quorum of 6000 was required for a meeting of the Assembly on the Hill of the Pnyx, while the *boulê* or Council was a rotating executive of fifty, and there were further assemblies in the 139 demes.[22] It is not clear exactly how many people gathered in the Theatre of Dionysus before the building of the great stone auditorium whose remains are visible today, and recent archaeologists have sought to bring the number down to something like the size of the Assembly on the Pnyx, challenging the idea that the Festival of Dionysus was a face-to-face encounter of the entire citizen community, which may have numbered some 50,000 men before the Peloponnesian War depleted the population.[23] Because tragedies were performed from a written text, they were reproducible, and it is clear that, just as there were assemblies in the different demes of Attica, so there was a network of performance festivals in the demes, allowing all citizens to participate in the theatrical culture of the democracy.[24] The centre nevertheless remained the place where important political decisions were made, and where most new tragedies were performed. Symbolically if not actually, the performance of tragedy at the City Festival of Dionysus was a gathering of the citizen body, and the presence of foreign visitors only enhanced the idea that tragedy was connected to political identity. The presence of dignitaries in the front row and a central block of seating for the presiding Council ensured that the theatre was visibly a democratic space.[25]

Though Athens was not an intimate community where everybody knew everybody, it was certainly experienced as a face-to-face culture by a loosely defined elite. Josiah Ober presents political oratory as a kind of dramatic game that allowed this elite to maintain its dominance. In Ober's account, the political orator

> had to persuade the citizens that he was both an average citizen ... and, simultaneously, that he possessed abilities and attributes that legitimised his assumption of political privileges, especially the privilege to stand before and even against the masses. The politician had to play a complicated double role and maintain credibility in both roles over a long period of time, all the while in the face of acute public scrutiny and the jibes of his political opponents.[26]

The political orator was therefore a man who

> wore a mask with two faces. On the one hand, he was the perfect exemplar of the norms of society ... On the other hand, he was superior to the ordinary citizen, an elite in terms of his ability, wealth, and status ... Maintaining this balance required ... consummate "acting" on the part of the speaker and a willingness on the part of the audience to accept the performance.[27]

When watching a tragedy in the theatre, the citizen spectator in Ober's understanding had a similar double awareness, for he

> knew that the man behind the mask was an actor, but that knowledge did not interfere with his enjoyment of the performance or with the power of the performance to affect him. Rather, the recognition of the actor behind the mask doubled and enriched the dramatic experience and made it consequentially more meaningful.[28]

Ober recognises here that neither theatre nor political rhetoric put a premium on sincerity. Democracy turned, in fact, upon collective recognition that all politicians were rhetoricians who wore metaphorical masks.

Aristotle distinguished the rhetoric which belongs to written documents from the rhetoric of a live *agon*, explaining that 'written language is precise, while agonistic language is performative (*hypokritikôtatê*)', and noting also that the agonistic idiom of the political assembly is more broadbrush than that of the law-court. To help distinguish agonistic language, he offered the example of repetitions that prove strong only in performance because performers endow each repeated element with a different character and tone. Aristotle classified agonistic language on the basis of how far it turns either on character (*ethikê*) or on emotion (*pathetikê*), observing that 'actors accordingly pursue plays of both these kinds, and such actors are pursued by playwrights'.[29] It is the overarching thesis of his *Rhetoric* that a speaker persuades his audience firstly through building trust in his own character, secondly through arousing emotions in the audience, and only thirdly through argument.[30] Whilst Ober focused on the presentation of character in Athenian public speaking, Victor Bers turned to emotion in an exploration of courtroom language, demonstrating that although Athenian litigants generally sought to demonstrate 'mastery of their own emotions under the stress of the trial', nevertheless in some circumstances 'unregulated emotion can be taken as an index of authenticity of feeling, and hence of the truth'.[31] Bers draws upon Aristotle's insight that although 'the listener shares the emotions of one who speaks with emotion, even when nothing is really being said', it is unwise for a speaker to accompany harsh words with an overtly harsh voice and face lest his strategy seem too obvious.[32] Aware that the language of tragedy must have played strongly on Athenian emotions, Bers remarks that courtroom speakers rarely adopt 'the vocabulary, phraseology, or delivery of tragic poetry as resource or inspiration', with litigants reluctant to make direct emotional appeals for pity in the manner of tragedy.[33] When he goes on to reject Edith Hall's claim that there is a fundamental equivalence between acting in the lawcourt and acting in the theatre,[34] Bers fails to reflect on the emotional literacy and understanding of character imparted by the courtroom to the theatre auditorium and vice versa, in a process of reciprocity.

The Mytilene Debate

Speeches in the Assembly were more broadbrush than speeches in the courtroom because the audience was larger and more volatile, and the stakes were higher. Thucydides illustrates the workings of democratic oratory in the Assembly through dramatising a debate which took place two years after Pericles' death. When the city of Mytilene on the island of Lesbos, or more exactly its oligarchic government, rebelled against the de facto Athenian empire which had emerged out of what was once an antiPersian alliance, Sparta came to the rescue too late and the city was captured. In fury, the Athenians rejected pleas for pity, and urged on by Cleon, Pericles' effective successor as the dominant voice in the Assembly, they decided to set an example by putting the entire male population to death, enslaving women and children. When tempers had cooled overnight, the Assembly reconsidered, and Thucydides distils the two days of debate down to a pair of balanced speeches by the otherwise unknown Diodotus and by Cleon, portrayed by Thucydides as a violent demagogue.[35]

Cleon begins by equating the rule of law with respect for decisions taken, praising the deep wisdom of the uneducated who 'place no trust in their own quick-wittedness, and presume that the laws know more than they do. Though incapable of analysing the arguments of an accomplished speaker, as impartial judges rather than contestants [*agonistai*] they generally reach the right decision.' Orators, he continues, have a duty to avoid rhetorical artifice 'and not get so caught up by our own energy and the battle [*agon*] to outwit each other that we ignore common sense in whatever policy we put to *you*.' Having skilfully established his own persona as the common man, Cleon goes on to discredit any intelligent argument that his opponent might launch against him:

> It's perfectly obvious: either he'll delight so much in his own powers of argument that he won't resist the challenge of proving that what manifestly *was* the case wasn't – or else, saying yes to bribery, he will deploy specious arguments as he sets out to seduce you. In this kind of contest, the city hands rewards to others, but runs all the risk herself. You are to blame for this horrible competitiveness, because you have gotten too used to being the spectators of words, and a passive audience to action. You picture future outcomes on the strength of fine talk, and rely upon your ears rather than your eyes to feel confident about what happened in the past, setting too much credit on grand words. You win the prize for heeding newfangled lines of argument, objecting to all that has undergone proper scrutiny, slaves to a paradox, dismissive of norms, and since what each of you wishes most is to hold the floor, but you can't, you race against every speaker to show how you have arrived at their conclusion one step ahead, quick to clap a pithy phrase, keen to be first in applauding a speech, but slowest to perceive the consequences of that speech, always searching for things that don't belong to, let's call it, reality, never mindful enough of the here and now. In a word, overwhelmed by the joys of listening, you are more like spectators at a performance given by sophists than men debating the future of their city.[36]

Compounds of the word *agon* appear four times in this passage to seal the connection between competitive performance and democratic debate. Criticising the theatricality of Athenian politics is a device that allows Cleon to conceal the theatricality of his own performance as he tries to win the political contest. His speech goes on to urge that Athens must avoid three snares if it is to maintain its authority over other states: pity, love of speeches, and moderation. Cleon argues for justice not pity, and for decisiveness not reflection.

In his response, Diodotos studiously avoids any appeal to the emotion of pity, but points to the folly of anger, exposing Cleon's technique of smearing an opponent so no one can ever be trusted:

> A good citizen does not intimidate the opposition, but delivers what may fairly be regarded as the best speech, and if he comes up with sound advice, a wise city will neither heap honours on him nor humble him, and should his proposal be rejected, he will neither be punished nor lose status. Were this to be the case, no talented speaker would ever be tempted to advance his career and, in hopes to please, propose motions that conflict with his own beliefs, nor would the defeated speaker in like manner try to curry favour and win control over the masses. Our practice is the opposite, and what's worse, should a speaker offering sound advice be accused of taking bribes, the very suspicion of bribery based on paltry evidence stops the city from taking advantage of a policy that is plainly beneficial. Our problem is

that good proposals set out in straightforward language are no less suspect than foolish ones, so just one tactic works: if you want to push a disastrous policy then you tell lies to win over the crowd, and conversely, if your policy is a sound one, you lie in order to be convincing. Ours is the only city which, thanks to its mental convolutions, will only accept clear-sighted advice through being deceived. It has become axiomatic that anyone open with good ideas must be secretly driven by money.[37]

Thucydides, through Diodotos, confronts the problem that neither speaking as you feel nor telling the simple truth works in a democracy. Democracy always requires a performance.

In the event, Diodotos won the argument and in a dramatic dash an Athenian ship reached Lesbos in time to countermand the order for genocide. Clemency might be too strong a word for the outcome, because a thousand prisoners were still slaughtered, and the island was colonised. The Mytilene debate presents the historian with a conundrum: should we regard it as a triumph of democracy, because reason triumphed over anger and the final outcome was the right one, or should we regard it as a travesty of democracy because both parties relied upon deception? Cleon is a palpable deceiver, using rhetorical skill to deny the presence of rhetorical skill, while Diodotos is a more subtle deceiver, using the language of reason in order to trigger emotions of pity. Thucydides makes it clear that the Council called a second assembly because there was a widespread understanding that the anger driving the initial decision had been too 'raw', and he describes how feeling in the two crews caused the first ship to row slowly, the second to row rapidly. Diodotos evidently grasps that a personal display of anguish would have been the least effective way to arouse collective pity, for this would have undermined his image as a man of authority. He dons the mask of reason in order to demonstrate that a mass execution would have no deterrent value because human beings do not behave rationally.

Reason in the Mytilene debate cannot be prised apart from emotion. As Aristotle explains in his *Rhetoric*, it is not simple reasoning that causes people to be swayed in a debate. The emotions that generate decisions 'are accompanied by pain and pleasure, and include anger, pity, fear, and so forth.'[38] In order to sustain Athenian rage, Cleon plays upon the emotion of fear, imagining future revolts, while in order to assuage anger Diodotos deploys the calming language of balance. The other key element of a political speech is character, which for Aristotle is a function of narrative.[39] Both speakers construct a character for the men of Mytilene: while Cleon's Mytileneans are calculating opportunists, Diodotos separates democrats from oligarchs and paints a picture of human fallibility. The two speakers also build a character for their audience, Cleon's Athenians being intelligent and strong whilst Diodotos' are only strong because they are wise. Finally, they stage their own characters because, as Aristotle explains, people's emotions are governed by their trust in the speaker, particularly in the political arena.[40] Asking the Athenians to accept that they are 'tyrants' over their fellow Greeks, Cleon shamelessly plays the strongman himself, chastising his audience for their weakness. In the passage which I have cited, Cleon builds up a long rhetorical period to ratchet up the emotions of his listeners, and my rendering 'sets out to seduce you' reflects the alliteration of the original. Diodotos' language is more broken, in keeping with his persona as a plain-spoken ordinary man, keen to lower the emotional temperature.

When Cleon and Diodotos argue about the fate of the Mytileneans, there is no thought that individual human rights are at stake, and no appeal is made to the conscience of the individual voter. In the Assembly, voting by show of hands was collective and public, and the aim of the speakers was to create what Aristotle called *homonoia*, common-mindedness. Aristotle cites Mytilene as a byword for *homonoia* at a time when the city had a charismatic populist leader.[41] The unspoken moral code in the Mytilenean debate is based on reciprocity.[42] Even though this was a religious society and when the Athenians took possession of Lesbos they donated one tenth of the captured land to the gods, neither speaker refers to the gods or to 'unwritten laws' relating to murder.[43] Tragedy addressed a subterranean area of collective human feeling that was excluded from the surface of political debate. Religion was an influential force much as it would be in the so-called 'Enlightenment' era when the foundations of modern democracy were laid down in Catholic France and Protestant America.

Reason and Emotion

In my first chapter I cited Jonathan Haidt who argues that 'Intuitions come first, strategic reasoning second', and that seen from the perspective of a social psychologist 'moral thinking is more like a politician searching for votes than a scientist searching for truth.'[44] Haidt is representative of the way scientific thought in the 21st-century has been reshaped by evolution and neurology in a new understanding of the human being that has only begun to percolate to the arts and political science. He challenges the 'worship of reason' initiated by Plato, sustained by the Enlightenment, and characteristic of much modern political thinking, along with its concomitant, the model of 'homo economicus', and maintains that as 'groupish' creatures we like to 'deploy our reasoning skills to support our team'.[45] While Plato portrayed the rational soul as a charioteer struggling to drive the two horses of positive and negative emotion, Haidt substitutes rider and elephant, with the controlled processes of the rider subservient to the instinctive processes symbolised by the elephant.[46] On the surface Cleon and Diodotos conduct a rational argument about tactics, but ultimately the vote had to be based on intuition and a sense of who 'we' are.

In the introduction to his *Politics* Aristotle sets out his premise that group identity is prior to collective identity, sharing Haidt's assumption about the 'groupish' nature of human beings, and in his *Ethics* he declares that: 'If the same good belongs to the individual and the city, the good of the city seems greater and more perfect to secure and conserve. The good of the individual must be prized, but more beautiful and divine is the good of the clan or the city.'[47] Not normally a man given to religious language, Aristotle voices here a spiritual intuition. In his *Rhetoric*, he makes no distinction between emotion and cognition, with anger, pity and fear understood to be modes of perception. Aestheticians have been much struck by Aristotle's analysis of the 'pleasure' provided by pity and fear in tragedy,[48] but have not often connected it to the 'pleasure' provided by an emotion like rage whipped up in the Assembly. In terms of Aristotle's analysis, Cleon purveyed pleasure because 'men linger on the thought of revenge, and the vision that then arises yields pleasure, as in dreams'.[49] Diodotos removes the source of pleasure by breaking down the object of the audience's anger, a generalised Mytilenean population.

The distilled speeches in Thucydides offer only a glimpse of their performative force, and Aristotle gives us some further insight in his history of the Athenian constitution:

> So long as Pericles maintained his standing with the *demos*, politics was conducted quite well, but once Pericles died things deteriorated badly. For the first time the *demos* acquired a leader who was not respected by men of competence ... After Pericles' death, the upper class were championed by Nicias who died in Sicily, and the *demos* had Cleon son of Cleainetos, who through his onslaughts badly corrupted the *demos*. Cleon was the first to shout and hurl insults from the rostrum, gathering up his cloak as he addressed the people, while all others observed decorum. After them, Theramenes son of Hagnon led the rest and Cleophon the lyre-maker led the *demos* ... From the time of Cleophon, those who wanted to embolden

the many with an eye to short-term gratification formed an unbroken line of demagogues.[50]

Cleon positioned himself as a leader of the people by using his voice and body in a new way, differentiating himself from the aristocratic Pericles. Greek orators wore a rectangular woollen wrap that had to be supported by the left hand if it was not to fall out of place, and Cleon threw the wrap over his shoulder in order to gesture freely. Plutarch records that Cleon 'stripped the rostrum of its decorum, and in the Assembly was first to shout and unwrap his cloak and slap his thigh and speak on the run as he made his pronouncements'.[51] Through breaking the rules of constraint, Cleon signalled both his disrespect for traditional leaders, and the authenticity of his embodied emotions. His mode of delivery allowed him to express emotion freely, and transmit those emotions to his audience. In the Mytilene debate he appealed to poor men whose regular incomes derived from the revenues of empire, and who feared losing them. Cleon's father made his money through a tanning business, and Aristotle places his successor Cleophon as a manufacturer in his own right. Athenian politics became polarised on a class basis, and the word 'demagogue' entered the political vocabulary.

Aristophanes and Cleon

The comic playwright Aristophanes is responsible for the first known use of the term 'demagogue' in his comedy *The Knights*, which caricatured Cleon at the height of his influence some three years after the Mytilene debate: 'Demagy is no longer for men of education and noble conduct, but for the ignorant and squalid.'[52] Aristophanes' Cleon is characterised by his yelling, likened to a rushing torrent, a dog's howl or a seagull's cry,[53] and he is vanquished by a near-illiterate sausage-seller used to shouting his wares in the marketplace, a man who pushes Cleon's methods to an absurd extreme. In the conceit of the play, Cleon is represented by the slave Paphlagon (a name implying both foreign origins and blusterer), whose manipulations have allowed him to take control of his master named Demos. The chorus represent the opposite pole of Athenian society, effete young men rich enough to supply their own horses when fighting for Athens, and it was men from this social group who took the lead in suppressing democracy thirteen years later.[54] The two demagogues compete in trading insults and battling to get the first word in, while the horsemen picture Athens reduced to silence by this verbal bombardment, and Demos, properly master of the state, can do no more than gape like a clown.[55] It is implied that Cleon did not just yell at the Assembly, but used to invade the Council where the agenda for debate was set.[56] Aristophanes' parodic version of Cleon does not just use his voice to dominate, but also challenges his rival to outglare him, and Aristophanes refers elsewhere to Cleon's flashing eyes.[57] One of Aristophanes' competitors dwelt on Cleon's fierce eyebrows in a parody of the Perseus story, and Aristophanes' claim in *Knights* that the mask-makers were too frightened to provide the playwright with a likeness of Cleon may refer to this earlier caricature of Cleon as a sea-monster.[58] Facial expression was a crucial part of Cleon's act. The comedy has a happy ending when Demos is magically rejuvenated and restored to his senses, recovering an identity that all members of the polarised Athenian audience might comfortably embrace, as the type that had fought off the Persians some sixty years earlier.

In his *Wasps* two years later, Aristophanes gives us a glimpse of the Athenians who supported Cleon. The protagonist is called Love-Cleon, an old man addicted to serving on a jury, and living off the jury pay funded by imperial revenues which Pericles instituted and Cleon enhanced.[59] Love-Cleon's son Loathe-Cleon tries to persuade his father to stop taking conspirators to court, and to recognise that he has become a slave to the leaders he worships. The *agon* or debate conducted in front of the chorus of waspish jurymen is a case study in how an audience can be moved to change its mind.[60] Loathe-Cleon takes notes while Love-Cleon delivers a rambling, anecdotal speech setting out all the perks that he enjoys as a juror, happy because Cleon the shouter never bites him but cradles him in his hand to keep the flies away. The jury declare Love-Cleon's speech clever and faultless, swelling with pride as they listen to their colleague, and they picture the heavenly moment when they will cast their ballots, warning Loathe-Cleon that only submission will soften their rage. Loathe-Cleon responds with statistics, appropriating Cleon's rhetorical methods to argue against Cleon's policy of maximising revenues, conjuring up all the secret benefits that Cleon and his fellow 'people-isers' purloin from state revenues with only a pittance left for the poor. He bombards the jury with cumulative lists, veering from long periods to short explosive phrases in a speech enriched by mimicry, demotic vocabulary and alliteration. Both speeches are peppered with interruptions, a reminder that the two speeches distilled in Thucydides would in practice have been interrupted by heckling and applause throughout.[61]

Love-Cleon is shocked to find himself won over by his opponent and describes his bodily sensations, a numb hand and a limp penis. To be moved in argument, he reports, is an experience similar to that of sands moving under the surface of the water. The transformation is, however, not complete, for a desire to convict remains and Loathe-Cleon has to find a domestic courtroom to satisfy his father's addiction to debate. The two *agon*s in *Wasps* and in Thucydides resemble each other, for in both cases the second speaker, less well known to the audience, calms the rage excited by the first in what looks like a triumph for democracy. The chorus of converted jurymen conclude at the end of the *agon* in Aristophanes:

> It was a wise man who pronounced: 'Before you hear both stories, never come to a decision." You [i.e. Loathe-Cleon] seem to me far and away the winner. You have eased our anger, so we shall lay down our sticks. And you [Love-Cleon], our age-mate and fellow-devotee, [*Here they start to sing.*] be persuaded, persuaded by his words, act sensibly, don't be so rigid, so obdurate. Ah, if only I had a parent or guardian like you to warn me off.[62]

This is democracy in action in the sense that the audience hears an argument and changes its mind, but it is also poor democracy because it turns upon bad statistics and unsubstantiated charges of corruption. Posterity has viewed Cleon harshly, but has rarely confronted the problem: leaving aside the much mythologised Pericles, what models do we have from antiquity of a 'good' democratic leader?

The plays of Aristophanes help us to understand Cleon's success in the Assembly, but comedy was also in itself part of the democratic system. Freedom of speech has always been recognised as a basic component of democracy, and Aristophanic comedy exemplifies what seems like an unparalleled level of freedom from censorship. So long as he was subject to public mockery in the theatre, Cleon could not morph into a tyrant or dictator. Critics have long pondered how the Athenians could have awarded first prize to *The Knights* before placing their trust in Cleon a few months later through appointing him to a generalship, and there are different answers to this conundrum, once one discards the idea that art and politics sit in separate mental compartments.[63]

Critics viewing Aristophanes through the lens of liberal democracy position him as an engaged dramatist speaking truth to power, and his campaign for peace rather than war has endeared him to modern radicals. Aristophanes' claim that he (or his producer) was prosecuted by Cleon for insulting the *demos* is a key piece of evidence for this liberal-democratic reading,[64] and the theatre on this basis becomes the pre-eminent Athenian site for the exercise of 'free speech'. The US Supreme Court in 1972 clarified the modern meaning of free speech when it interpreted the provisions of the First Amendment: 'To permit the continued building of our politics and culture, and to assure self-fulfillment for each individual, our people are guaranteed the right to express any thought, free from government censorship.'[65] In the early years of Athenian democracy, the watchword was *isegoria*, the *equal* right of each and any citizen to speak in public, and it was only in the time of Aristophanes that the emphasis shifted to *parrhesia*, the right and duty to speak out and say *everything*.[66] What mattered in Athens was the active public challenge rather than individual freedom of expression. The generous use of obscenity and insult in Aristophanes created a context in which it seemed that anything could be said, and although there were laws of defamation Creon had no easy way to defend himself before a mass jury without making himself seem ridiculous.[67] Those who applaud Aristophanes as the embodiment of progressive thinking tend to pass over his implicit support for the land-owning classes who had most to gain from a peace-treaty. Dramatists belonged to the leisured classes, and were closely connected to the rich *choregoi* who funded the chorus and all the production expenses,[68] while the urban poor may have been less dominant in the theatre than they were in the law-court since there was less financial incentive to attend.[69]

An alternative line of argument, noting that Cleon and Aristophanes belonged to the same Athenian deme, holds that both were showmen, and masters of verbal insult with a shared interest in public controversy. The caricature of Cleon as a tanner who worked with his hands did no harm to a rich politician seeking to position himself as a man of the people.[70] Words that seem angry and personal when we read them on the page had a different ring when voiced by a masked figure with a padded stomach and large hanging phallus.[71] It is clear that Aristophanic parody relishes the way Euripides broke with convention in his tragedies, and since Cleon broke the rules governing rhetorical performance no less radically and deliberately than Euripides broke the rules for tragic performance, he may have been content enough with the attention he received in the theatre.

A judge in the Constitutional Court of South Africa pronounced in 2005: 'Humour is one of the great solvents of democracy. It permits the ambiguities and contradictions of public life to be articulated in non-violent forms. It promotes diversity. It enables a multitude of discontents to be expressed in a myriad of spontaneous ways. It is an elixir of constitutional health.'[72] If the slave Paphlagon was indeed a characterization of Cleon that both friends and enemies could laugh at with pleasure, then the contradictions and competing perspectives of public life were articulated in a non-violent way that aided mutual understanding. However, the disappearance from comedy of attacks on politicians after the end of the Peloponnesian War forces us to ask whether Aristophanic comedy really was an 'elixir of constitutional health'. Aristophanes' ridicule of Socrates contributed, according to Plato, to the public hostility which culminated in his execution.[73] How to balance freedom of speech against the need to suppress hate-speech has always been a conundrum of democracy, and there is no lack of debate today about humour as a vehicle for racism and misogyny. One of the methodological issues for the historian trying to understand Aristophanic free speech is Golden Age thinking. The reality of democracy was constant change, with power relationships always having to be rebalanced. Like the conventions governing drama, the rules governing democracy had to be kept under constant review if democracy was to survive. Neither Cleon nor Aristophanes could repeat their performances without those performances losing their efficacy.

Plato and Rhetoric

Without public persuasion democracy cannot function. The term 'rhetoric' relates to an indispensable political art, but has been tarred by imputations of mendacity and manipulation. To describe the rhetorical art of Pericles, Plutarch borrowed Plato's term *'psychagogia'*, a 'leading on of men's souls', and defined it as the technique of identifying 'character and emotion, which like the strings and stops of the soul need a musician to touch and play them'.[74] Plato came from a rich family and grew up during the long Peloponnesian war that culminated in military defeat. His great-uncle, a noted playwright, was one of the anti-democratic 'tyrants' imposed on the city by Sparta, killed in the uprising that followed. Plato's philosophical works raise fundamental objections to theatre, to democracy and to rhetoric, and his arguments need to be confronted in any defence of democracy and any defence of theatre. Political rhetoric is the theme of Plato's early dialogue *Gorgias*, where the unspoken context is the impending execution of Plato's mentor Socrates in a politically motivated trial.

The dialogue takes its name from the famous rhetorician Gorgias who first visited Athens in the year of the Mytilene debate, soon after Plato was born. Gorgias came from a democratic town in Sicily that lay just north of a more powerful democracy, Syracuse, and it is an accident of our historical sources that perceptions of ancient politics have been organised around Athens to the exclusion of Syracuse.[75] Both rhetoric, as a learned system for swaying a crowd, and comedy, which entailed the freedom to speak freely, seem to have been children of Sicilian democracy.[76] Gorgias came to Athens hoping to persuade the Athenians to ally themselves with his home town against Syracuse, and his new manner of arguing proved so successful that he quickly set himself up as the first professional teacher of rhetoric in Athens. Gorgias demonstrated how the persuasive power of words rested upon stylistic devices such as antithesis and repetition, driving a wedge between the meaning of words and their style, and forcing people to conceive political speeches in the same terms as poetry. He became in his later years a kind of performance artist, doing set-piece displays of his rhetorical art, either speaking in a fictional situation or improvising in response to challenges from the audience.[77]

At the start of Plato's dialogue, Gorgias has just completed a private demonstration of his skills when he encounters Socrates, who challenges him to engage not in speechmaking but in dialectical debate.[78] Gorgias defends political oratory on the democratic ground that it is 'the source of human freedom, and the means by which anyone can achieve power over others within their city', and he defines rhetoric as the ability 'to use words to persuade jurors in the courtroom, councillors in the *boulê*, the public in the Assembly, and any other sort of political gathering'.[79] Socrates complains that Gorgias' command of language does not involve knowledge of the real world, and forces him into a contradictory stance on ethics: the power of words is held to be value neutral, a force that can be used equally for good or ill, but Gorgias as a teacher acknowledges responsibility for the moral well-being of his students.

At this point Gorgias' student Polos, another Sicilian, comes to the rescue, and celebrates the fact that an orator wields more power than anyone else in the city, equivalent to the power of a 'tyrant'.[80] Young Polos is a more hard-nosed character then his mentor, and it transpires that he has written a book about the art of rhetoric. Socrates unpicks his argument, starting from the premise that the city, the *polis*, is an organism comparable to the human body. Socrates refuses to glorify rhetoric with the label of 'art' when it is merely opportunistic, and likens rhetoric to a fashion item which conceals the natural shape of the body, or to the tricks of a fancy chef whose sauces conceal the natural taste of meat. Such devices flatter the wearer or diner, hiding a flabby body.[81] In terms of Plato's philosophical theory of 'forms', rhetoric offers a mere image, idea or illusion of true political leadership. Just as the body needs a gymnastic trainer or a dietician, Socrates argues, so the mind needs expertise of a kind that no mere wordsmith can provide. Unimpressed, Polos reiterates that rhetoric is the route to political power and thus happiness. The pair mull over various demagogues or 'tyrants' who have risen to power by violent and corrupt means, and Socrates insists that these men are never actually happy, for although they may appear powerful, they are ultimately impotent, trapped by circumstance and unable to do good in the world.[82]

Socrates' third interlocutor is Gorgias' host, Callicles, a rich young Athenian with political ambitions who is learning from Gorgias how to play the democratic system. Callicles mocks the philosophical life as something with no relevance to the adult world of political reality, and launches into a 'might is right' philosophy on the basis that nature favours the fittest. He sees democracy 'moulding the best and healthiest of us, snaring us like cub lions, then using songs and enchantments to enslave us', and sneers at the poor with their demands for redistribution of wealth. His name has vanished from the record, but his extreme views and abrasive manner suggest that the real Callicles may have died in the counterrevolution that followed the war.[83] Callicles' boyfriend is conveniently named 'Demos', allowing Plato to play upon the orator's courtship and flattery of the Athenian masses. Socrates again pulls apart his opponent's premisses: Does 'fittest' refer to strength, intelligence, or bravery? And is not the *demos* manifestly stronger than the elite? Comparing rhetoricians to spiritual doctors, Socrates refuses to accept that any recent political leader has succeeded in making the body politic healthier. Pericles, for example, merely gratified the desires of the people, reflecting their own views back to them, and through his welfare measures he left them lazier and more mercenary than they had been before, much like a herdsman unable to tame his unruly flock.[84]

While Callicles is a hedonist accepting no higher value than personal pleasure, Socrates argues for self-discipline, and his critique of the pleasure principle leads him to cite dramatic performance as an example of collective self-gratification. Performances on the reed-pipe or stringed cithara, choral dancing and song are all designed to please the public rather than turn them into better people, he claims, and the same applies *a fortiori* to the art which combines these elements:

SOCRATES That most sacred and magical thing, tragedy, what is its aim? Is its end and purpose, do you think, just spectator pleasure? Take a scene that is delightful and pleasing but also harmful, isn't bit better to balk the spectators by keeping silent? Or take a situation that is unpleasant yet instructive: shouldn't it be played out in word and song whether it please or no? For which of these two reasons is tragedy performed?

CALLICLES The answer is clear, Socrates. It is driven by pleasure and gratifying the spectators.

SOCRATES	Did we not agree just now, Callicles, that this can be termed flattery?
CALLICLES	Yes we did.
SOCRATES	Now, if we strip tragedy of song, rhythm and metre, is anything left but the words?
CALLICLES	Nothing.
SOCRATES	These words being delivered to a massed public?
CALLICLES	Indeed.
SOCRATES	So tragedy is a mode of public speaking?
CALLICLES	Seemingly so.
SOCRATES	Public speaking, which is to say 'rhetoric'. Or do you consider tragedians something other than orators?
CALLICLES	No.
SOCRATES	So here we see a kind of rhetoric addressed to a *demos* that includes alongside children both women and men, enslaved and free, a rhetoric that we dislike since we have labelled it 'flattery'.
CALLICLES	That's right.
SOCRATES	Well then. What of rhetoric addressed to the Athenian *demos*, or to an assembly of free citizens elsewhere, how should that be regarded? Do you hold that politicians always speak for the best, with the sole aim of bettering the public through their speeches? Aren't they motivated instead by a desire to ingratiate themselves with the *demos*, concerned for self rather than community, treating the public like children, with the one aim of providing gratification, whether for good or for bad.[85]

From this Socratic viewpoint, tragedy and democratic speechmaking are parallel practices that use language not to help the audience but to make them feel good. There is a slippage in this passage from the form of tragedy, where speeches are commonly addressed to a chorus of women and/or slaves, to the broader reality of a theatre audience more diverse than that in the assembly.[86] Plato suggests that tragedy infantilises, feminises and enslaves its audience through creating situations that are absurd, tear-jerking and mesmerising, and that rhetoric in the law-court and Assembly does the same. Just as Gorgias dresses up his language in flowery figures of speech, so tragedy uses verse and song as superficial forms of beautification, concealing its underlying purpose of gratifying desire.

Democratic politicians, according to Plato, have to make their audience feel good, and they use performance techniques in order to succeed. Although the word 'democracy' has always been negotiable, its range of meaning cannot possibly embrace the authoritarian regime described in Plato's *Republic*. Plato's argument challenges ancient democratic ideals and modern liberal values alike, but his case for meritocratic rule by men of wisdom stumbles on the problem that no-one will ever agree what constitutes wisdom. At the end of the *Gorgias*, Socrates turns to religion in order to find a source of absolute ethical authority that will counter any challenge to his own ultimate rightness, and in a striking anticipation of Christianity he imagines souls stripped of their bodies before coming to the court of judgement and being assigned either to heaven (the Isles of the Blessed) or to hell (Tartarus).[87]

In his *Republic*, Plato modelled his typical 'tyrant' upon Dionysius the ruler of Syracuse, describing how he (nominally Socrates but actually Plato) was qualified to portray such a figure after living in his house and witnessing not only the tyrant's public behaviour but also his private dealings when 'stripped bare of his tragic garb'.[88] Syracuse illustrates Plato's principle that by a remorseless logic democracy always slides into populist dictatorship: Dionysius succeeded in becoming a 'tyrant' because he acquired the support of the *demos*, turning them against the monied classes through persuading them that the elite had appropriated public funds dedicated to theatrical entertainment.[89] Plato attempted to turn theory into practice by imparting his own wisdom to Dionysius while transforming Dionysius' son into a budding embodiment of virtue, and he failed.[90] Dionysius cultivated a flamboyant style, and a court historian celebrated his funeral 'as though it were the closing procession in the great tragedy of his tyrantship'.[91] Dionysius learned no moral lessons from his distinguished Athenian guest, but, since one of his tragedies secured victory in a theatre competition in Athens, he may have learned something about dramaturgy.[92] Theatrical skills were of more use than philosophical skills in the real world of ancient politics.

Plato had no viable political answers, but his analysis remains crucial. He reveals how mistaken it is to suppose that if a wise man tells the truth to the masses, frankly and honestly, then that truth will prevail, for democracy turns upon rhetoric. The people have to be persuaded by means of a performance, which is to say by theatre. Theatre and democracy are interwoven. The Athenians had a deep and creative understanding of these twin performance arts, which was key to the durability of their social system. Today theatre has been marginalised as 'art' or 'culture', and in the school curriculum little value is placed on dramatic performance. In a world with no satisfactory forum for political encounters or culture of collective watching and listening, it is scarcely surprising that democracy struggles to function.

CHAPTER 2

Acting versus Sincerity
Aeschines versus Demosthenes

My focus in Chapter 1 was a debate in the Assembly in 427 BCE, presented by Thucydides as a contest between the man of reason and the demagogue. In this chapter, I move forward a century to a battle fought in the law-court between the sometime tragic actor Aeschines and the trained rhetorician Demosthenes (Figure 2.1). The Mytilene debate belonged to an era traditionally thought of as the Athenian golden age, so defined by the Parthenon, the great tragic dramatists and the wealth of the Athenian Empire. The later period is often conceived as the twilight of Athenian democracy on the basis that absolute sovereignty was soon to be lost.[1] In 427 BCE democratic Athens was pitted against Spartan oligarchy, and in 330 BCE against the kingdom of Macedon. Aeschines argued for compromise with Macedon, while Demosthenes, in a speech much admired by posterity, urged Athenians to stand firm against the advancing northern empire. In front of a mass audience this was a test of strength between two men who voiced and embodied two different understandings of democracy.[2] As we saw in Aristophanes' *Wasps*, the law-court was an essential component of the democratic system, where relations of power were negotiated.

Aeschines was not from a moneyed background, and he entered political life at the late age of forty-two. His career as a tragic actor brought him a degree of wealth and status, reinforced by his reputation as a courageous soldier, and established political figures sponsored him because of his physical ability to command the attention of the volatile thousands gathered in the Assembly. Born into a much wealthier family, Demosthenes received an expensive training in rhetoric, which allowed him to start his career writing speeches for others. His core skill was in essence that of the playwright not that of the actor, and speaking in the courts gradually taught him the bodily craft of commanding the Assembly. In the battle between these two figures, Aeschines was a physically imposing figure who relied on the seductive power of his voice, while

39

Figure 2.1 Aeschines (a) and Demosthenes (b): Roman copies of Greek bronze originals.
Source: Statue of Aeschines, from Villa of the Papyri in Herculaneum, now in the National Archaeological Museum, Naples. Photo by Paolo Monti, 1969. Bust of Demosthenes, after a statue by Polyeuktos (c. 280 BCE). Louvre, Paris. Photo placed in the public domain by Eric Gaba.

Demosthenes, ten years his junior, was a slighter man who relied on his exceptional ability to put words together.[3] Demosthenes needed to highlight his opponent's bravura vocal technique and Aeschines the younger man's verbal dexterity, each portraying his opponent's performance skills as barriers to the representation of truth.

The key word for Aeschines was *demokratia* as he urged the jurors to respect the rule of law, while the key word for Demosthenes was *patris* as he told them to put legal niceties aside and behave as patriots. I shall argue in this chapter that Aeschines' background as a tragic actor was bound up with his commitment to the dialogic and provisional values of democracy. In tragedy there are two moral sides to every question, and theatre is always of the moment because the inflections of the actor's voice cannot be preserved. Greek actors needed to be adept in switching masks, maintaining a distance between themselves and the roles they played. Demosthenes, by contrast, championed the timeless values of nationhood in language that has withstood the test of time, and his success lay in persuading the audience that they saw no gap between the person and the public role.[4] He performed his own authenticity in order to sustain his patriotic message.

In the short term, Aeschines lost the vote by a huge margin, and was obliged to leave Athens; and in the longer term, since his voice could not be recorded, it was the published words of Demosthenes that became the centrepiece of a rhetorical education in the Roman Empire and again in the years from the Renaissance to the nineteenth century. Yet Aeschines was also in a sense the winner. He lived to develop a successful career as a teacher of rhetoric in Rhodes, while Demosthenes was hunted down by the Macedonians and committed suicide. Aeschines had a shrewder sense of how things would turn out, although we must not assume that the way history unfolded was inevitable. Demosthenes won the debate because he made the Athenians feel good about themselves, putting fear to one side, while Aeschines asked them to admit they had made a mistake. In the language of today, we might say that Demosthenes looks like a populist, Aeschines a conservative stickler for democratic procedure. Neither, certainly, was a liberal.

The Demosthenes Myth

Demosthenes' reputation has undergone many changes. After his death, Demetrius of Phaleron, who governed Athens on behalf of the Macedonians, portrayed Demosthenes as a decadent, but when democracy was restored his nephew set up a statue to honour him as a democratic hero. In the Roman period rhetoricians welcomed Demetrius' picture of Demosthenes as a master of artifice because it allowed them to market rhetoric as a technique which students could pay to acquire.[5] One of these teachers was Dionysius of Halicarnassus, who used Demosthenes to show his students that political oratory needed to deploy melody, rhythm and metre in order to move an audience, insisting that Aeschines was wrong to criticise his rival's calculated style. Rome was an oral culture, and it was axiomatic for Dionysius that students studying Demosthenes' texts needed to find the intonations, facial expressions and gestures that belonged to the words.[6] Demosthenes worked long and hard not only to hone his language but also to overcome the physical limitations of his body and voice.

In the Renaissance, Demosthenes became an icon of political liberty. The future Queen Elizabeth I, for example, learned Greek and made a close study of *On the Crown*, Demosthenes' speech of 330 BCE, and this training must have helped her compose and then deliver her famous address rallying the troops at Tilbury in face of the Spanish Armada. Protestant England mapped easily onto Athens, Philip II of Macedon onto Philip II of Spain and 'the body but of a weak and feeble woman' onto the physical frailty of Demosthenes.[7] Demosthenes' patriotic agenda made him comfortable reading for the English elite well into the nineteenth century. In the Enlightenment era, however, the Scottish philosopher David Hume was more interested in Demosthenes' emotionalism than his style or patriotism. Demosthenes once galvanised huge audiences, Hume lamented, but in his own day parliamentary orators, even in the extreme case of Robert Walpole's impeachment, seemed incapable of generating the same excitement as an old stage ham like Colley Cibber. What Hume admired in Demosthenes was his fusion of emotion with reason, a result of the orator himself being perceptibly moved by the passions he sought to impart. The eloquence of Antiquity, which Hume took to mean 'the sublime and passionate, is of a much juster taste than the modern', which is to say 'the argumentative and rational'. Although he was happy to endorse the democratic principle that ultimately the 'lowest vulgar of Athens' ruled Demosthenes, Hume added the proviso that in reality 'orators formed the taste of the Athenian people'. The educated elite, in other words, retained control of the podium and the power to shape how people thought.[8] Demosthenes' modern biographer Ian Worthington tells his readers that

> rhetoric as a formal art developed in tandem with democracy, enticing ambitious men to exploit it for their own political advancement. The downside was that very often an Assembly was swayed not so much by the content of speeches (and thus the validity of propositions) but by the speakers' rhetorical performance.[9]

From Hume's perspective, Worthington's separation of 'content' from 'rhetoric' exemplifies the prejudice of an academic. Reason can never be extrapolated from feeling, and democratic politics has always relied upon what Hume calls 'eloquence' to move the heart.

In revolutionary France, Aeschines' political sponsor Phocion seemed a more heroic figure than Demosthenes, an embodiment of tight-lipped stoic values martyred for his devotion to the city.[10] At the end of the Reign of Terror the Jacobin leader Saint-Just nevertheless invoked Demosthenes when trying to exonerate Robespierre from the charge of demagogic tyranny, in a desperate speech prepared for the Convention that was silenced before he could get started:

> Those who have swayed public opinion were always the foes of oppression. Was Demosthenes a tyrant? If so, it was his tyranny that preserved for so long the freedom of Greece. Jealous mediocrity likes to drag genius to the scaffold. If the gift of oratory, now practised by yourselves, is the gift of a

despot, then the accusation will soon come that you are likewise tyrannizing thought. The right to influence public opinion is a natural right ... Have you ever seen an orator stood below a royal sceptre? No. Around thrones, silence reigns. Only amongst free peoples has the right to persuade one's peers been granted.[11]

Saint-Just went to his death in denial about the ancient problem of the demagogue that was always a feature of democratic Athens.

It was only in the nineteenth century that a 'democratic' Demosthenes came into fashion. The Whig politician Thomas Babington Macaulay rescued Demosthenes' political reputation in 1823, likening him to Washington and Franklin who in their day endured much British abuse, and contrasting him with Aeschines 'the orator of aristocracy'. Democracy, Macaulay believed, is always a better form of government than aristocracy even though 'it is but one step that separates the demagogue and the sovereign', and he hailed the way Demosthenes at a distance of two thousand years still 'stirs our blood and brings tears into our eyes'. Seeing that democracy relies on an educated electorate, Macaulay idealised the Athenians as men who benefited from seeing the Parthenon sculptures, grasping the arguments of Socrates, hearing recitations of Homer and attending the theatre. Macaulay's Demosthenes, unlike modern politicians who skim pamphlets, acquired wisdom through copying out Thucydides six times.[12] George Grote in his twelve-volume *History of Greece* (1846–56) elaborated Macaulay's idea that Athens was a model for libertarian democracy, arguing that the Athenian jurors who supported Demosthenes against Aeschines displayed 'fidelity and steadiness of mind'.[13]

Plutarch's Demosthenes

Whether democrat or patriot, Demosthenes was fixed by Plutarch's biography as a flawed hero, a man of magnificent words but not always magnificent action. In Plutarch's account of Demosthenes' death, Demosthenes takes refuge in a temple after the fall of Athens, and is hunted down by a Macedonian who was once a tragic actor, which prompts him to dream that he is participating in a theatrical competition; although in Demosthenes' dream he out-acts his rival, he fails to win the prize thanks to the inadequacy of his *choregia*, that is, the supporting chorus, costumes and scenery supplied by a wealthy sponsor. Next day, when the Macedonian bounty-hunter makes a string of seductive promises, Demosthenes complains that he was never convinced by this man's performances on stage, and when the Macedonian loses his temper, Demosthenes responds that acting has now been replaced by the oracle, that is, truth. Granted permission to write a last letter, Demosthenes discreetly sucks poison from his reed pen. When he is accused of cowardice because of the way he hides his face, Demosthenes looks up and likens his opponent to the tyrannical Creon in Sophocles' *Antigone*, himself the corpse that will prove Creon's undoing.[14]

Plutarch's biography makes much of the story that Demosthenes had a speech impediment and needed a tragic actor to tutor him in taking command of the *demos*,[15] and the tale of his death catches the underlying reality that tragic acting and political debate were twin forms of competitive rhetorical performance.[16] Aeschines came into politics because professional actors made natural ambassadors, thanks not only to their vocal skills but also to their knowledge of how different audiences in different parts of Greece tended to respond.[17] Plutarch notes that any politician needs to understand the particular character of his public, contrasting the volatile but tolerant nature of the Athenians with the dourness of the Carthaginians.[18] While Aeschines came to public attention as an actor, Demosthenes established his profile through deploying his personal wealth strategically, sponsoring theatrical events alongside fortifications and warships. The dream narrated by Plutarch reflects a famous controversy when the young Demosthenes went to court to complain of how, when serving as funder of the performance and leader of the dance, he had to put up with his chorus being intimidated, his costumes tampered with and then physical assault when he paraded through the theatre, humiliations which led to defeat in the theatrical competition.[19] Theatre was an integral part of democratic life, and Demosthenes was frustrated in this early attempt to justify his wealth by giving a fine gift to the people.

Aeschines and Demosthenes were fellow ambassadors at the Macedonian court at a moment when the fate of Athens hinged on whether the king's oracular promises were to be trusted, so the question of trust resonates when Demosthenes tests to see if the bounty-hunter is merely acting.[20] This lie-detector test echoes a tale earlier in the biography where Demosthenes provokes a prospective client to anger in order to establish his honesty, and it is clear that his own particular skill lay in his ability to communicate through word, face and body something felt to be authentic emotion.[21] Plutarch's Demosthenes goes to his death as a tragic hero who avoids polluting the god's altar, and here again anecdote is a vehicle for symbolic truth. In *On the Crown*, Demosthenes positions himself as a tragic victim of the gods' will, with the Athenian people his sympathetic chorus, demanding that heroism be chosen over mediocrity.[22]

The Setting

The debate in 330 BCE was effectively a rematch. Thirteen years earlier Demosthenes failed to convict Aeschines of taking bribes from Philip, but did enough damage to neutralise him as a political opponent. Five years after that, the allied forces of Athens and Thebes were defeated by Macedon in the decisive battle of Chaeronea.[23] Philip acted ruthlessly against Thebes, demolishing the city and enslaving the population, but did not try to attack the larger city of Athens. Although Aeschines, Phocion and others had long argued for compromise, their influence was eclipsed by the militant Demosthenes, whose hold over the Assembly proved so strong that after the battle, far from enduring a backlash, he was asked, like Pericles, to deliver the funeral address over the bodies of the slain. Aeschines threatened prosecution two years after Chaeronea, and it was probably the death of Philip that stopped him proceeding, but by 330 Philip's successor Alexander the Great was growing too powerful, and Aeschines must have judged that the public mood had turned against Demosthenes.[24]

These political battles intertwined with personal animosities were fought out in the law-court, where more sustained listening was possible than in the hurly-burly of the Assembly.[25] The case in 330 turned on the legality of a proposal to honour Demosthenes with a crown of gold at the Dionysia, the great annual theatrical festival, in appreciation of his political services. Here art sat in a complex relation to politics. When serving as *choregos* or 'sponsor', Demosthenes could legitimately sport a crown in the theatre because he was gifting the Athenian people with a performance, but an overtly political coronation strayed across a symbolic threshold. For Aeschines this was more like the crowning of a demagogue than the crowning of a public servant, and in the place where tragedy normally confronted moral uncertainty the Athenian people were being asked to applaud a public hero with no questions asked. Technically, Aeschines was prosecuting the man who proposed the crowning, but everyone knew that Demosthenes would be called to the rostrum, and Demosthenes seized the occasion to rally his supporters and set out his career as that of a lifelong patriot.

The law-court was a cornerstone of the democratic system, a place where hasty proposals could be thrown out as unconstitutional in a vital check upon the unpredictability of the Assembly.[26] This trial was probably an all-day affair, and the jury could have numbered 1001, but 501 and 1501 have also been suggested.[27] Athenian jurors were chosen by an elaborate process of sortition to minimise the risk of bribery and lobbying, and were assigned seats so there could be no question of claques as in the Assembly. Voting was by secret ballot, and not as in the Assembly by a show of hands, so everything was done to ensure that jurors would hold to the terms of their oath, vote impartially and follow their personal sense of natural justice when the legalities were unclear. Jurors were paid for their work, and thus in practice were representative members of the common *demos*, although they had to be over the age of thirty in another check on the impulsiveness of the Assembly. Architecturally, courts were no more than fenced-off areas in a corner of the marketplace, with twin rostra set up for prosecutor and defendant, who were each framed by their separate entourages, and in this informal space protocols lent solemnity to the proceedings.[28] Staging was always crucial. Aeschines anticipated that Demosthenes would seek to exploit class divisions, pointing to a supposed oligarchic faction gathered around Aeschines' rostrum, and he countered by identifying his supporters as the only true democrats.[29] Because this trial had a high political profile, a crowd of spectators stood outside the fence that enclosed the benches and rostra.[30]

The magistrate assigned to the case was responsible for procedure but not for guiding the jury, and there were no lawyers to speak on behalf of the plaintiff and defendant. All Athenian citizens had to be capable of defending themselves in court. As a civic culture, Athens placed a high value not only on public speaking but also on the active process of public listening. The spontaneous outbursts of a divided audience reinforced the obvious fact that beneath its legal technicalities this trial was a political fight, and part of the democratic process. The jurors were both spectators and performers, playing out their citizen role under the watchful gaze of fellow-citizens and visitors outside the fence. Plato describes the infectious power of a *thorubos*, the standard Greek word for a noisy crowd response:

> When the *hoi polloi* crowd together in assemblies, law-courts, theatres, musters, or some such gathering of the masses, they complain in a *thorubos* about parts of what they see and hear, applaud the other bits, never in moderation but shouting and stamping, with the noise of their complaints and applause amplified by echoes from the rock or walls. In such circumstances, what young man could, so to speak, hold his heart in check? What sort of private tutoring could ever equip him to hold firm, and not be overwhelmed by all the protests and cheers which sweep him along in their flow, until he comes at last to accept these same views about what is noble or vile, strives for the same thing, becomes the same.[31]

It was not easy for speakers who faced a hostile *thorubos*, and Demosthenes begins one of his speeches with an apology, saying that a person sometimes gets it right, sometimes gets it wrong, and so deserves a silent hearing.³² From a modern liberal perspective, *thorubos* seems deeply undemocratic, an interference with the freedom of the individual to form an independent opinion. In Athens, however, the ability to shout and stamp and ultimately boo a speaker off the stage enhanced rather than damaged the ability to listen, and was experienced by many citizens as a democratic freedom.³³ Taking issue with Plato's elitism, Aristotle saw some wisdom in crowd responses, arguing that crowds can coalesce into a single human entity with effectively one set of legs, arms and sense organs, one character and one intellect, but although a unified crowd was better than a handful of individuals in judgements about performances, he thought collective wisdom too dangerous when it came to democracy.³⁴ Though it may seem to us paradoxical, particularly in northern cultures which have learned to suppress public emotion, the intensity of an Athenian *thorubos* was bound up with the intensity of listening accorded to the spoken word. Freedom of *thorubos* meant that a speech delivered from the rostrum or in a play was not a communication transmitted in a single direction from speaker to listener but was a speech-act jointly created by both parties. The actor or orator had to gauge every word spoken in relation to the response feeding back to him.

The historian has to rely on texts assembled after the event by Aeschines and Demosthenes on the basis of memory, notes and drafts, reflecting what in retrospect they would like to have said bearing in mind the arguments of their opponent. In his early years as a writer of speeches for others, Demosthenes learnt the art of creating an illusion of spontaneity, and that illusion is built into the text of *On the Crown* transmitted to posterity. We glimpse the power of *thorubos* when he mimics Aeschines's complaint that Demosthenes will charge him with being Alexander's friend:

> Quite the opposite. You are in his pay, first hired by Philip then by Alexander – as all these men will confirm. If you doubt me, ask. Or I will do it for you. Men of Athens, what do you reckon? Is Aeschines in the pay (*misthôtos*) of Alexander, or his friend (*xenos*) . . .? You hear the answer.³⁵

Demosthenes could count on the hiss and long vowel of *misthôtos* drowning out the competing *xenos*. Many of the first readers of these published texts would have been present at the trial, so we can take them as being at least reflections of what was actually said. Alcidamas, a student of Gorgias, likened written texts to bronze statues that merely imitate the live human body, arguing that only a tyrant would force citizens to sit through memorised renditions of scripted speeches.[36] Orators, he explained, need to focus on arguments rather than a precise form of words so they can adapt themselves to the ploys of opponents. Nor can written speeches deal with the challenge of timing:

> It is hard, maybe impossible, for the human mind to predict the future, and thus foresee precisely what an audience will think is the right length they should speak for. Those who improvise their speeches can manage their words according to their hold over the spectators, cutting short longeurs, and laying out what they had planned to omit.[37]

From this perspective, improvisation is inherently more democratic than speaking from a script, for it does not tyrannise listeners but keeps responding to them in an interactive process that involves the eye as well as the ear. When transposed into written form, speeches obscure what Erika Fischer-Lichte has called the 'ever-changing feedback loop' characteristic of live performance.[38] Demosthenes was more skilled than Aeschines in using his pen to create the retrospective illusion of interaction.

The Politics of Personality

Aeschines begins his speech by insisting on the rule of law, and his underlying message is simple: 'when citizens observe the laws, democracy is safe'.[39] He traces this axiom back to the great lawgiver Solon, who at the start of the 500s BCE established a democratic structure in Athens which reconciled rich and poor, allowing poor citizens to serve on juries and vote in the Assembly.[40] The principle that jurors are bound by an oath to vote in accordance with the law sounds simple enough, but in reality laws are often contradictory. Rightly anticipating that Demosthenes will sidestep questions of legality, Aeschines warns the jurors about rhetorical tricks that will divert their attention. The battle for hearts and minds would be won by stories rather than technicalities, and Aeschines knew full well that he had to construct an account of Demosthenes' career that would prove more compelling than Demosthenes' counter-narrative. In the picture he paints, the Athenian Council and the Assembly have been reduced to chaos, subverted by the likes of Demosthenes so that decisions are made in anger, and Aeschines holds up a functioning law-court as the only protection for the constitution.[41]

Aeschines did not need David Hume to explain to him about the driving importance of emotion in any rhetorical contest. Thirteen years earlier, he successfully eliminated Demosthenes' key supporter with an outrageous exercise in character assassination, making accusations that were evidently untrue but funny enough to raise a laugh from the jurors at the expense of the victim. Demosthenes' riposte on that occasion was to charge Aeschines with bribery, never producing a scrap of evidence but reiterating the charge so often that it came to seem believable.[42] The challenge now for Aeschines was to generate the emotion of fear as he reminded the jurors of their recent humiliation in battle, and he did his best to convince them that they risked their own and their families' lives by continuing to support Demosthenes. His solution to the problem of making his listeners think the unthinkable and imagine their own downfall was to evoke the world of tragedy where pity and fear were legitimate emotions, and where it was possible within the frame of art to visualise the fate of a fallen city like Thebes. He reminds the jurors of the parade of war-orphans that used to take place in the theatre at the time of the Peloponnesian War, contrasting this public recognition of loss and death with Demosthenes' arrogant insistence on being crowned in the same location.[43] Demosthenes ultimately won because he knew how to make the jurors feel good about themselves, pumping them up with pride in the achievements of their ancestors and blaming Aeschines for letting 'his hatred of *me* lead him on to demean and dismiss *your* finest moments'.[44]

Ultimately this was a battle between two personalities standing before an audience and competing for its trust. Both men needed to prove that on the one hand they were common Athenians just like the jurors, and on the other were exceptional individuals endowed with natural authority. Their characters emerged through their manner of speaking. Here is Aeschines, who playfully claims authority by pretending he has had a preview of Demosthenes' speech, and knows that Demosthenes plans to set out a four-stage career.

> When he [Demosthenes] has listed these, he intends – I gather – to call me forward and put the question: to which of these four phases does my prosecution relate? Precisely when do I claim he failed to act in the best political interests of the *demos*? Supposing I won't reply, but will cover my face and cower, he plans to rip off my cloak, and drag me to the rostrum, and force me to respond. So *he* doesn't get above himself, so *you* can be forewarned, so *I* can reply, in front of this jury, Demosthenes, and all these citizens beyond the fence, and all those other Greeks concerned enough to come along to the trial – in greater numbers than any can recall attending a court case – my answer is 'guilty' in all your four stages however you chop them up, and if the gods be willing, and the jury listens without bias, and if all those many things I know about you don't overwhelm my memory, I have utter confidence I shall prove to this jury that the city owes her

> survival to the gods, and also to men with humane and moderate political views, while each and every disaster stems from Demosthenes.[45]

Aeschines organises his thinking in triads, each of which builds up to a miniature climax, and can be marked by gesture. The three-part structure, easy to recall and easy for the jurors to grasp as they listen and watch, testifies to the oral roots of Aeschines' speech.

> When he [Demosthenes] has listed these, he intends – I gather – to call me forward and put the question: to which of these four phases does my prosecution relate? Precisely when do I claim he failed to act in the best political interests of the *demos*? Supposing (1) I won't reply, but will (2) cover my face and (3) cower, he plans to (1) rip off my cloak, and (2) drag me to the rostrum, and (3) force me to respond. So (1) *he* doesn't get above himself, (2) so *you* can be forewarned, (3) so *I* can reply, in front of (1) this jury, Demosthenes, and (2) all these citizens beyond the fence, and (3) all those other Greeks concerned enough to come along to the trial – in greater numbers than any can recall attending a court case – my answer is 'guilty' in all your four stages however you chop them up, and (1) if the gods be willing, (2) and the jury listens without bias, and (3) if all those many things I know about you don't overwhelm my memory, I have utter confidence I shall prove to this jury (1) that the city owes her survival to the gods, (2) and also to men with humane and moderate political views, (3) while each and every disaster stems from Demosthenes.

The long final sentence illustrates the amplitude of the voice for which Aeschines was famous, as it builds without a perceptible pause for breath to the final word with accompanying pointed finger: 'Demosthenes'.

Here is a sample of Demosthenes, who is characteristically more succinct:

> Cunning plan, Aeschines, but it's proof you are some idiot, to dream I would stop discussing past events and politics and let your insults divert me. Never will I do that. I am hardly so gullible. As far as my political record goes, I shall refute each and every lie and accusation; and as for your dingdong comic turn, once I'm done, and should I be asked, don't imagine I'll let it go.[46]

Demetrius of Phaleron recalled how training techniques helped Demosthenes overcome shortness of breath and an inability to sound his 'r's. Familiar with this account of Demosthenes' weak constitution, Dionysius of Halicarnassus explained to students 300 years later how the orator's literary style was a product of his physical body, entailing a constant switch of moral and emotional registers with all their accompanying gestures, intonations and rhythms. Understanding what it must have felt like to experience Demosthenes in the flesh, he told his students that to read Demosthenes was to be caught up in a swirl of emotion that felt like participating in a Dionysiac dance.[47]

In his first contest with Aeschines, Demosthenes exploited his own physical limitations:

> Who has, do you think, the strongest bellow in Athens? Whose voice displays the best elocution? Aeschines here, of course! Who do these men [the jury] say is the shyest, most nervous of a crowd, or as I'd put it the most 'reticent'? Me. Because I never bullied you or forced you to act against your will ... So how come then the biggest brutes in Athens, the loudest bellowers, find that I, with no bravery about me, and a voice no bigger than anyone else's, cut them to size? Because there is strength in truth, and a corrupt conscience cripples. That's what stops their bravado, curbs their tongues, shuts their mouths, chokes them, reduces them to silence.[48]

Demosthenes regularly draws a line between Aeschines' base character and the beauty of his powerful voice, and in *On the Crown*, he accuses his rival of going to law with the sole purpose of displaying his word-craft and vocals.

> The words of an orator, Aeschines, have no value, nor does the timbre of his voice, but only choosing what the many choose, saying no or yes to the same men as the country [*patris*] does.[49]

Although the sentiment is profoundly undemocratic, Demosthenes successfully exploits here the ordinariness of his own voice to position himself as the voice of the fatherland and thus the true democrat.

Aeschines' voice was the product of a powerful physique, and he uses it to capture the slightness, instability and deviousness of Demosthenes with a vignette of the orator 'circling about on the rostrum'. Demosthenes' rapid switching from 'you Aeschines' to 'you the jurors' helps us to imagine the physical reality of this 'circling'. Aeschines' caricature of his opponent is the preamble to an extended comparison between the democratic and the oligarchic human being. As we saw in Chapter 1, an Athenian politics of the body began a century earlier when Cleon broke decorum by freeing his arms and deploying the language of insult.[50] When prosecuting Demosthenes' supporter Timarchus, Aeschines asked his audience to recall a famous statue of Solon which portrayed the great lawgiver standing with his hands clasped beneath his cloak, and went on to picture the scene when Timarchus 'throwing off his cloak, naked, gave a kind of boxing display in the Assembly, and made such a revolting and shocking spectacle of his body, so drunk and bestial he was, that decent men covered their eyes, ashamed for our city, ashamed of *us* for heeding such specimens as this.'[51] Aeschines kept working away at the idea that Timarchus was a man who sold his body, inviting the jurors to draw their own conclusions. 'Can't you see who he is, Timarchus, this old fart? We may never visit the gymnasium, but we can still recognise athletes from the healthy way they hold themselves; and as for tarts, we might never catch them in the act, but from their flaunting, their bravado, their little ways, we know just who they are.'[52] To be a democrat, Aeschines argues, is to practise bodily self-restraint, while sexual freedom paves the way for tyranny.

Aeschines' evocation of Solon's statue was part of a strategy to align himself with traditionalist values, a posture that was punctured when Demosthenes pointed out that the statue in question was a modern one, joking that Aeschines liked to poke his own hands out of his cloak to collect bribes, before turning Solon back on him in order to mock the way he liked to strut about the marketplace.[53] Aeschines in response pursued the same line of attack that worked against Timarchus, accusing an effete Demosthenes of seducing a youth for money, while holding up his own military record as proof of manliness.[54] Though Demosthenes was able to afford a stronger intellectual education, Aeschines goads the audience to laugh in acknowledgement that Demosthenes clearly never trained in any gymnasium.[55] When prosecuting Timarchus, Aeschines succeeded in embodying an old-fashioned, disciplined and virile version of democratic man that stood its ground against the fluid democratic body of Demosthenes. In *On the Crown*, Demosthenes changed his tactic and focused not on the democratic body, but on the democratic voice in its complex relationship to truth. It was more straightforward for Demosthenes to separate Aeschines' voice from his words, than for Aeschines to separate Demosthenes' words from what lay behind them, words that Demosthenes knew how to frame with a startling directness.

The challenge for the speaker was always to *other* the performance of his opponent, reaching out to the audience to create a common 'we' that could be distinguished from the 'he' who stood on the opposite platform.[56] Aeschines knew how to spin a good tale, but he could not get away from the difficult story that 'we' were men who had failed:

> The *demos*, traumatised by recent events, like victims of dementia or delusion, cling only to the label 'democracy', while the real thing has departed elsewhere. When you come away from the Assembly, you have not been debating, it's more like a banquet where you have been fed nothing but scraps.[57]

They the people turn into *you* the men who have failed to engage in proper democratic debate. Cleon displayed a savage wit when throwing this challenge at his audience, but for Aeschines, Chaeronea was a man-made catastrophe, and the vision of Athens which the ex-tragedian offered was essentially tragic. Demosthenes' response was brilliantly circular: *you* the *demos* awarded me a crown because the award reflects glory back on *you*. Defiantly he blamed military disaster on the gods. 'Yet you [Aeschines] reject that, put the blame on me, my policy being the same as these men's here, as you full well know, and your slanders are also an attack upon one and all, and "all" includes yourself.'[58] While Aeschines the former actor urges the jurors to think how to perform their democratic duty as they cast their individual ballots under the eyes of others,[59] Demosthenes the former *choregos* choreographs the jury as natural heroes, a more comfortable role to play.

Acting and Sincerity

"Sincerity. If you can fake that you've got it made." For literary critic Jerome McGann this was 'one of the most notorious proverbs of post-Modernism'.[60] Theatre director and pedagogue Peter Hall cites a variant, replacing 'sincerity' with 'honesty' and, in common with many, attributes the axiom to the comedian George Burns.[61] In the contest between Aeschines and Demosthenes, sincerity, or its synonym honesty, is the central issue. In 330 BCE it was not the wisdom or usefulness of the politician's advice that mattered, but the sincerity of his devotion to the *demos*, with charges of insincerity always tied to financial corruption. Though Demosthenes keeps reverting to Aeschines' background as an actor, he does not follow the modern line of argument derived from Plato which holds that acting is inherently a form of pretending. The Athenians knew that acting was a rule-governed form, a rhetorical art of persuasion, and that democracy needed skilled public speakers, but Demosthenes succeeded nevertheless in opening up a gap between the authentic person of Aeschines and the words he spoke in order to undermine the authority of his voice. Cleon and Diodotos in Thucydides focused their argument on policy, but Demosthenes and Aeschines bring everything back to personal honesty in what seems part of a bigger cultural shift.

A new tendency to psychologise is clear in the visual arts but most conspicuous in the theatre. This was no longer the age of Aristophanes where the emblem of the phallus attached to a bodysuit certified that all human beings are driven by animal instinct. The new comic dramatist who emerged in the late 300s, and whose plays remained classics for centuries to follow, was Menander, and in Menander's love stories everything turns on the sincerity or emotional honesty of the heterosexual bourgeois lovers. This new genre, a precursor of twentieth-century naturalism, used theatrical masks that had to be deciphered for clues to psycho-physical characteristics.[62] In *The Hated Man*, for example, one of Menander's most popular plays, a handsome mercenary purchases a Greek war captive and falls in love with her, treating her as his wife. On account of a captured sword, she believes he has killed her brother and rejects him. The comedy is poignant in its portrayal of despair, exemplified by the lover's opening monologue to the night sky, his suicidal thoughts and his decision to release the enslaved heroine in an attempt to convince her of the depth of his love. Homosexual love was bound by social rules and Aeschines contrasts his own regulated courtship of young men with Timarchus' wild abandon,[63] but Menander's world sits outside the domain of civic scrutiny, and it is only true love that restrains the mercenary from raping his legal property. It is not the body of his beloved that he wants her to give him but her *nous*, her 'mind'. Tears and flaming eyes testify to the authenticity of his feeling, and he wonders if drink will help him acquire a *psyche* made of stone, while an Asiatic slave measures the heroine's behaviour against the norm of what is *anthropinon*, 'human'. There is a formulaic happy ending when the girl's brother turns up and her father puts down a dowry to permit legal marriage.[64] Just as the values of Hollywood were locked into those of twentieth-century US democracy, so the values of Menander were locked into those of Greek democracy at the end of the 300s BCE. The personal values of sincerity and honesty counted for more than the value of political action in a world torn apart by Macedonian warlords.

Since actors were not held to be inherently dishonest and insincere, Demosthenes had to develop a different line of attack. Firstly, he homed in on the child performer. Since the acting profession was attached to the religious cult of Dionysus, Demosthenes pictures the boy Aeschines ululating in a hocus-pocus initiation ceremony, undermining any charisma created by the music of the actor's voice.[65] Secondly, since Aeschines liked to caricature Demosthenes as 'Batalos' ('arse-hole'),[66] Demosthenes counter-attacked by linking Aeschines to the drunken Dionysiac ritual of trading insults with bystanders.[67] Thirdly, he built an association in the mind of the audience between Aeschines and the anti-democratic roles which brought the actor to fame. Having joked about Creon in the earlier contest, he turns to another doomed Sophoclean tyrant, basing his joke upon some humiliation that befell Aeschines at a performance in one of the local demes.[68] Since Greek tragedy was performed in masks, there could be no direct linkage of the stage tyrant to the face of the man who now spoke from the podium, but the voice was a constant. Demosthenes pictures naïve foreigners who were once taken in by Aeschines the ambassador on account of the actor's plausible stories and 'words with fine masks', confident that Athenian jurors will be able to read through the face to penetrate Aeschines' 'soul, his thoughts, his judgement'.[69] Demosthenes invites them, so to speak, to read Aeschines' character without reference to the plot. This was the new cultural idea, that a person can be separated from what they do.

Plato shifted the paradigms of Western thought with his persuasive account of a disconnect between the material body and the soul or *psyche*. Demosthenes responds to a new way of thinking about human beings when he implies that Aeschines' soul is legible beneath the surface of his words: 'What greater crime could be committed by any public orator', he asks, 'than failing to speak as he thinks? You have been discovered now. To ramble on, while looking these men in the face, how dare you?' Demosthenes claims that he was chosen over Aeschines to deliver the funeral speech after Chaeronea because the Athenians did not want a speaker who would 'act with his *voice* tears over the fate of the fallen, but one who in his *soul* would grieve with them'.[70] Aeschines meanwhile 'neither voiced the sentiments of a decent fair-minded citizen, nor did he weep, nor did he feel anything in his soul, but in a loud voice, full-throat, he crowed, thinking of course, because in face of the catastrophe he wasn't moved like everybody else, that this was evidence against *me*, not an indictment of himself'. Demosthenes concludes that Aeschines may claim to care about legality and constitutionality, but if he cannot feel the same sorrows and joys as the many, then he is not on the side of the community.[71] In short, when choosing a leader, the Athenians should be guided by the authenticity of the speaker's emotions.

Demosthenes goes on to compare the blasting voice of Aeschines to a gale: 'well trained, no pause between phrases, each word joined to the next without any intake of breath – but all to no avail ...'. The technique has no value, insists Demosthenes, if the words are not produced by a 'just soul', while his own qualification to lead Athens rests upon an 'upright, just and uncorrupted soul'.[72] In his peroration, Aeschines opens up the tragic stops to declaim: 'Earth and Sun and Virtue! Intellect! Education! We have these things to tell good from bad ...' Demosthenes caricatures his language, mocking its staginess to imply that such words do not bear witness to sound political judgement, which should turn on something more intuitive, a feeling that the speaker is sincere and sees the world through the selfsame eyes as the democratic listener.[73] Aeschines' tragic voice may have served well to evoke the heroes of a bygone age, but it does not belong to the present. By positioning himself as a man of the here and now and not a product of history, Demosthenes works to create a sense of intimacy, as a man who is not set apart as a performer but is at one with his audience.

Aeschines' skill as a masked actor was to fill the theatre with the richness of sound, so the audience could respond to the power of the story and the poetry, but Demosthenes was a man who knew how to bring tears to his eyes so that his performed emotions seemed to emerge directly from his soul. Aeschines tried to inoculate the jurors against Demosthenes, asking them to imagine themselves seated in the theatre, pondering why they cry over the fiction of a tragedy yet fail to weep over Athens' real mistakes. Tears are the essence of the problem since they appear to betoken emotional truth, and Aeschines points to the danger of responding to Demosthenes' weeping and to the raised pitch that accompanies tears.[74] When he charts Athens' mistakes, Aeschines warns the jurors to beware of Demosthenes' lies as he 'steals your ears, and imitates men who tell the truth, which is why he deserves to be scorned as a villain who tramples all signs of nobility.'[75] The issue becomes one of representation when Aeschines complains that Demosthenes wants to create a performance without *signs*.[76] But the question turns also upon class. The heroic body language of Aeschines was tied to an elite system of values, and the moral categories of villain/noble (*poneros/chrestos*) slide into class distinctions. In reality a much richer man than Aeschines, Demosthenes presented himself to the jurors as a spontaneous human being uninflected by class. The triumph of Demosthenes' rhetorical art was to efface the signs of his art.

The twentieth-century theories of Brecht and Stanislavski offer a lens through which to view the contest between these two orators. Aeschines gives the jurors his view of democratic spectatorship:

> Just as you watch boxers during their bouts struggle to position themselves, so should you do now, battle all day long to place yourselves in relation to the argument. Don't let him step outside the bounds of the legal point at issue, and stay on your guard, listen if you can catch him out, prod him into discussion of the law, watch out for diversionary chat.[77]

Brecht advocated a similar critical attitude, envisaging a smokers' theatre where the audience might puff at cigars like aficionados watching a boxing match.[78] Aeschines does not simply ask the spectators to sit back and judge but wants active engagement in order to keep Demosthenes to the point, for the two orators were not confined to a script but kept adapting to the noisy responses of the audience. E. R. Hapgood's 1937 translation of Stanislavski's *An Actor Prepares* was a seminal text which encouraged the English-speaking world to think that the first job of actors was to develop a 'psycho-technique' and concentrate on internal rather than external methods, the key message being that '[t]ruth on the stage is whatever we can believe in with sincerity, whether in ourselves or in our colleagues'. In a claim borrowed from Cicero, Stanislavski maintains that inner conviction is visible through the eyes, for '[t]he vacant eye is the mirror of the empty soul. It is important that an actor's eyes, his look, reflect the deep inner content of his soul'.[79] Brecht worried about actors who use tears to force spectators into a surrender of judgement, and challenged the axiom of the Roman poet Horace: 'If you want me to weep, first show me your own eye full of tears.'[80] Demosthenes deployed his glistening eyes to communicate what supposedly lay in his *psyche*, using broken sentence structures to create a direct and apparently spontaneous connection to the breath, causing Aeschines to complain that Demosthenes was a liar who knew how to 'swear an oath by means of his shameless eyes'.[81] Stanislavski's method was in reality complex, and so was that of Demosthenes, who according to Plutarch not only worked on his vocal and physical technique but also studied the behaviour of others in a state of emotion, and could when necessary push himself into a state of Dionysiac possession.[82] Stanislavski helps us understand how Demosthenes could be both sincere and insincere at the same time.

Was This Democracy?

Demosthenes and Aeschines provide a test case if we want to debate whether Athens remains a beacon for modern democracy. On this occasion the Athenians were persuaded and public policy turned, and at a later date Demosthenes lost his hold over the people, convicted of bribery. With the benefit of hindsight, should we see the contest in 330 BCE as a model of good democratic practice, or a testament to failure? To evaluate this trial, we need to reflect on how we ourselves are products of history. Queen Elizabeth I, David Hume and Thomas Babington Macauley all came to Demosthenes with historically conditioned assumptions, and judged accordingly.

In Chapter 1, I focused upon Cleon and Diodotos arguing over the punishment of Mytilene. Historians have broadly painted Cleon as the villain of the story, while Demosthenes is more often portrayed as a hero, but Cleon and Demosthenes both argued for war rather than compromise, both were associated with the *demos* rather than the elite in a murky divide, and both men developed a politics of the body to dissociate themselves from tradition. Both, in short, trod the same fine line that divides the democrat from the demagogue. Almost a century apart, both debates attempted to reverse a decision of the *demos*, giving people a chance to reflect back on choices that might have been too hasty – to annihilate the people of Mytilene, to crown Demosthenes as a public hero. By 330 BCE the law-court had emerged as a counterweight and corrective to an Assembly that succumbed too easily, always subject to public frenzy. A more important shift, however, was not institutional but cultural. Aristotle complained that in his day 'actors have become more powerful than poets, and the same thing happens in political contests because of the decay of polities'.[83] Demosthenes and Aeschines critique each other's performances in the knowledge that political decisions will turn upon who performs best, but this does not necessarily imply decay of the democratic polity. Aeschines complained that constitutional principles were being overlooked, but from the perspective of Demosthenes Aeschines had the same goal as Aristotle, to allow an educated elite to continue discreetly managing the *demos*.

Like most biographers Plutarch tends to develop a sympathy with his subjects, and he praises the nobility of the Athenian jurors who acquitted Demosthenes after a pro-Macedonian party had taken control.[84] Plutarch's biographies were themselves contributions to a rhetorical education which preferred dialogic principles to any quest for ultimate truth, and he also penned a sympathetic biography of Phocion, contrasting Phocion's incisiveness with Demosthenes' verbal flummery.[85] Phocion was Aeschines' political mentor, standing as his witness and advocate in the prosecution of Timarchus,[86] lacking Aeschines' verbal fluency but cultivating the same dignified manliness. Plutarch's Phocion is both a pragmatist and a patriot, never afraid to speak his mind to the people, brave in battle but even more courageous as a lone political voice saying no to war. Plutarch thus offers us a usefully balanced take on our modern judgements. He tells how Phocion once mocked an overweight emissary who needed to drink water while urging the Athenians to fight Philip, for this was not the body of a true soldier. And in another anecdote, when urged to speak up for a Sparta-style constitution, Phocion declares that the speaker's taste in perfumes will never convince anyone of his commitment to the Spartan way of life. Plutarch's biographies are packed with incidental details of this kind which remind us that for Athenian citizens ideology was never separable from material and gendered bodies.

Athenian democracy was a physical exchange between an orator and a crowd, and some of this dynamic remains in Parliamentary democracy. The future Whig Prime Minister William Gladstone in 1836 drew on his experience in the House of Commons to explain how, like the conductor of an orchestra, the orator 'flings himself at once upon the sea of passion and sentiment around him, expecting to be sustained by its buoyancy', adjusting continually to 'great rises and falls in the thermometer of feeling'. Speaking from benches packed with fellow party members, Gladstone's parliamentary speaker finds that he is transformed by 'the animating consciousness that he is as it were discharging for the time the functions of many minds by the machinery of his own' and this awareness 'stimulates his own force'.[87] Gladstone learned to declaim Demosthenes at Eton, voting for Phocion against Demosthenes when their respective moral worth was debated, and he picked up his schoolboy Demosthenes again when he was elected to Parliament.[88] Athens did not, however, provide Gladstone with a straightforward template for the House of Commons. He assumed that the size of the Greek audience must have forced orators to shout, imposing a coarseness of emotion that effaced the true *ethos* of the speaker along with the 'finer shades of intonation and delivery'.[89] Put another way, Demosthenes did not orate like an Etonian.

As I noted in the Introduction, my perspective as a British theatre historian has been informed by discussions of 'Brexit', where one narrative held that the referendum of 2016 was a triumph of democracy, the other that this was a travesty of democracy because the *demos* were fed with lies, and perhaps also because direct and representative democracy are incompatible principles. In this context I find myself instinctively alienated by Demosthenes' heroic go-it-alone national story. It is clear that the vote to leave the European Union turned not upon economic calculus but upon questions of identity, and identity was likewise at stake in the contest between Aeschines and Demosthenes. Brexit was supposedly produced by lies, but in the political arena evidence tends to be elusive. When documents were produced as evidence in the Athenian courtroom in 330 BCE, their purpose was to jog memories, not clinch a reasoned case. In order to conjure up his preferred version of the heroic past Aeschines quotes inscriptions that sound like examples of documentary fact, but facts tell according to how they are framed and Aeschines relied on his vocal skills to animate the solemn archaic language and create the mood he wanted. Truth is never easy to pin down because it can only be expressed in a form of words.

Factual answers were not available for the many questions that mattered in 330 BCE. Did the Athenians lose the battle of Chaeronea because of military incompetence, or because that was the will of the gods? Was the late King of Macedon benevolent or malevolent in his intentions towards Athens? It is hard to imagine that any modern recording technology could have provided factual answers to these questions. Demosthenes tells the jurors that they will have to form a judgement based on their sense of intent, and insists that any human being can distinguish willing from unwilling action.[90] This faith in the consciousness of choice remains today an enabling fiction for modern courts of law, but is hard to reconcile with theories of mind that reject a central decision-making ego. The debate of 330 BCE illustrates a general democratic principle: in the most crucial decisions, reasoning based upon the facts alone is not an option because the questions that finally matter are questions of value, questions about feeling.

Gladstone's attitude to truth is instructive. Starting from the classical assumption that any orator needs to balance 'the inviolable law of truth' against 'the defective and deteriorated mind of the hearer', his essay changes its tone when he goes on to explain how the orator passes via the 'fancy' to reach that deeper level of the human being called 'feeling'.[91] Convinced of his own ultimate rationality, Gladstone proffers the key proposition of Romanticism that truth lies not in reason but in feeling. Athenian sensibilities were not informed by romantic poetry, with its insistence on interiority and the supremacy of the individual, but by tragedy, which made it easier for them to accept that there is no final truth available to humankind either on earth or amongst the quarrelsome gods. It is my contention in this book that in the twenty-first century we have much to learn from seeing how Athenian democracy was grounded in the dialogic medium of theatre.

Competing narratives are the stuff of tragedy, and the crowning of Demosthenes was the finale for two competing accounts of the Athenian past. For Aeschines, the foundation stone of democracy was Solon the lawgiver who bestowed voting rights on all citizens, even though he did not allow all to take office, and his name was invoked by men like Phocion for whom the franchise was not a priority.[92] The defeat of Persia was a defining heroic moment for all Athenians, but rather than Salamis, a victory won by ships rowed by the poor, Aeschines celebrates Marathon, a battle won by foot-soldiers, men like himself who could afford to arm themselves. The third pivotal moment in Aeschines' story is the return of a resistance army to restore democracy after the city's defeat by Sparta and reinstate the rule of law.[93] In contrast to these strong, silent and heroic soldiers of the resistance, Aeschines gives his audience an effete Demosthenes directly responsible for Chaeronea. In Demosthenes' counter-narrative, the key moment in the Persian war was the decision to abandon the city and take to the water rather than surrender, the Athenians being a people who value liberty above all else.[94] In the fight against Philip, Demosthenes aligns himself with Themistocles at Salamis, and the defeat at Chaeronea was an act of the gods in accordance with the law of fate. On the basis of this tragic narrative, Demosthenes stands before the audience as a hero, inviting their empathy in his suffering. Aeschines becomes the authoritarian, a version of Creon in *Antigone*, a man who attends to the law of the city while blind to the higher laws of nature and the gods, unable or unwilling to listen to the voice of the people. As Sophocles knew, it was a good story.

Towards a Definition of Democracy

In 1968 Peter Brook published a minimalist definition of theatre which discarded old assumptions about the grounding of theatre in impersonation: 'I can take any empty space and call it a bare stage. A man walks across this empty space whilst someone else is watching him, and this is all that is needed for an act of theatre to be engaged.'[95] Though it has been critiqued for its gender bias, the problematic 'I' who establishes an aesthetic framework, and the assumption that space can somehow ever be empty, Brook's definition was widely welcomed for its emphasis on 'presence'.[96] His vision stimulated a rich body of modernist creativity through discarding red curtains and the 'deadly' assumption that theatre is just an act of pretending. His text can be adapted to yield a helpful minimalist definition of democracy: *We can take any bounded space and set up a stage. Two people stand on the stage and speak, whilst a crowd is watching and listening, and this is all that is needed for an act of democracy to be engaged*. My notion of boundedness derives from Arendt, who insisted that democratic communities need borders, and a stage creates physical separation between the actor/orator and the audience, allowing the performer to be seen and heard. The pairing of two performers forces the audience to compare and contrast, to recognise greater affinity with one rather than the other, and ultimately make a choice. When the democratic impulse waned in the age of Macedonian dominance, solo song became more important in tragedy than dialogue.[97] The trial in 330 BCE turned upon the crowning of Demosthenes in the theatre, which cast him symbolically as a solo performer, an unopposed demagogue, and I follow Mouffe in regarding the 'agonistic struggle' as 'the very condition of a vibrant democracy'.[98]

A theatrical *agon* produces a story, an outcome, but Brook's modernist aesthetic made him reluctant to conceive theatre in terms of narrative, focusing instead on the quality of the individual actor's encounter with the audience. Stories matter in my understanding of theatre, and to elaborate them past a certain point requires speech. When Aeschines offered his grey hair as a reason for preferring him over his opponent, he needed vivid language to explain why.[99] Speech is a production of the material body tied visibly to gesture and the performance environment, and the sound of speech touches everyone at the same moment, drawing them into the speaker's rhythm and binding them into a group.[100] Democracy, according to this Brookian definition, is not a matter of evaluating abstract arguments and ideologies, but turns upon the triangular interaction of bodies. Brook was content to imagine an individual spectator but most theatre, like democratic speechmaking, relies on the energy that stems from being part of a crowd.

In the Chapters 3–5, I shall look at the beginnings of three liberal democratic cultures which kept reformulating their relationship to classical antiquity. The complicating factor was Christianity, itself a product of the Greco-Roman world. The Christian *agon* of good versus evil, true versus false, has never sat comfortably with the tragic *agon* of democracy which pits good against good. The mask was a foundational component of Greek tragedy, rejected by the Christian tradition because it prevented people from seeking out the wearer's inner soul.[101] Greek actors demonstrated their flexibility as human beings, and their democratic capacity for change, by swapping masks to play young and old, male and female, free and slave, often in different scenes of the same play. Athenian democracy hinged like theatre on the principle of the mask: you could reject someone's arguments without rejecting them as human beings, you could deplore Cleon the man but vote for his policies. The dangerous step taken by Demosthenes was to remove the mask, so the man became the argument, the *hypokrites* became the hypocrite. Once you identify yourself with Demosthenes the patriot, there is no further room for argument.

CHAPTER 3

Puritan Democracy
The English Revolution

The English puritan revolution culminated in 1649 when King Charles I was executed and England became a republic. Although monarchy returned, the long-term consequence was a regime where the monarch was subordinate to the authority of Parliament. In the course of the 1640s, proposals were put forward by so-called Levellers for a constitution that entailed religious tolerance, regular elections and voting rights for all male heads of household irrespective of their wealth. This would have been 'democracy', rule by the people, as the term was understood in the UK at the start of the twentieth century. The enfranchisement of women was the crucial addition, yet to made.

The Athenian religious system was polytheistic, with the different gods embodying different human drives, and it was left to human beings to determine the nature of justice and tell right from wrong. When men argued about moral principles in democratic assemblies, they echoed the debates of Homeric gods on Olympus. Debates conducted in the Assembly on a secular ethical plane were complemented in the theatre by the recognition of natural laws that sat outside the rationalising language of male debate, like the overriding duty to bury corpses, or the obligation to honour one's mother. Theatre and Assembly were symbiotic in the way they allowed the Athenians to reflect upon themselves and to adapt. Although Christianity had a strong egalitarian strand in its early days, with its story of the carpenter's son turned son of God born in a stable appealing to slaves and women as much as free men, it was taken for granted that God rather than the wisdom of ordinary people was the final arbiter of right and wrong. As Christianity became institutionalised in the Roman Empire, it lost its egalitarian foundations, and a hierarchical structure of popes, bishops and ordained priests left no space for anything we might recognise as democracy. All this changed with the Protestant Reformation, and members of congregations free to choose their own pastor felt they should also be free to choose their political leaders.

In his classic study of 1905, *The Protestant Ethic and the Spirit of Capitalism*, Max Weber explored the relationship between religion and economics.[1] Unlike Marx and Engels, for whom religion was just a reflection of economic activity, Weber allowed belief systems some autonomy in shaping political behaviour. For Weber a key feature of the Protestant and more specifically Calvinist mindset was its rationalism, tied to 'disenchantment' of the magical Catholic world where wine transformed itself into the blood of Christ, and this rationalism was tied to individualism. Weber saw the Calvinist as a lonely figure forever scrutinising the inner workings of his or her soul in an effort to establish whether he or she was predestined for damnation or was one of God's elect. Calvinism called for a disciplined life since any surrender to pleasure built up fear you might find you were not one of the chosen, and preoccupied with their own salvation each individual pursued their secular calling with little value placed on local historically defined communities. For Weber, although Calvinism did not call directly for the accumulation of capital, the drive to accumulate was a logical consequence of the Protestant spirit.

The Austrian-American economist Joseph Schumpeter took Weber a step further in 1943 when he argued that the 'classical' eighteenth-century theory of democracy was a product of Protestantism, meeting the needs of a bourgeois class and substituting its ideals for those of religion. He doubted that electoral democracy could ever really mean rule by the 'people' because the 'people' cannot now be anything more than the sum of voting individuals. For Schumpeter the Christian principle whereby each individual soul has equal and intrinsic value paved the way for what he called the democratic 'gospel of reason and betterment'.[2] As a migrant to the USA, Schumpeter observed not only Hitler's manipulation of the crowd and rise through the ballot box, but also the new power of advertising to mould group decisions. Under capitalism, he believed, democracy could be no more than an 'institutional arrangement for arriving at political decisions in which individuals acquire the power to decide by means of a competitive struggle for the people's vote'.[3] More cynical than Mouffe, Schumpeter takes us back to the public *agon* as democracy's defining principle. For both Schumpeter and Weber, the Puritan revolution was less a precursor of Enlightenment democracy than a pointer to its essential nature.

Weber had the English revolution in mind when he addressed revolutionary students in Munich at the end of World War I on the theme of politics as a vocation or "calling".[4] People are *called* by God, in Calvinist thinking, but are also bound to pursue some secular profession or *calling*.

The problem of democracy for Weber as he faced the reality of revolution was one of leadership, and he saw three possible ways to legitimise the leader's role or calling: there was the ruler validated by tradition, such as the discredited Prussian Kaiser; the bureaucratic ruler whom we might today label the 'expert', 'technocrat' or party 'apparatchik'; and the ruler who commands authority on the basis of his or her 'charisma', a metaphor drawn from the 'grace' bestowed on individuals by the Christian God. As a demagogue who convinced the masses of his personal rightness, William Gladstone provided Weber with a vivid example of charisma, securing Home Rule for Ireland not because he won the argument but because the 'political machine' had come to trust him and follow wherever he went.[5] A less reductive thinker than Schumpeter, Weber brings us back to the necessary theatricality of democracy through focusing on the elusive quality that makes people follow a demagogue because they perceive this individual to be 'called' by a higher reality such as God, the nation, or socialism. There is an analogy between charisma and what theatre analysts tend to describe as 'presence', a mysterious personal force that compels an audience to attend.[6]

In this chapter I shall focus on debates that took place in Putney in October and November 1647 within the General Council of the New Model Army, where radical soldiers and a couple of civilians debated England's constitutional future with two generals, Oliver Cromwell and his son-in-law Henry Ireton. The event matters not just because of the constitutional framework it envisaged, but also because it was in its own right a democratic encounter. Three days of argument were recorded in shorthand and have come down to us in a form that reads like a three-act drama. Through subjecting this text to a dramaturgical analysis, I will show how seventeenth-century democracy actually worked. To contextualise the 1640s, I will begin by looking at the period through the rationalistic eyes of Thomas Hobbes, the greatest political thinker of the age, and then offer the counter-view of a puritan. Since puritanism was defined by its hostility to the theatrical aspect of religion, I will take the case of William Prynne, who in 1632 published a lengthy, learned and thunderous book castigating stage actors, and who later became an eminent parliamentarian. I will use Prynne's *magnum opus* to ask: Can you have any kind of democracy without theatricality? I will finish laying the ground by turning to a key Christian foundation myth, the story of Adam and Eve. This was a contested story in the seventeenth century because it could be read either as a parable about obedience or a parable about equality, and the principles of government turned upon how primal human nature was understood.

Thomas Hobbes

Hobbes was the first man to translate Thucydides into English, and this labour shaped his view of democracy. He understood the Greek historian to hold democracy the worst possible form of government because of the way 'he noteth the emulation and contention of the demagogues, for reputation, and glory of wit'. The desire of these demagogues to dominate the common people led to inconsistent and damaging policies, and Athens worked best, Hobbes thought, when ruled by the tyrant Peisistratos or when 'it was *democratical* in name, but in effect *monarchical* under Pericles'. Thucydides might himself have been a political leader, but opted for the quiet life of a historian because 'in those times it was impossible for any man to give good and profitable counsel for the commonwealth and not incur the displeasure of the people'.[7] Hobbes made the same decision because his own times did not seem so very different. For him democracy was a primitive form of government that preceded the more sophisticated forms of social contract entailed by monarchy and aristocracy. Democracy for Hobbes could never be any more 'than an aristocracy of orators, interrupted sometimes with the temporary monarchy of one orator'.[8]

In 1640 Hobbes fled England for France, fearing the Presbyterian orators who now controlled Parliament, and he returned to England only when the benevolent dictatorship of Cromwell had brought in tolerance for men of independent religious views. Towards the end of his life he followed Thucydides, also forced into exile by 'democrats', and penned *Behemoth* as a history of the times through which he had lived. Hobbes argued for a single source of absolute political authority because he had lived through anarchy and mass bloodshed, and much of the blame for this, he thought, lay with educated gentry, nourished on the 'democratical principles of Aristotle and Cicero' whose speeches set them 'in love with democracy'; in his *Leviathan* he described the result of reading these subversive ancient texts as 'tyrannophobia', a disease akin to rabies.[9] He was even more angered by Presyterian preachers who set the public against the established church and against the new prayerbook imposed by Archbishop William Laud. The translation of the Bible into English had paved the way for this urge to democratise religion because now, Hobbes lamented, 'every boy and wench, that could read English, thought they spoke with God Almighty, and understood what he said'.[10] These preachers drew their support from city-dwellers who had lost their roots in tradition.

Puritan Democracy: The English Revolution

For Hobbes, these radical preachers were artful demagogues:

> And first, for the manner of their preaching; they so framed their countenance and gesture at their entrance into the pulpit, and their pronunciation both in their prayer and sermon, and used the Scripture phrase (whether understood by the people or not), as that no tragedian in the world could have acted the part of a right godly man better than these did; insomuch as a man unacquainted with such art, could never suspect any ambitious plot in them to raise sedition against the state, as they then had designed; or doubt that the vehemence of their voice (for the same words with the usual pronunciation had been of little force) and forcedness of their gesture and looks, could arise from anything else but zeal to the service of God. And by this art they came into such credit, that numbers of men used to go forth of their own parishes and towns on working days, leaving their calling, and on Sundays leaving their own churches, to hear them preach in places, and to despise their own and all other preachers that acted not so well as they. And as for those ministers that did not usually preach, but instead of sermons did read to the people such homilies as the Church had appointed, they esteemed and called them *dumb dogs*.[11]

These preachers, in other words, succeeded thanks to their mastery of theatre, offering what seemed to be authentic performances. With the prayer book and printed homilies cast aside, they extemporised prayers before their sermons in order to demonstrate how their words were 'dictated by the spirit of God within them, and many of the people believed or seemed to believe it'. These sermons rarely addressed social injustice, Hobbes notes, for the doctrine of predestination meant that 'men were to be assured of their salvation by the testimony of their own private spirit'. Through developing a deep hatred of Catholicism, and through memorising sermons in order to internalise them, individual listeners convinced themselves they were amongst the chosen Saints. Passing lightly over commercial greed, Hobbes notes, Presbyterian preachers tiraded against lust to win themselves authority as spiritual doctors, since no young person could help discovering within themself the guilt of sexual desire.[12]

Hobbes was drawn to Thucydides because he found in him a rare combination of 'truth' and 'eloquence',[13] and he likened 'eloquence' to witchcraft, citing Medea's success when she persuaded the gullible daughters of Pelias to chop up their father and cook the pieces in a cauldron in absolute trust that this would make him young again:

> Eloquence is nothing else but the power of winning belief of what we say; and to that end we must have aid from the passions of the hearer ... And

such is the power of eloquence, as many times a man is made to believe thereby, that he sensibly feeleth smart and damage, when he feeleth none, and to enter into rage and indignation, without any other cause, than what is in the words and passion of the speaker ... For the faculty of speaking powerfully, consisteth in a habit gotten of putting together passionate words, and applying them to the present passions of the hearer.[14]

For Hobbes, Presbyterian preachers manufactured emotion and exploited human instinct in order to engender a democratic rebellion, and his observation of crowd behaviour reinforced his objection to democracy. In *Leviathan* Hobbes explained how the passions of individuals gathered together 'in Assembly are like many brands, that enflame one another, (especially when they blow one another with Orations) to the setting of the Commonwealth on fire, under pretence of counselling it.'[15] To illustrate crowd behaviour, he repeated the tale of how a Greek audience watching *Andromeda*, a romantic tragedy by Euripides, went collectively mad so no-one could stop repeating lines spoken by the lovers. This epidemic of passion was not authentic but 'proceeded from the passion imprinted by the play', exacerbated by the extreme hot weather.[16]

In much the same terms, Hobbes psychologised religion and showed how it functioned as a tool of social control. God, he claimed, never spoke directly through the dreams of Old Testament prophets, and tales about Christ casting out devils were fictions. There was no place for spiritual experience in his material universe, and no way to tell what other human beings truly believed in their hearts. He refused to condemn those secret thoughts 'holy, profane, clean, obscene, grave, and light, without shame, or blame' which run randomly through people's minds, and believed you could never tell if someone has genuinely repented his sins 'further than by external marks, taken from his words and actions, which are subject to hypocrisy'. In other words, repentance can always be simulated.

The ultimate unknowability of the inner world and the spiritual domain led Hobbes to a theory of the mask, which made sense in a world where elite men were starting to wear powdered wigs, cosmetics and skirts in order to mask their natural physiques and perform their public identities.[17] *Persona* is the Latin term for a theatrical mask, leading Hobbes to interpret the three 'persons' of God in the Trinity as three masks, and he argued that the monarch needed likewise to adopt a facade:

Persona in Latin signifies the disguise, or outward appearance of a man, counterfeited on the stage; and sometimes more particularly that part of it, which disguiseth the face, as a mask or vizard: and from the stage, hath been translated to any representer of speech and action, as well in tribunals, as theatres. So that a Person, is the same that an Actor is, both on the stage and in common conversation; and to Personate, is to Act, or represent himself, or an other ...[18]

Just as actors play roles on the stage, representing some other person, so the monarch needs to 'represent' his people, and his royal mask should not be confused with his natural being. Hobbes' answer to civil war was to unify the diverse multitude through causing them to be 'represented' by a single royal mask. Charles I's claim to rule by divine right became unsustainable because every Presbyterian now claimed to speak with divine authority, and a social contract was now required to maintain public order, an agreement to accept the theatricality of kingship. David Runciman shows how 'hypocrisy' for Hobbes was quite different from 'acting', because there is nothing hypocritical about acting in a mask on stage. As Runciman frames the paradox, Hobbes wanted 'an honest performance' where monarchs and subjects would 'play their parts truthfully'.[19] Though Hobbes could imagine a system where multiple representatives made decisions through majority voting, a single representative *persona* was always going to be more conducive to peace, and a king could not be driven by private self-interest if in some way he *was* the people whom he represented.[20]

William Prynne

Hobbes argued for a theatrical monarchy, and lambasted hypocritical Puritans who claimed to be sincere on the basis that God spoke through them. William Prynne was just the kind of man whom Hobbes hated most, and is known to theatre historians for his *Histrio-mastix, the Player's Scourge* (1633), running to 1006 pages + analytic index. Prynne was not a pastor but a barrister, and his text is supported by copious footnotes, causing his implacable foe William Laud, Archbishop of Canterbury, to deny that Prynne could ever have consulted so many sources.[21] *Histriomastix* provided intellectual foundations for the defence of a cause that seemed under attack. The book is a feat of scholarship and does all it can to compensate for the fact that Scripture has nothing directly to say about theatre. During the many years it took him to compile his great work, Prynne published controversial pamphlets arguing the Calvinist case to counter Laud's move towards Catholicism.[22] In his classic study *The Antitheatrical Prejudice*, Jonas Barish rightly observes that *Histrio-mastix* exemplifies a Puritan desire for 'absolute sincerity', but Barish de-politicises the book when claiming that Prynne must have written it 'to work off a staggering load of resentment and anxiety'.[23]

Direct competition between plays and sermons to attract Sunday audiences and related book sales drove Prynne on to see theatre as the centre of a wider system of values and practices.[24] He lived in the barristers' community of Lincoln's Inn, where he was proud that the ancient tradition of Christmas revels had recently been abolished. Gambling, dancing, cosmetics, May-games, love songs, drunkenness, excessive laughter, and long hair all seemed to him related to the problem of the actor.[25] It is not easy to empathise today with the Calvinist conviction that led Prynne to insist that his critique of theatre was undertaken to bring souls to salvation, 'to endure the cross, and ... to assuage ... these inveterate, and festered ulcers, (which may endanger Church, and State at once,) by applying some speedy corrosives and plasters to them ...' He claimed that *Histrio-mastix* was itself a kind of tragedy that would have neither 'clown, nor actor in it, but only bare, and naked truth, which needs no eloquence, nor strain of wit to adorn, or plead its cause'.[26] Such truth claims are a time-honoured classical ploy, but Prynne's puritan urge to mortify the body for the sake of the soul is entirely un-classical. He saw church and state as conjoined parts of a national body politic that needed harsh physical discipline. As the son of a West Country farmer, Prynne had separated himself from his community of origin in order to become a London barrister, and he is representative of the social atomisation that fuelled religious assumptions about personal salvation, and in the longer term democratic assumptions about the civic rights of all individuals. The lure of London with its career rewards and low life expectancy meant that Prynne was not alone in his cast of mind.

In his book Prynne adopts the Platonist argument that acting is by definition 'hypocrisy', a form of counterfeit,[27] and he complains about the many practical consequences of theatre, confining his list to twenty: theatre is a waste of time, time now being viewed as a commodity; it is a waste of money; it induces lust; also actual fornication; it corrupts minds; it invites excess; has no shame; causes riots; and so forth, all culminating in death and damnation.[28] Sex is critical in this system of values, and Prynne appeals to actors and playgoers alike to search their consciences: 'Do not your own hearts experimentally inform you, that there are many sinful swarms and flames of lust, many lewd unchaste affections oft kindled in your breasts by the very acting, sight and hearing of lascivious stage plays?'[29] The presence of brothels next to theatres reinforced the message that Prynne drew from early Christians: to watch a representation of whoredom is to play the harlot in your mind, in preparation for actual fornication.[30] Underlying everything is the disconnect between a corrupt external body and a vulnerable God-given soul.

Prynne moved into political territory towards the end of *Histrio-mastix* when praising a conspiracy against the 'infamous playerly emperor' Nero, who loved to sing, dance and act on the stage. Charles I and his Catholic Queen Henrietta Maria had a well-known taste for masques, and it is obvious that they were Prynne's target.[31] When the book landed Prynne in the Star Chamber, a tribunal controlled by the Crown rather than Parliament, on a charge of sedition, he refused to apologise, and had the pleasure of hearing long passages read aloud in court. Charles' struggle for dominance over Parliament and the City was bound up with what we have today come to call a 'culture war', and Prynne's trial proved a significant moment. His prosecutors attacked his character in the effort to win a moral victory and avoid charges of tyranny, but by playing the role of dedicated scholar Prynne undermined all attempts to portray him as a fanatic. After a long trial that attracted huge publicity, he was put in the pillory, his ears were clipped, and in an unprecedented gesture his book was burnt under his nose. He was also fined, expelled from the Bar, stripped of his degree, had his library confiscated, and was locked indefinitely in the Tower of London.[32] With little left to lose, Prynne fixed on the path of rebellion, and from the Tower he smuggled out writings which landed him back in the Star Chamber with two fellow rebels. This time the assault on his ears was more brutal, and when the initials S L (for Seditious Libeller) were crudely branded onto his cheeks he declared that they stood for Stigmata Laudis, 'stigmata' being the wounds of Christ nailed to the cross, and Archbishop Laud his persecutor. Three wooden pillories were erected for the three rebels, and when the victims held their arms aloft, the scene resembled the crucifixion in a medieval passion play. The preacher Henry Burton seems to have been the star of the show, given a separate stage for his pillory, but all three men saw the analogy with Christ. Herbs were strewn on the ground as the trio walked to their surrogate crucifixions, the crowd cried out at each lopping of an ear, and devotees held back the surgeon so they could dip their handkerchiefs in the blood to keep as relics.[33]

This was a performance event, and a public relations disaster for the royalist regime. Prynne played his role with impassive dignity, much as Charles would do on his scaffold twelve years later. It is hard to read the account of how part of Prynne's ear was left dangling as he fainted in the pillory without questioning Hobbes' reductive portrayal of puritan hypocrisy. In front of the crowd Prynne performed a role which we may or may not judge to have been 'sincere', but he was palpably not driven by economic self-interest. He did not believe himself to be Christ, but had plainly convinced himself he was one of God's elect. Hobbes' materialist account of the world allows no space for identity or spirituality to become drivers of human and thus democratic behaviour, and this limited his ability to explain the English revolution. Notions of hypocrisy and sincerity break down in performative environments where conviction and showmanship are interwoven. It is hard to draw a clear line between pretending and believing because brain and body are interconnected systems, as theorists of stage acting have begun to recognise.[34] In the pillory, Prynne playing the role of Christ with emotional commitment but no pretence to be Christ.

The crowds of supporters who waved Prynne and his colleagues off into exile welcomed them back three years later when Charles was forced to set up what became known as the Long Parliament. Restored to his money and offices by Parliament, Prynne became active in political life, and something of a political theorist. He believed that Parliament rather than King was ordained by God to control the church, but saw no constitutional alternative to the enforcement of order by a monarch.[35] The high point of his new political career was the impeachment of William Laud, and Prynne secured all the Archbishop's private papers for the purpose. At the trial, the clash of two incompatible views came to a head: Laud believed in an external religion of the body, which required people to bow before the altar, and accept that the communion wafer became the body of Christ, while Prynne believed in the supremacy of the pulpit, and the sacrosanct nature of God's word preserved in the Bible.[36] Centred upon ritual, Laud's corporeal religion supported the ideal of community, while Prynne valued the Word as it penetrated the soul of each responsive individual. While communities rarely escape hierarchies, Prynne's religion had an egalitarian basis because every individual has a soul of equal worth. Although Prynne spoke much about liberty in the sense of freedom from the rule of kings and bishops, he was far from being a liberal or libertarian in the modern sense.

Parliament was dominated by Presbyterians, puritans who rejected the rule of bishops and wanted the church to be governed by elected local presbyters or 'elders' rather than by 'brethren', and it is clear that Prynne was an instinctive authoritarian. Like Lenin and many a later crusading socialist, he was too convinced of his own rightness to allow his egalitarian ideals to be complicated by the vagaries of democracy. Cromwell's army was dominated by 'Independents' who broadly believed in religious toleration and the separation of church from state, and on their behalf Colonel Pride 'purged' Parliament of its Presbyterian majority, allowing only a 'rump' to remain in the Chamber. Recently elected to the Commons, Prynne seems to have been the only parliamentarian to put up physical resistance, and after Charles' execution he paid the price with three more years in prison.[37] In his new role as defender of the royalist establishment, Prynne had no hesitation in recanting *Histrio-mastix* and declaring the stage to be an honest 'calling'. The young firebrand had come full circle, confessing that when he wrote that book he 'had not so clear a light as now I have; it is no disparagement for any man to alter his judgement upon better information'.[38] Prynne changed his judgement but not his nature, merely updating his perception of the relevant tyrant. When his conscience told him he had got it wrong, he had no way of coming to terms with the fact that God's voice had previously led him to condemn theatre. When attacking Cromwell's 'tyrannical, abominable, lewd, schismatical, heretical army'[39] with the same fury he had directed at the stage and at Laud, he could not easily accept that he himself had always been a rhetorician, a species of performer, his performance skills honed by extemporal sermons and enthusiastic crowds. Being a performer is not the same as being a hypocrite. Performance is a necessary means of acting on the world in order to change it.

Adam and Eve: The Dream of Human Equality

Richard Bancroft, later to be Archbishop of Canterbury, complained in 1593 that 'The world nowadays is set all upon liberty'. Anxious that a version of Calvin's Geneva might be established in London, he feared the popular cry: 'the *first institution, the first institution*, everything must be brought to the *first institution*'. He associated these words with the notorious priest John Ball, whose sermon about Adam and Eve helped stir the Peasants' Revolt of 1381 and included the rhyme '*When Adam digg'd and Eve span, who was then the Gentleman?*'[40] Half a century later, Prynne complained about the idealisation of 'Adam's younger days' which encouraged the idea that there should be 'no Nation, Kingdom, City, Republic, Catholic or Parish Church now. No man will be so void of sense or reason to argue thus.'[41] The Adam and Eve story resonated in the seventeenth century because it could be a story about free will and equality, or it could taken to mean that humans are condemned by their nature to sin and may only be saved by God's grace.[42] The royalist John Filmer portrayed Adam's 'patriarchy' as the principle which justified Charles I's claim to rule by divine right, and a generation later John Locke, commonly seen as the founding father of political liberalism, framed the first of his two *Treatises of Government* as a critique of Filmer. For Locke, the story of Eden showed how God made all human beings equal (with the proviso that males are naturally abler and stronger), granting them reason which in itself constituted the voice of God.[43] Locke's God gave Adam and Eve property to manage in Eden, along with the right to transmit their property to their heirs. For Locke, property is the foundation of law, contract the foundation of marriage, and people find true freedom in the rule of law after giving their direct or tacit assent to living in political communities.

At the beginning of Elizabeth's reign, the Guild of Drapers in Chester was still presenting the medieval play of Adam and Eve on a pageant wagon. In the Catholic world, the truth of the story was expressed by its corporeal re-enactment, not by the precise Hebrew or Latin words of Scripture. Any member of the Guild was by definition a son of Adam condemned by sin to a life of labour. Humans needed clothing and drapers sold cloth because Adam and Eve's sin made nakedness intolerable. The Drapers were part of a corporate community, and by tradition every newly married couple in Chester presented a gift to the Guild, which lent another dimension to the story of the primal married couple, symbolising the way personal identities were inseparable from social identities in the pre-Reformation city.[44] Although Max Weber saw the guild-based medieval city as a foundation of modern democracy because it was in an important sense ruled by the people, guilds were in themselves hierarchical organisations.[45] The proclamation which announced the Chester pageants contrasted the 'wealthy' Drapers with the 'simple' Water-drawers, the 'honest' Smiths and the 'worthy' Vintners, declaring that the Drapers' play would be set out 'wealthily'.[46] The Drapers evidently created a spectacular pictorial representation of Eden commensurate with their place in the urban hierarchy.

Theatre does not pose any existential threat to personal identities when identities are in the first instance social. The Chester actors were known members of the Guild paid for their labour, and the representation of nakedness was symbolic rather than erotic.[47] The draper representing Satan put on in front of the audience a spectacular outfit that included an adder's tail, bird feathers around the body and the mask of a girl to make his theatricality overt. Enlightenment democracy turned upon individual acts of decision-making, but in the Chester play dramatic interest did not lie in the anguish of decision-making, since Adam and Eve were doomed to eat the apple, but in the fateful consequence of their action. In pre-Reformation Chester people's identities were defined not by themselves but by the locality and situation into which they were born. However, by the time William Prynne passed through under armed guard in 1637, these medieval plays were no more and Chester was part of a national community. Prynne was lionised in the city as a heroic individual, a fighter against tyranny, and his portrait was painted and circulated, though later, on orders from London, the frames that once housed his iconic portrait were burned at the High Cross.[48]

John Ball's sermon about Adam helped inspire the figure of Jack Cade in Shakespeare's *Henry VI Part Two*. Shakespeare's Cade is a carnivalesque rebel who storms London at the head of illiterate craftsmen, promising to abolish gentry and private property so food and beer can flow. When the head of the militia condemns the rebels as the 'filth and scum of Kent' and Cade as a mere cloth-worker and plasterer's son, Cade retorts: 'And Adam was a gardener.'[49] The rebellion comes to a head in a strikingly democratic moment, when the King's representative addresses 'the commons' and calls for patriotism. The commons are won over, but Cade wins them back by evoking their 'ancient liberty' and present slavery. In the end, however, Cade has no answer when the nationalist card it is played and the crowd are reminded of Henry V's victories in France. Before making his escape Cade laments: 'Was ever feather so lightly blown to and fro as this multitude?'[50] The scene reveals why Shakespeare, like almost all his educated contemporaries, could never be a democrat. There was too much fear of the mob, and too much awareness of how easily crowds were swayed by oratory. The 'Adam' theme comes to a head in Shakespeare's play when a starving Cade climbs into a symbolic Garden of Eden – the garden of Alexander Iden Esquire – in search of food.[51] Shakespeare anticipates Locke in trumping the demand for equality with the claims of private property, idealising Iden as a bourgeois individual who is neither a scheming aristocrat nor an anarchic plebeian. Iden prefigures Shakespeare's own final destination in life as the owner of a large walled garden and a gentleman's coat of arms, complicit in the enclosure of common land.[52] Like Greek tragedy, Elizabethan theatre represented a morally ambivalent world that could be recognised as truthful by a socially diverse audience, and despite Iden's property rights, Cade's failure remains tragic. As the theatre gravitated into the orbit of the Crown, forbidden to engage with pressing religious issues, it lost much of its relevance to bigger cultural and political battles that were fought out through the performative medium of the sermon.

John Lilburne, the most famous of the 'Levellers', followed Ball when he declared in 1646 that all men and women are alike with no natural right to authority because they are children of Adam and Eve.[53] Robert Everard, a common trooper in Cromwell's cavalry regiment, was another Leveller and one of the protagonists in the Putney debates.[54] As a Baptist Everard believed there was no need to baptise infants because children were not born contaminated by any inherited sin of Adam. He published a pamphlet about Adam in 1649, arguing that God endowed human beings with free will, and 'the principal part of man, his soul or spirit, was not dependent upon Adam, but had his dependency ... even from God himself.' Religious opinion could not be separated from political opinion. If all men are God's creatures, 'how cometh it to pass that one should be in subjection to another's will?' Everard asked, and he concluded: 'Rulers are to be obeyed so far only as they bring the Word.'[55] Everard's language as a pamphleteer derives its energy from orality, and we know he was giving sermons on the topic of Adam three years later. He sometimes took the pulpit in an afternoon in order to reflect on the text that another preacher had used that same morning, in what we might see either as a breach of protocol or as a brotherly exercise in democracy with the aim that 'by a loving conference differences might be ended in love'.[56] Like Prynne, Everard was an instinctive rebel, and in his later years he converted with equal enthusiasm to Catholicism.[57] The Protestant conscience was never a reliable guide to truth, but it was powerful in its effect on individual behaviour, and in the oratory that it generated.

The most famous treatment of the Adam and Eve story is Milton's *Paradise Lost*. Milton believed like Everard in the principle of free will, but his faith in democracy was shaken when the people failed to choose rightly and support the execution of Charles I.[58] Thomas Jefferson found inspiration for the American revolution in Milton's famously sympathetic Satan, though John Adams had more concerns about Satan the demagogue.[59] Milton's seducer is not an actor dressed up in exotic finery as in pre-Reformation Chester, but an accomplished public speaker, and in the climax of the seduction scene:

> The Tempter, but with show of zeal and love
> To Man, and indignation at his wrong,
> New part puts on, and as to passion moved,
> Fluctuates disturbed, yet comely, and in act
> Raised, as of some great matter to begin.
> As when of old some orator renowned,
> In Athens, or free Rome, where eloquence

> Flourished, since mute, to some great cause addressed,
> Stood in himself collected, while each part,
> Motion, each act won audience ere the tongue,
> Sometimes in highth began, as no delay
> Of preface brooking through his zeal of right:
> So standing, moving, or to highth upgrown,
> The Tempter, all impassioned, thus began: ...[60]

Milton's Satan is the ultimate political orator with all the eloquence of Demosthenes, able to play a part and in a controlled manner communicate a sense of unrestrained emotion, assisted by the ancient technique of standing still for a moment before speaking. As Cromwell's propagandist, Milton knew that he had to use rhetorical skills in order to move the *demos*, in a fallen world where people could not be persuaded by reason but needed words to be inflected by musicality, passion and the body. How to communicate truth without the intervention of the body was for Puritans an insoluble conundrum, and preachers repeatedly castigated the body whilst using their voices and bodies to optimum effect. Milton couched *Paradise Lost* as a poem not a play partly because he had no forum for performance, but in part because eating the apple was a prelude to the sexual act which could not be represented through the carnal medium of theatre. The puritan world had a horror of performance, but it could not escape the legacy of Satan.

Modern liberal or electoral democracy turns on the assumption that the individual exercises free will when choosing how to vote, equivalent to the choice made by Adam and Eve to eat the apple. In practice that act of choosing could never be distilled and separated from the body and its biological desire for sweet tastes, sex and new experiences. It is easy for the modern liberal to look back disdainfully at Calvinism and its commitment to predestination, but today's widespread democratic belief in free will is no less an act of faith. Democrats of the Enlightenment era like Jefferson operated on the basis of a creed no less than their puritan predecessors, and the problem has not vanished in the twenty-first century. The philosopher Saul Smilansky argues that free will is merely an illusion necessary for sustaining civilised life, while the social psychologist James Miles suggests that in the modern political environment 'the myth of free will is inextricably linked to contempt for the poor and the unlucky'.[61] Greek democracy was grounded in a more collectivist view of human nature, and Aristotle, for example, saw choice as ultimately a function of habit.[62] Modern Western democracy owes more to the Protestant Reformation than to antiquity, and if free will is indeed a modern myth, however fondly cherished by the popular imagination in defiance of cognitive science, then we can see why the theatrical lens is helpful for understanding democracy. Theatre complicates and interrogates the I who performs the act of choosing.[63]

The Putney Debates

The debates in Putney in the autumn of 1647 give us a close-up of the human interactions involved in trying to make democracy work. It is on the face of it surprising that such fundamental discussions of political principle should have taken place within the army and not within Parliament, since armies are commonly associated with hierarchy and obedience. Parliament at the time was preoccupied by its fight with the King, bishops and aristocracy, and had less interest in challenging the property rules which denied the poorest members of society any representation. Cromwell's New Model Army was something new, a standing professional army with commanders appointed on the basis of merit rather than feudal entitlement, and soldiers often driven to enlist by an ideal rather than personal loyalties or penury. Having unhooked themselves from the communities in which they grew up, many common soldiers developed new regimental and sectarian loyalties, and were in that sense newly minted as individuals.[64]

The General Council of the Army was set up in 1647 as a forum to allow senior officers and the ranks to interact, and the conversations that took place in Putney were driven by mounting urgency. Fighting had stopped, and the king was held under house arrest in nearby Hampton Court. Parliament wanted to disband the army, or launch an invasion of Ireland, but had no money for substantial arrears of pay, and forced to live off the land the army found itself increasingly unpopular. After a royalist mob had invaded the House of Commons, the army entered London to take control, and then withdrew to Putney a short way upriver while Londoners started to transform their own militia into a viable fighting force. Parliament was dominated by Presbyterians who wanted to see a single national church answerable to the state but not to the King, while most of Cromwell's soldiers were Independents who believed in a high level of religious toleration – sadly for Ireland, a tolerance never extended to Catholics. The two leaders of the New Model Army, Thomas Fairfax commander-in-chief and his lieutenant Oliver Cromwell, needed a political settlement, but the king was unreliable and duplicitous and the idea that England could become a republic was not at this point on their horizon. At the time of the debates, one regiment was in a state of mutiny, and discipline was breaking down. The army's successful military record reinforced the idea that God was on its side and had predestined its victory, but it was not at all clear what kind of settlement God now wanted the army to impose to ensure peace.[65]

A month before the debates in Putney, Fairfax published recent documents as a public relations exercise, and the frontispiece communicates the feel of a General Council meeting as Fairfax wanted it imagined, with himself larger-than-life in the centre (Figure 3.1).[66] He seems to be silencing the commander on his right, while pointing to the text that will be sent to Parliament. The officer on his left also points to it, while two men in the foreground have their hands raised to speak, and the body language of each figure has a distinctive attitude. On the table are the pen and ink that belong to the secretary John Rushworth who stands in the centre foreground. A striking feature of this print is the hierarchical divide between the officers, seated at table with hats and sword belts, and the so-called agitators, common soldiers elected by their regiments and huddled bareheaded in a corner. The one seated figure without a sword belt must be the Chaplain Hugh Peter. The image conveys a traditional hierarchical order that disappeared in the privacy of the Putney debates, where the agitators were studiously addressed as 'gentlemen', implying permission to wear hats. The picture captures the importance of documents within a religious culture that was focused on the written word, and looked for deliberation rather than speechmaking.

A shared puritan faith allowed dialogue to take place across class boundaries, in an attempt to resolve the old conflict of the *demos* versus the property-owning classes. At the heart of the conversation lay a timeless problem: *your* sense of freedom is not the same as *my* sense of freedom. There could be no rational way to resolve this difference of perception, and one of the strengths of puritanism lay in its recognition of the limits to human reason. Prior to morning prayers on the second day of debate, Captain John Clarke invited his colleagues to seek out an inner silence in order to remind themselves of these limits: '[L]et us but search our own spirits with patience, and look by the light of God within us, and we shall find that we have submitted the Spirit of God unto the candle of reason, whereas reason should have been subservient under the Spirit of God.' In order to discover the true light of Christ, Clarke went on, the glimmering candle of reason must be removed, and 'our lust, which doth seduce and entice us to wander from God, must be eaten out of us by the spirit of God, and when there is no place for lust, there is place enough

80 Democracy, Theatre and Performance

Figure 3.1 A meeting of the General Council of the Army, with Thomas Fairfax presiding.
Source: *A Declaration of the Engagements, Remonstrances, Representations, Proposals, Desires and Resolutions from His Excellency Sir Tho: Fairfax, and the general Councel of the Army.* London, 1647. British Library Board G.3861.

for the Spirit of God'.[67] The idea that reason is a species of lust, essentially a source of human pleasure, flies in the face of modern Enlightenment assumptions about democracy. Clarke tries to open up a route to consensus through calling for a silence that unites rather than words that divide.

Because of its focus on the individual's responsibility for their own human soul, puritanism generated a notion of individual human rights. The most memorable discussion in Putney pitched Henry Ireton – a general, Member of Parliament, and husband to Cromwell's daughter – against those who argued the Levellers' case for universal male suffrage. While Ireton's position was essentially that of John Locke, linking property to the rule of law, what the Levellers were proposing was not Shakespeare's nightmare of Jack Cade but an attainable Garden of Eden free of the divide between gentry and commoners. Many Levellers hooked this biblical utopia to a historical utopia, the Anglo-Saxon England destroyed by the Norman conquest, and their argument was underpinned not by any idea of 'universal' human rights but by the 'birthright' of a 'true Englishman'. Popular nationalist sentiment fed on the fact that King Charles was the son of a Scot and a Dane, married to a Catholic Frenchwoman, and many legal proceedings were still couched in Norman French. Englishness was not an abstraction but a way of living and speaking that did not sit comfortably with Ireton's educated Latinisms.

Three days of debate were transcribed, and it may be that Cromwell and Ireton called off the stenography when they lost faith that the conversations were yielding results. What has come down to us takes the form of a structured drama with a rich cast of characters.[68] These include: Cromwell in the chair, older than most of the other participants, measured in his speech and set on consensus; Ireton, legally trained and determined not to be out-talked; his nemesis John Wildman, also legally trained, a young and eloquent London radical sent in by less articulate soldiers as their spokesman; Colonel Nathaniel Rich, educated, with a classical frame of reference; Colonel Thomas Rainborough, seaman and entrepreneur from East London, a doer rather than a man of education; Lieutenant-Colonel William Goffe, with the Bible always on his lips; Commissary Nicholas Cowling, preoccupied with the Norman yoke and recent author of a utopian pamphlet arguing that modern saints can be as perfect on earth as Adam once was; Edward Sexby, a trooper and polemicist who began life as an apprentice grocer; and his Baptist comrade Robert Everard.[69] Thomas Fairfax, commander-in-chief and a man who preferred war to politics, was a notable absentee, pleading illness. The text is richly polyphonic, like the drama of Shakespeare and Jonson which a generation earlier engaged a socially diverse audience.[70] The Putney drama contains no obvious heroes and villains, and according to political taste a modern historian could represent each of these characters as a man of vision, or each as a hypocrite. As in Greek tragedy, what mattered was not the face of the actor behind the mask, but the consequences of what they said and did.

Act I. The regular Thursday meeting of the General Council took place in an improvised arena in the nave of Putney church. The planned business was to discuss a manifesto that had emerged from the ranks of the army, brought forward by Sexby, Everard and eight others, calling for government by a reformed House of Commons, and appealing less to religion than to the idea of a free-born English people.[71] The precipitating incident which set the plot in motion (to use the language of dramaturgical analysis) was a reworking of that manifesto into a more focused 'Agreement of the People', presented by the former soldier John Wildman who acted as an intermediary between the troops and London Leveller politics.[72] This proposed Agreement declared that sovereignty was vested in the people and defined their fundamental rights: freedom of worship, freedom from conscription and equality under the law, along with an amnesty for recent war crimes. The document was too cogent to allow a fudged response, and a crisis threatened to break apart this army that had hitherto seemed to be the vehicle of God's will.

Ireton had a perfect grasp of the intellectual issue at stake, the nature of Justice. Does justice lie in contract law, in this instance abiding by promises made, he asked, or does it lie in natural law, that is, what is inherently right? The problem, as he rightly saw, was related to a difference between positive and negative concepts of freedom.[73] There could be no definitive moral answer, and as theoreticians such as Aristotle, Hobbes and Hume all set out in their different ways, democratic decision-making must in the last analysis turn upon emotion. Through giving a performance of his own intellectual prowess, Ireton did himself no favours in his attempt to win over men who lacked his own education. The real battle in Putney was for moral authority, and although final authority lay in principle with God, God was an elusive touchstone of rightness. When Cromwell sets up parameters for discussing the Agreement, he argues that practicalities have to be addressed and it can never be enough to trust in faith, for 'a man may answer all difficulties with faith ... but we are very apt, all of us, to call that *faith*, that perhaps may be but carnal imagination, and carnal reasonings ... God hath given us our *reason* ...' Having dismissed faith, Cromwell rapidly changed gear, speaking of what 'as before the Lord I am persuaded in my heart', and what 'I think in my heart and conscience', hoping that all participants will try to speak *'honestly* and *sincerely* and to approve ourselves to God as *honest* men'.[74] Cromwell needed a particular performance style to convince the assembly that he himself spoke conscientiously and sincerely, with a rationality uncontaminated by desires of the flesh. Everard commented later that he was willing to trust Cromwell because 'When I heard the Lieutenant-General speak I was marvellously taken up with the plainness of the carriage'.[75] To be seen as a 'plain man' was always Cromwell's first aim.

When Cromwell first entered Parliament, John Hampden, famous for campaigning against royal taxation, reportedly prophecied: "That slovenly fellow which you see before us, who hath no ornament in his speech; I say that sloven if we should come to have a breach with the King (which God forbid) in such case will be one of the greatest men in England."[76] Cromwell neither dressed nor spoke with elegance, and his voice was described as 'sharp and un-tunable'.[77] His route to supreme power lay in being master of the anti-theatrical idiom in his language, dress and manner, and people trusted him because, rightly or wrongly, they felt he was not acting a part. There is nothing in the recorded debates to suggest that Cromwell was experienced as a 'charismatic' leader, the carrier of God's 'grace', but the bare written record of words spoken deprives us of all those nuances of timing, intonation and body language that may have communicated special authority when he made claims about what lay in his heart. A royalist who visited Cromwell close to the end of his life commented that he was 'not handsome, nor had he a very bold look with him. He was plain in his apparel, and rather negligent than not. Tears he had at will, and was, doubtless, the deepest dissembler on earth'.[78] Whether today we judge Cromwell to be a species of Tartuffe is a matter of political taste.

Wildman steered clear of protesting his faith at Putney, and simply insisted that the new draft constitution accorded with natural law. Cromwell and Ireton were clearly grateful when Goffe rescued them with the statement that 'there hath been a withdrawing of the presence of God from us that have met in this place', and proposed a prayer meeting next morning.[79] As they saw it, they themselves were willing to scrutinise their hearts, whilst Wildman and his colleagues spoke to a script, being tied to a mandate from those they represented. When Wildman insisted that he spoke for natural principles of right and freedom espoused by many in the ranks, Ireton became emotionally 'affected', claiming to see 'venom and poison' in the document before him, and declaring: 'I am afraid and do tremble at the boundless and endless consequences of it.'[80] The lines of battle were drawn when Everard spoke up in the language of a soldier as a professed man of God, and Cromwell began to see possibilities for open-minded dialogue, with the proviso that he could never concede a universal franchise.[81]

Wildman was the probable author of a diatribe against Ireton circulated to sympathisers that night. The printed version begins with a text from St Matthew: 'Woe unto you Scribes and Pharisees, hypocrites; for ye are like unto whited Sepulchres, which indeed appear beautiful outward, but are within full of dead men's bones', before moving on to a direct threat of mutiny, proclaiming that 'you have men amongst you as fit to govern, as others to be removed, AND WITH A WORD YE CAN CREATE NEW OFFICERS, necessity hath no law, and against it there is no plea.' Ireton is attacked on the grounds that '[o]ne of the surest marks of deceivers is to make fair, long and eloquent speeches, but a trusty or true-hearted man studies more to do good actions than utter deceitful orations'. Ireton becomes a Machiavelli, a man in a mask, a serpent, full of art and cunning, skilled only in the art of delusion, with a cold legal manner that contrasts with the vehemence of colleagues whose passionate claims to godliness 'both deceive the world and bring their wicked designs and self-interests to pass'.[82] Cromwell was too much loved by the troops to be attacked directly, and is therefore portrayed as a victim exploited by his son-in-law.

The document is not a comfortable one to read for those keen to hold up the Agreement as a precursor of modern enlightened democratic principles, because its account of the conversations at Putney is so manipulative, designed to whip up emotion in a crowd of soldiers listening to the words read out. It helps us grasp why Cromwell and Ireton were desperate to reach an agreement, and insistent that a fine-sounding constitution would never guarantee civil order. Based on the art of the sermon, Wildman's open letter gives us a glimpse of a different kind of politics based on oratory rather than deliberation that continued behind the scenes. Its claims raise again the theoretical question: How do you ever break out of the circle whereby anyone can accuse anyone of being a hypocrite? This game can be played by modern historians as much as persons present in 1647. A performance-based analysis escapes that circularity when it shifts the focus from motivation to consequences.

Act II. In dramaturgical language, this is the *peripeteia*, the turning around of the situation.[83] The day centred on the franchise, and the question whether, in a land where the poor outnumbered the rich, universal male franchise could be reconciled with the secure holding of property. The whole day of debate was impromptu, forced upon Cromwell by group pressure when he had hoped to commence with committee work, and it took place in a crowded room in the Quartermaster's house. Either at the end of the day or else at the next formal meeting of the General Council, the question was pushed to a vote and Cromwell and Ireton – privileged as generals, landowners and Members of Parliament – were comprehensively outvoted.[84] The debate was driven forward by Thomas Rainborough, a military man of action, rather than John Wildman, the lawyer and man of words.

Rainborough's ringing challenge has been much quoted by historians of democracy: 'For really I think that the poorest he that is in England hath a life to live, as the greatest he; and therefore truly, sir, I think it's clear, that every man that is to live under a government ought first by his own consent to put himself under that government.' These words are a triumph of the monosyllable. Ireton's lengthy speeches, full of qualifications, parentheses and enumerated points were no match for Rainborough's command of sarcasm, story and metaphor, as he pitched the language of a soldier against that of a man trained in the law. Rainborough concluded his famous challenge to Cromwell with the claim that his proposition was self-evident 'insomuch that I should doubt whether he was an Englishman or no, that should doubt of these things',[85] winning a victory for Englishness over godliness in the battle for rhetorical dominance. Ireton's command of rational argument sat uneasily with his self-image as a man of God, a man of transparent sincerity, while Rainborough's Englishness correlated with muscularity, plain uneducated speech, and a particular vision of Eden.

Edward Sexby was equally forceful, speaking for the determination of fellow soldiers who have 'ventured our lives, and it was all for this: to recover our birthrights and privileges as Englishmen'. As he developed the point, Sexby's syntax broke down, taxing the modern editor tasked with reconstructing a coherent flow of argument, but this inability to articulate only increased the force of feeling as he built to a veiled threat: 'I shall only sum up this. I desire that we may not spend so much time upon these things. We must be plain. When men come to understand these things, they will not lose that which they have contended for.' Ireton did his best to deconstruct the notion of a 'birthright', but nothing could undermine the force of Sexby's simple demand, which drew resonance from the biblical story of how Jacob stole his older brother's birthright. Cromwell attacked Sexby's speech 'because it did savour so much of will', in other words because it smacked of personal emotion rather than God, but

Rainborough immediately objected: 'I wonder how that should be thought wilfulness in one man that is reason in another.' There could be no intellectual answer to Sexby's simple insistence on how the soldiers felt. They seemed to have fought for nothing, and Sexby regretted that 'the Lord hath darkened some so much as not to see it'.[86]

Act III. A committee worked over the weekend to hammer out compromise proposals, and the General Council reconvened on Monday to vet them. Cromwell began by asking everyone to say what God had told them in their prayers, but was quickly reminded of his unfair attempt to quell Sexby, and it was clear that God should not be allowed to become 'the author of contradictions'. As Sexby put it, they were now all in the wilderness, or in Babylon, and Cromwell had to settle for a consensus that the presence of the Lord could be determined only through the 'outward evidence' of mercy, love and the 'desire to do good to all', and the meeting would proceed with the aim to 'avoid bringing of a scandal to the name of God, and to his people upon whom his name is bestowed'. In other words, no one could any longer simply appeal to the authority of an inner voice, or a truth that lay beyond appearances. When Wildman insisted that the God of mercy was also a God of justice, any recourse to divine authority for political answers was self-evidently hopeless.[87]

The day was dominated by the offstage presence of the King, who as it happens was poised to escape from house arrest and launch what became known as the 'Second Civil War', and the question turned upon whether he should be allowed to retain a role in constitutional government. Little more than a year later, Cromwell and Ireton signed the warrant for Charles' execution, but at this point they were determined to keep negotiating, knowing how much symbolic power the monarchy had over most English people, and a few days later Ireton lost his temper and stormed out of the General Council because of mounting pressure to stall these negotiations.[88] The recorded debate on Day Three turned into a face-off between Ireton, who wanted protected constitutional status for the monarch, and Wildman, who took the republican view that any role for the King was a threat to the people, and the climax resembled what in Greek tragedy is called *stichomythia*, a tense line-against-line dialogue where two incompatible positions are distilled to their essence.[89] Their exchange, if I boil it down further, can be reduced to the following:

w: Justice!
i: Kings rule by contract.
w: Mere superstition.

1: We must honour the bargain.
w: It's a fraud.
1: For public security.

After a senior committee member intervenes saying that the royal role will be honorific, the dialogue finishes:

w: Is this what we fought for?
1: Law will guarantee your rights.
w: The King will ignore the law.
1: He won't dare.
w: Convince me and I will concede.

Historical events rarely have the structural elegance of art, and the debate continued for over a week, poorly documented, until Fairfax intervened as a kind of *deus ex machina*, calling the bluff of the radicals by assembling the troops in mass gatherings and testing their loyalty to himself and his fellow generals.[90] Then war against the King broke out again, and changed circumstances put the search for a workable constitution on hold. The recorded debates in Putney are much like a Greek tragedy in the way they pitch against each other two incompatible goods: on the one hand, the ideal of a democratic constitution that would give a voice to all 'free Englishman', and on the other, the practical constraints of public order and creating peace. At stake were two views of humanity, the utopian view that humans are naturally good as they once were in Eden versus the realist or cynical view that humans are inherently sinful and bound to keep fighting amongst themselves. Also at stake were two views of justice: an absolute justice grounded in nature versus a legal code grounded in mutual contracts and understandings. There did not seem to be any compromise position available, nothing equivalent to John Rawls' liberal doctrine of perceived 'fairness' which satisfied many theorists in the latter part of the twentieth century.[91]

It is hard not to be impressed by Cromwell's patient efforts to achieve consensus, if we bear in mind that the radicals had little support in the country at large, and no means of persuading a broad public to sign their names to the proposed new social contract. The Putney debates were a genuine exercise in democracy in the sense that they brought elected representatives of the *demos* into real dialogue with officers who were affluent landowners, a more diverse group than the fifty-five lawyers, merchants, physicians and planters who met to frame the American constitution. In the surrogate parliament of the General Council soldiers debated the first principles of government with a rigour that can be scarcely imagined in the British House of Commons with its traditions and protocol. Fighting and roaming the country together had built up a bond of trust amongst the soldiers that made their conversations possible, permitting in Mouffe's terms an agonistic politics to keep overt antagonism at bay. From one point of view, the puritanism of those who spoke at Putney was, as Hobbes perceived it, a cover for hypocrisy and a means of claiming moral authority on behalf of personal or class interests, but from another point of view these professions of faith set up a frame which allowed people to look each other in the eye as equals, and talk about common ends that were not merely material. The religious frame disposed of the illusion that reason will ultimately yield justice, throwing participants back on the need to build relationships.

Cromwell functioned as a kind of stage director at Putney, managing a cast of actors who each came with a script which they claimed God had set down for them. Since part of the Calvinist legacy was the idea that people unwittingly lived out predestined behaviour, uncomplicated by the romantic and modern cult of self-expression, God lurked in the background as the ultimate dramaturg. Just as a modern stage director working in the Stanislavskian idiom may look for 'emotional truth', so Cromwell sought out a quality of sincerity which proved that the speaker's soul was voicing God's truth. Most of the soldiers seem to have done their best to give what Runciman terms paradoxically an 'honest performance', and democratic engagement became easier when their godly language started to sound more like theatrical artifice. Unlike William Prynne, always better at speaking than listening, the men of Putney were committed to some operation of free will, and to the corollary that both speakers and listeners were capable of changing their minds.

With the benefit of hindsight, it is easy enough to make out the participants at Putney as a bunch of hypocrites with malleable consciences. Cromwell and Ireton had to reconcile two different identities, as soldiers and parliamentarians.[92] Cromwell preached religious tolerance, but later became the butcher of Irish Catholics. Rainborough had just elbowed his way into a naval appointment, and at the time of the debate was fighting to maintain a double salary.[93] Cowling believed himself one of the saints, but preferred to speak about history. Sexby, after rising to the rank of colonel, was court-martialled for withholding pay from his men, and turned royalist.[94] Everard turned Catholic. Wildman by the end of his life was rich, knighted and a London alderman, and his career is summed up in the *Dictionary of National Biography* in damning terms: 'His irresistible attraction to political intrigue, which proved to be his defining characteristic, overrode both political convictions and friendships.'[95] The problem with this summation of Wildman lies in its premise that a person can be defined by their overarching 'character'. In respect of theatre and the work of the stage actor, this assumption belongs to romanticism and modernity. In the theatrical jargon of the early seventeenth century an actor was said to 'personate' the figure they were playing, in other words to wear their mask, with no binding need to be of the right gender, ethnicity and age group in order to trace a line of inner consistency from scene to scene.[96]

Judith Shklar describes Molière's *Tartuffe* as 'the matchless black comedy of the Puritan culture of fear and of the opportunities it offers hypocrisy'.[97] Written four years after Charles II left Paris and brought the English Republican dream to an end, Molière's comedy portrayed the unmasking of a greedy puritan, quashed in the end by another *persona*, that of Louis XIV in the person of an officer who arrives improbably, like a Greek *deus ex machina*, to arrest the hypocrite and restore the domestic regime of patriarchy, inheritance, and class difference. In Putney, Wildman tried to be a Molière, and set up Ireton as a Tartuffe whose cloak of godliness and humility allows him to deprive decent people of their inheritance. In the wake of the debates Wildman published a pamphlet entitled *Putney Projects – or the Old Serpent in a New Form*, where he declared that as a patriot he would continue to 'impartially communicate the actions of Cromwell, Ireton, and their adherents in their continued series, and when your eyes shall behold them naked, I shall submit them to your censure'.[98] In reality no narrative can ever be impartial, nor any human mind be stripped naked, and when Wildman tried to lift the masks off Cromwell and Ireton to expose them as incarnations of Satan, he refused to acknowledge his own mask. When Wildman later plotted to assassinate Cromwell, it is impossible to say whether in his private, muddled inner self he was driven by patriotism, personal hatred or opportunity, and most likely he did not know himself.[99] The man behind the mask is unknowable. Wildman emerges from the Putney debates as the classic demagogue, brazenly whipping up emotion, but only able to do so because of a widely felt sense of historic injustice.

CHAPTER 4

Oratory in the French Revolution

'I have studied much history, and I dare affirm that I have never met with a revolution where one could see at the start, in so many men, a more sincere patriotism, more disinterest, more true greatness.' So wrote De Tocqueville. Although on the face of it the Revolution of 1789 collapsed within five years, those idealists spawned, as De Tocqueville put it, a new 'race which has perpetuated itself, and spread among all civilised parts of the world, which everywhere has kept the same appearance, the same passions, the same character'.[1] The few short years of revolution had an impact far beyond France in establishing the principle that to be civilised equated with being a democrat.

The 'Terror' that brought so many idealistic revolutionaries to the guillotine was no simple aberration, and might seem to confirm Plato's observation that democracy will sooner or later always slide into dictatorship. The clinical efficiency of the guillotine could be likened to slavery, colonialism and exploitation, forms of violence that have long sustained liberal democracy, hidden as far as possible from the eyes of a bourgeois public. Two different ideals were at stake in the French Revolution: Roman-style 'republicanism', which declared that all free Frenchmen with a minimum of property were citizens whose views must be represented in a sovereign assembly, and Greek-style 'democracy' which demanded for each and every Frenchman an active voice in government. This tension was exemplified in the places of political assembly, where elected representatives sat in the body of the hall while vociferous onlookers in the viewing gallery claimed to be an embodiment of the *demos* and shaped the direction of debate.[2]

De Tocqueville attributed the collapse of the revolution to its insistence on dismantling the church alongside the old constitution, and he saw the revolutionaries as men driven by a new species of religion. The Catholic Church enjoyed a near monopoly of French education under the Old Regime, and many of angriest anti-clerical voices in the National Assembly were products of that system. In the last chapter, I showed how the seeds of modern English democracy lay in a radical Protestantism which hated hierarchy and insisted that people were in the first instance individuals who should be free to follow their private conscience. The Catholicism embedded in French culture meant that the revolutionaries of 1789–1794 were more sympathetic to ritual, collectivity and in the broadest sense theatre. They set up elaborate quasi-religious festivals in the streets, and in commercial if not aesthetic terms metropolitan theatres were a success story. However, Jean-Jacques Rousseau, a product of Calvinist Geneva, fed into the culture of post-Catholic France a Protestant sensibility that put a premium on emotional truth and moral transparency, condemning the essential fakery of theatre.[3] There was no way to resolve the tension between these two ideas.

The study of classical oratory was a cornerstone of elite French education, and most of the leading revolutionaries were well trained in the art of marshalling persuasive public arguments while concealing the rhetorical techniques they deployed. Catholic educators were always happy for their students to immerse themselves in pagan Cicero because of Cicero's insistence on civic virtue in the speaker, and Cicero alongside Plutarch planted in French radicals a conviction that heroism lay in civic virtue, and must count for more than any obligation to home and family. The exclusion of women from public life sustained this republican creed.[4]

The causes of the French Revolution have been much debated, with the economic rise of a new bourgeoisie weighed against the impact of new ideas, and the power of the mob weighed against the power of the pen.[5] Paris in the mid eighteenth century was a place of intellectual ferment and, as De Tocqueville observed, philosophers like Voltaire had no practical interest in how politics worked.[6] Under the Old Regime there was no forum equivalent to the British Parliament where politics could be seen at work, and this blank slate allowed radical social changes to be imagined that might never in practice be viable. Whatever the transpersonal causes of the Revolution, the question of agency arises when particular human beings try to persuade others to follow a given course of action, which is what had to happen once the collective frenzy of the attack on the Bastille subsided. I will ask in this chapter: What makes for a persuasive performance? Logical argument? The display of emotions like anger, fear, pity and loyalty? Telling an alluring story? Or a quality of physical presence? In their recent book *Messengers: Who We Listen to, Who We Don't, and Why*, the behavioural psychologists Stephen Martin and Joseph Marks demonstrate how people are swayed less by facts and ideas than by the individuals who deliver them, and they isolate qualities such as status, attractiveness and most problematically 'charisma' in an attempt to explain the power of particular messengers.[7] I shall frame this chapter around six messengers, each of whom shines light on a different aspect of political performance. I begin with the playwright Philippe Fabre d'Eglantine in order to see how the Revolution related to the civic institution of theatre.

Fabre d'Eglantine: Politics and the Public Theatre

Parisian theatres under the Old Regime, as in Stuart England, were formally controlled by the Court but served as a conduit for public opinion. Calling for organizational change at the start of the Revolution, the playwright Jean-François de La Harpe explained that theatres mattered because of the contagious nature of emotion. Actors and playwrights, he claimed, responded to the collective mood before giving public opinion a nudge in the direction of progress.[8] In the years building up to the Revolution, the abolition first of privileged seats on stage and then of standing places in the pit created the illusion of a homogeneous auditorium that was the single voice of bourgeois opinion.[9] We should not of course confuse this 'public opinion' with the feelings of the *demos*, the so-called *sans-culottes* or 'no britches' who lacked the time or money to visit the theatre.[10]

When the Revolution began, Fabre had education behind him, but as an actor, playwright and manager he had not yet made good on the Paris stage, and the Revolution offered him a route to status and income. He entered politics through becoming secretary to the charismatic Parisian orator Danton, and worked his way to a dominant position first in Danton's Cordeliers Club and later in the Jacobin Club. The Cordeliers district was home to the Comédie Française, the most important theatre in Paris, and this gave Fabre leverage over the actors who controlled the repertoire.[11] His assumed surname 'd'Eglantine' alluded to a pure white rose supposedly won as a prize for a poem to the Virgin Mary, a bold choice given his reputation as a sexual predator.[12] At the height of the Terror, Saint-Just complained of how Fabre 'managed the revolution like a theatrical plot ... He played on minds and hearts, on prejudices and passions, in just the way a composer plays notes on a musical instrument.'[13] Although Fabre was a man of diverse intellectual and creative skills that included painting and singing, there is no obvious reason to place him amongst De Tocqueville's sincere and disinterested patriots.

As a man of the theatre, Fabre finally made his name with his play *The Philinte of Molière* performed at the Comédie Française in 1790. Rousseau was the apostle of the Revolution, appealing both to the affluent bourgeoisie who liked his emphasis on personal emotion, and to radicals who liked his theory of the General Will that envisaged government via consensus of the masses. Rousseau's *Letter to d'Alembert* of 1758 was a passionate manifesto attacking theatre as a corrupt medium that could never provide the moral education dreamed of by philosophers such as d'Alembert, Diderot and Voltaire, and at the centre of this manifesto was an analysis of Molière's masterpiece *The Misanthrope*, where the comic hero Alceste tries to be brutally honest and never hide his thoughts, refusing to oil the wheels that make social life possible. Rousseau's *Letter* envisages the possibility that one day a genius might reverse Molière's narrative, positioning as the ultimate egotist not the forthright Alceste but Philinte the voice of conciliation and white lies. For Rousseau, Molière was a writer of personal integrity forced into moral compromise by the need to win laughs from the pit.[14]

Fabre boldly aspired to be that writer of genius, and he was fortunate that the actor François-René Molé, familiar to the public in the role of Molière's comic hero, was able to render Fabre's new, selfless version of Alceste as a warm and sympathetic figure.[15] Reflecting the public mood, Baron von Grimm pronounced that although the play had less finesse than Molière's original, it was more important and useful.[16] The comedy and poignancy of Molière's original Alceste derives from the character's sexual attraction to a flirt, but in line with Rousseau's stipulations no love interest was allowed to contaminate Fabre's sequel. One critic lamented that Fabre's writings 'charm the mind and never reach the heart'.[17] *Philinte* was scarcely a revolutionary text, for, as Mechele Leon points out, the play was written before the Revolution and had 'radicalism thrust upon it',[18] borrowing its plot motifs, character types and verse form from the Old Regime. Fabre's subsequent plays endorsed the principle of monarchy, in accordance with the prevailing mood of the audience before the King's execution, but he took a step too far when writing a play that satirised proceedings in the Jacobin club: it was promptly closed and the text has vanished.[19] Humour was dangerous, and the theatre was now no place for the free expression of opinion.

Serving well-heeled audiences did not sit altogether comfortably with Fabre's role of Danton's sidekick. Mme Roland painted a savage portrait of the pair when they attended her salon in 1792. 'As for Fabre d'Eglantine, decked out in his vestments, armed with a quill, caught up with weaving a plot to denounce or ruin the rich innocent whose fortune he covets, he is so perfectly into his role that if anyone wanted to paint the most nefarious

Tartuffe, dressed like that he could have sat for a portrait.'[20] Fabre's preferred self-image was Alceste, a role which he himself used to play in his touring days, and in the prologue to *Philinte* he created a persona for himself as an angry straight-talking version of Alceste, waving a copy of the *Letter to d'Alembert* at the audience, and offering his anger as proof of his integrity.[21] 'Do you take my *Philinte* for mere play? Is theatre nought but an idle pastime? When freedom dawns, let theatre turn classroom.'[22] When he had to defend *Tartuffe* against the clerics, Molière also claimed that theatre was educational. Rousseau's *Letter* was an elegant demolition of this argument, and Fabre's moral posturing lacked foundation.

Fired by the success of *Philinte*, Fabre wrote another homage play inspired by *Emile*, Rousseau's treatise on education. One pupil educated *à la mode* presents his aunt with a bouquet of artificial flowers and then delivers florid verses of equal artifice, gesturing copiously 'with all the affectation common in children trained in declamation, his voice two tones above the harmony of childhood', switching to a sentimentally sweet voice when the rose is made to speak. His cousin educated *à la Rousseau* responds with flowers gathered on the mountainside in an image of nature and authenticity.[23] By implication, Fabre claimed he was offering his own audience a natural and authentic representation of the world, but his play was of course shaped by stage convention and performed by actors trained in declamation. Denying its own artifice, the play also denied the existence of moral contradiction, and in a world of political chaos the audience must have found comfort in Fabre's easy certainties.

Unlike Danton, Fabre was not one of the Revolution's finest orators, too much of a chameleon to persuade the crowd of his personal authority and integrity, but he was a master of using language to weave stories and build characters, with a professional expertise in unmasking the performances of others. Robespierre seems to have been slower than most in recognising the political operator behind the façade, realising only belatedly:

> No mechanic positions his cogs better than this crafter of plots sets up passions and characters to make his stories work. No-one has better studied the art of dropping his own thoughts and feelings unnoticed into others, so to embed in people's minds ahead of time, quite casually, ideas kept for use later, when they can be linked to other circumstances freshly established, so it will seem as if facts, reason and never his own doing have swayed those against whom he has been plotting, so poor a patriot, yet so proud of his talent.[24]

Fabre's narrative skills kept trouble at bay when, suspected of embezzlement, he invented a plausible English conspiracy to fend off the accusation.[25] And his powers of character building are illustrated by his tribute to Marat, where a vivid description of the populist orator's looks, voice and delivery build a compelling portrait of a flawed genius, a man who was neither hypocrite nor charlatan but loved the People with all his heart and soul.[26] It was a character that Fabre conjured up for Marat more easily than for himself, with Tartuffe constantly breaking through the mask of Alceste. Like Aeschines, he could never escape being seen as an actor.

Hérault de Séchelles: The Matter of Technique

An aristocrat and high-flying lawyer in favour with the Queen, Hérault de Séchelles threw up his inheritance to become a revolutionary. When the King reluctantly convened an assembly of the three Estates on the eve of the Revolution, the nobility rejected Hérault but the commoners chose him as one of their representatives, and he went on to become one of the most effective orators in the Assembly, where he was three times elected to the challenging role of president.[27] The particular interest of Hérault lies in two short books where he analysed the rhetorical skills that he brought to the political arena, secrets of his art published only after his death.

Hérault turned to actors to understand the performance aspects of oratory traditionally discussed under the Latin heading of *actio*, and his *Reflections on Declamation* sounds more like the work of an actor than a lawyer.[28] The book documents lessons which Hérault received from the retired classical actress Clairon, widely celebrated as an exponent of calculated artistry, and contains further material from a fellow pupil, the actor J. Mauduit-Larive. Hérault makes it clear at the outset that 'a man who speaks in public plays a character of some sort. The first care of the orator must be to make only his character visible. The illusion is ruined if he fails to keep concealed the lessons he has learnt.'[29] Since the political orator plays a role just as much as a stage actor, there can be no question for Hérault of personal sincerity, but this does not imply any stepping back from emotion. Hérault admires the technique of the great actor Lekain who in impassioned roles used to produce gestures and broken sounds that allowed the audience to surmise subterranean emotions in the depths of the actor's soul.[30]

Taking it for granted that you convince nobody by reading out a text, Hérault begins with ways of training the memory in order to give every sign of spontaneity. Learning 'by heart', Hérault explains, does not mean learning by rote because an affective dimension is never absent. From memory he passes to the voice, and recalls Clairon's question at their first encounter: "Do you possess a voice?... Well, we'll have to make you one."[31] Using Clairon as a model without parroting her, Hérault develops a middling voice relaxed enough not to obstruct the force of emotion, and learns to slow his pace so he has a foundation on which to build. Voice is tied to person, Clairon explains, and a strong voice implies determination. The attention which Hérault gives to voice production might seem of small relevance today, but acoustics in the National Assembly, a hall originally designed for equestrian displays, were notoriously bad, and the orator needed both learnt skills and the right physical endowment to make himself audible (Figure 4.2).[32]

In eighteenth-century theatrical practice, finding specific emotions was the starting point for expressivity of both voice and gesture. Clairon taught Hérault to isolate and identify the emotions that belonged to each phrase in a sentence, not emotions that he the orator was supposed to feel within himself but those which had to be implanted in the listener, and she demonstrated her own ability to run through a repertory of feeling using nothing but her face. In the matter of gesture, a term which refers primarily to arms, hands and face, Hérault lays out what he has learnt from watching actors in the theatre, commenting that none of this knowledge can be found in standard manuals. Clairon explained to him that as a lawyer he needed to be minimalistic, using smaller and sparser gestures than those of stage actors to create the strongest effect, and Hérault notes for himself how few movements are in fact deployed by the best actors on stage. In the course of the eighteenth century the art of acting had increasingly detached itself from the skills of the law court and pulpit, and Hérault effectively reunited those arts under the pressure of swaying a democratic assembly subject to few protocols of deference.

Clairon was famous for her regal manner, and a key quality that Hérault learns from her training is 'nobility'. Keeping the head raised above the shoulders, preserving muscle tone and relaxing the hands all chimed with his aristocratic upbringing, and contributed to the desired quality of 'grace'. What Hérault learned from actors was to stand in a way that felt comfortable and authoritative rather than artificial and class-bound. Hérault slips into a footnote an anecdote about Clairon's great rival, Mme Dumesnil, lauded by the revolutionaries for her spontaneous and authentic passion.[33] The philosopher d'Alembert, Hérault reports, was a brilliant mimic, and when he offered Dumesnil an impression of her style, she instantly stopped him and lamented that he had caught so brilliantly the awkwardness of her left hand, a fault that she had spent ten years trying to rectify.[34] Dumesnil's spontaneity, in other words, was a carefully crafted illusion. Hérault sought to acquire a perfect posture that would arrest an audience's gaze through its representation of naturalness, creating the quality described today as 'presence'.

In his *Theory of Ambition* Hérault's concern is the psychology of persuasion. He draws heavily on Antoine La Salle, a materialist philosopher whom he took under his wing in the 1780s, responsible for the theory set out in the *Reflections* that the musical scales of the voice match onto a moral scale.[35] La Salle saw the human being as a complex machine which had to be kept in equilibrium,[36] recognising that the surface meaning of words is often contradicted by movements and gestures which allow character to be decoded.[37] Hérault sounds much like Fabre when he advises speakers that in order to act upon others they should 'not try to convince or persuade, but plant your devices in the feelings and thoughts of our listeners'. Since people never like to feel that a speaker is working on them, it is more effective to show that one has oneself come to an overwhelming realisation. To this end, before engaging in any sort of conversation, Hérault advises his reader to 'step back for a moment in order to stage yourself properly [*se bien mettre en scène*]'. To move others, the novice speaker must learn to 'give strength and flexibility to his voice, his looks, his face, and his whole performance, so he can at will propel his marionettes this way or that.'[38]

Since Hérault was inspired by materialist philosophy, it is worth comparing him to the Abbé Maury, a champion of Church and Monarchy in the early days of the National Assembly. As a man of the cloth, despite his own powerful build and reputation for shoving opponents from the rostrum, Maury said little about the body beyond the need for lungs and a piercing voice. In his essay on preaching published before the Revolution and again in an expanded edition afterwards, Maury developed a dialogic theory of oratory influenced by the theatre as he pursued his aim of making a thousand people share a single thought.[39] The key to successful oratory, he argues, is to create an imaginary interlocutor, and focus all your attention on that listener, never calling attention to self except to foreground personal failings, and avoiding any sense of acting or 'declamation'. It was a technique that generated striking silences as the speaker paused to listen for an imagined reply. With legal rhetoric bogged down by facts, Maury argues, and preaching in decline since the rise of neo-puritan Jansenism, the preacher learns from playwrights about how to construct characters and storylines, since the theatre is a place where people come to have their emotions moved. Personal faith and sincerity have little part to play when the churchman describes his art of persuasion.

The art of both Maury and Hérault was grounded in antiquity. Maury told how the great Demosthenes hid is own feelings beneath different characters, like general, prophet or king, and beneath the passions of his listeners as he subjugated them in the political arena.[40] Hérault in 1792 delivered a passionate tribute to the translator who knew that eloquence is tied to liberty and brought Demosthenes back to life for modern Frenchmen. Hérault himself drew on Demosthenes' tirades when convincing the Assembly, against the wishes of Robespierre, that France should go to war.[41] Whether he really believed in the strategic wisdom of this move, or whether he was seduced by the excitement of stirring up his audience, can never be known, but a hint of his inner world appears in a footnote where he protests that political celebrities who surround themselves with admirers should not be criticised for vanity because it is company that feeds their genius.[42]

The high point of Hérault's career came when democratic politics fused with theatre on 10 August 1793. As president of the Constituent Assembly, Hérault was charged with delivering speeches in front of giant effigies at the Festival of Unity and Indivisibility.[43] The aim was to commemorate ordinary Parisians who had died a year earlier in the assault on the Palace that brought monarchy to an end. Hérault was personally responsible for drafting the new democratic constitution that had been approved but not implemented, and this celebration of unity papered over bitter divisions now that hardline Parisians had ousted the once-dominant Girondin faction. Hérault found himself at dawn amid the ruins of the Bastille before an audience of thousands, standing in front of a huge statue of Nature flanked by lionesses with the pure water of regeneration streaming from her breasts (Figure 4.1), and it was his job to proclaim:

> Sovereign over Savage and over Enlightened Nations, O NATURE! This vast People gathered, at the sun's first rays, in front of your image, is worthy of you: it is free. In your bosom, in your sacred springs, it has recovered its rights, it has been reborn. After enduring so many centuries of error and servitude, it had to go back to your simpler ways to regain liberty and equality...[44]

A communal song of peace was sung to the martial tune of the Marseillaise as Hérault administered pure water from Nature's breasts to eighty-six old men who represented the newly established *départements* of France in a solemn pastiche of the communion service. The procession moved on to five other evocative locations with more speeches for Hérault to deliver.

The demotic, improvisatory oratory of a Danton or a Maury would not have served. Revolutionary festivals, choreographed by the painter David,

Oratory in the French Revolution

Figure 4.1 The Fountain of Regeneration: Hérault de Séchelles receives water from the statue of Nature.
Source: *La Fontaine de la Regeneration sur les debris de la Bastille, le 10 avril 1793*. Detail of an etching by Antoine-Jean Duclos after an original by Charles Monnet, c. 1794. Rosenwald collection, National Gallery of Art, Washington, DC.

had a classical aesthetic, and Hérault was trained by a classical tragedienne. Paradoxically, it was his aristocratic bearing that allowed him to stand as a symbol of the great democratic French nation. Like Demosthenes, Hérault knew how to confer heroic status on ordinary citizens deemed to have given their lives for their nation. Martin and Marx identify 'attractiveness' as one of the features of a successful political messenger, and Hérault was famed for exceptional good looks, which clearly fed into his political charisma.[45] Hérault's invocation of Nature did not need to convey sincerity. Its job was to create a compelling narrative about human nature and about the history of the French people, using the symbols of the old religion to stir a new politicised religious faith. Hérault's task was to sell a vision, and this has always been a part of democratic politics, too easily dismissed with words like 'propaganda', 'spin' or 'rhetoric'. Without rhetoric there would have been no revolution, and whether based on the external methods of an Hérault or the internal methods of a Maury, rhetoric has always been a learnt theatrical art.

The Marquis de Condorcet: The Perils of Liberalism

Condorcet was, like Hérault, an aristocrat turned political radical.[46] A former associate of Voltaire and an eminent mathematician, he was in a sense the resident philosopher in the Assembly, and he seems to tick all the boxes of modern liberalism. He believed in the political equality of men and women, and became President of the Society of the Friends of the Blacks at a time when the slave population of Haiti was rising in rebellion to demand citizen rights. He opposed the death penalty and foxhunting, argued for care for the elderly and some redistribution within a context of free-market economics, and he was an internationalist friendly with Paine and Jefferson. He hated the irrationality of monarchy and religion, and an experience of childhood sexual abuse may have given special animus to his loathing of Catholicism.[47]

The revolutionary cause to which Condorcet committed himself most profoundly was education, grasping that democracy turns upon an informed electorate, and he chaired the committee responsible for educational policy. Education shaped his thinking about slavery, and he developed a scheme for graduated emancipation because he believed that the experience of slavery was so corrupting, both intellectually and morally, that freed slaves would not instantly be in a position to exercise citizen rights.[48] In his *Sketch of a Historical Picture of the Human Mind*, he envisaged a final era of human development when 'that moment comes when the sun will no longer shine upon the earth save upon free men who recognise no other master but reason; where tyrants and slaves, priests and their unwitting or hypocritical instruments, will nowhere exist save in history or upon the stage'.[49] In Condorcet's utopian vision of a rational world, theatre survives as a tool of education to expose any Tartuffe who might still be lurking. It is ironic that Condorcet penned his *Sketch* while in hiding from the Terror, and he killed himself rather than face the guillotine. His quasi-religious faith in human reason flew in the face of the immediate facts.

Because Condorcet believed in reason rather than eloquence, he was slow to get elected to the Assembly. Unlike Fabre and Hérault, he was also a poor seducer of women, and the happy consequence was that he ended up in middle age as a devoted husband and father, married to a woman who became his intellectual collaborator. Sophie de Grouchy, through translating Adam Smith's *Theory of Moral Sentiments*, became expert in the domain of emotions and their connection to physiology, the aspect of human life that her husband seems to have found most difficult.[50] As a mathematician, Condorcet was a pioneer in grasping the contradictions in any simple system of majority voting, and to achieve a more democratic constitution he constructed a pyramidal scheme grounded in local assemblies to ensure popular participation, to filter representatives, and to generate consensus rather than conflict, but in another irony he was not eloquent enough to persuade the Assembly of the virtues of his plan.[51] It fell to Hérault, trained in the art of persuasion, to devise a simpler and thus more acceptable scheme, celebrated in the Festival of Unity but never adopted because a State of Emergency caused democratic principles to be set aside.

As a believer in progress, Condorcet rejected the model of Antiquity, arguing for a system of education based on modern science where words had precise meanings, and not on classical rhetoric as imparted by the Catholic Church to men like Fabre and himself. He wanted a progressive politics, as he reported to the Assembly in April 1792:

> I shall take just one example: Demosthenes, up there on the rostrum, addressing an assembly of the Athenians. Thanks to his speech a resolution was approved by the nation itself, with copies of his text passing down to orators and their pupils. Today we deliver a speech not to the People, but to its representatives, and in print the speech circulates to as many cold and severe judges as there are French citizens taken up by politics. In the past, when an engaging, passionate, seductive rhetoric might lead assemblies of the people astray, those who were deceived then merely adjudged on their own interests, and the mistake redounded only upon themselves. Should representatives of the People, however, allow themselves to be seduced by an orator, and yield to a power other than reason, then they will be failing in their duty, for they adjudge the interests of others, and will soon lose public trust, the sole basis on which any system of representation rests. That same rhetoric which was so needful in ancient systems of government would, in ours, become the seed of disastrous corruption. In those days it

was allowable, maybe useful, to move the people; today, our sole task is to try to enlighten.[52]

Rational thought, for Condorcet, was produced not by speech but by the written word, and the people had to be educated accordingly. Wary of populism, he considered that big assemblies were dangerous things:

> There could be exceptions: maybe an assembly of 1200 persons, divided into groups whose bonds are weak and uncertain, with nobody marching under any single leader's banner; or an assembly where the members are strangers to each other, known only to the electors who chose them.

Anti-Catholic prejudice in the House of Commons was an object lesson in the dangers of collective emotion.[53] Condorcet's personal lack of performance skills amplified his wariness of audiences given to responding as a collective rather than as individuals.

Theatre was a dilemma, for as a liberal Condorcet believed in freedom from censorship, but the power of the stage can too easily be misused. The tragedies of Voltaire demonstrated the potential value of theatrical performance because they had acted powerfully on French public opinion. Not only through the text but also through shocking stage images, they had 'helped release the spirit of youth from the chains of a servile education, and those whom fashion pointed towards trivia were forced to think.' Addressing Rousseau's vision of civic festivals, he commented that these needed to be 'genuinely popular' rather than spectacles gifted to the people by the authorities, and proposed a completely new genre: miniature tragedies in verse with plenty of physical action, but also words that would linger in the mind.[54] Yet the dilemma remained. His concept of democratic citizenship revolved around personal choice, and he was wary of theatre stirring up 'blind enthusiasm that renders citizens incapable of judging. If you say to them: Here is what you need to cherish and believe! – then that's a kind of political religion you are trying to create, chains you prepare for the mind.'[55] Political orators might in theory seek to enlighten rather than move their listeners, but it was hard to ask a playwright or actor to make the same distinction.

When La Harpe in the aftermath of the Terror set about reshaping the educational system, he reversed Condorcet's position on rhetoric, challenging an imaginary rationalist who might have been Condorcet: 'Eloquence is reason in armour, and reason needs to be armed for it has so many enemies. *He* claims that reason is sufficient to guide men, forgetting that men have passions, and that the aim of eloquence is to rouse noble passions against low passions.'[56] Stephen Pinker is a modern liberal champion of 'Enlightenment' values who echoes Condorcet's faith in reason and human progress, maintaining that according to all available data the world is steadily if unevenly becoming a better place. Writing in the age of Donald Trump, however, Pinker had to concede: 'There is, of course, a flaming exception: electoral politics and the issues that have clung to it. Here the rules of the game are fiendishly designed to bring out the most irrational in people.' Pinker traces the conundrum of democracy back to Plato and has no solution to offer.[57] Democracy has always been and can only be a form of theatre, subject to the vagaries of human emotion.

Joseph-Marie Lequinio: Observer of the Assembly

Lequinio was a Breton lawyer elected to the Assembly in 1791.[58] Like Fabre and Condorcet, he was trained in rhetoric by churchmen, an experience which turned him into a rationalist with an aversion to religion, and like Condorcet he was committed to the cause of education. Not a gifted public speaker, he was a fluent writer and a man of action, ruthlessly effective in putting down rebellion in the Vendée. At the age of fifteen he went to live among Breton peasants, admiring their directness though not their religiosity, and this sparked his lasting commitment to the cause of the rural poor. His *School for Labourers* of 1790 set out to be a plain man's guide to the revolution in far-away Paris. And in his *Prejudices Destroyed* (1792), he set out to give a countryman's view of the National Assembly. The latter was republished to coincide with the opening of the newly constituted 'Convention' in 1793, and he clearly hoped that the main failings of the earlier 'Constituent' and 'Legislative' Assemblies would now be avoided.

In his chapter on oratory or *éloquence*, Lequinio defines oratory as an art of deception which makes people fall in love with error, a tool for manipulation, and the scourge of liberty, with no real difference between three types of despot: king, priest and demagogue. Much like Plato, Lequinio pictures himself as a philosopher writing for mental slaves, 'you whose eyelids stay sealed, weighed down by passions'.[59] Like Aristophanes he argues ironically that the only way to beat demagogues is to join them:

> In your turn, become the mountebank. Begin by flattering your listeners; overwhelm their senses; try your best to deceive; produce a mighty flow of words so they can have no clear view of anything; let each new thought chase away the last so your audience never lingers, reflects, judges; search out pompous phrases, sonorous words, rhythmic periods; then finish with grand gestures that strike to the heart and kill reason. Hear it now – the

Figure 4.2 A meeting of the National Assembly in 1793, with an artistic representation of the way all eyes are focused on the speaker.
Source: *Présenté et dedié à la Convention Nationale l'an 2ᵉ de la République.* Detail of an engraving by A. Duplessis, 1793. Gift of Dorothy Braude Edinburg to the Harry B. and Bessie K. Braude Memorial Collection, Art Institute of Chicago.

bravoes, the clapping, the stamping of feet, applause of every kind, a complete triumph for you, and for your listeners surrender of their liberty.[60]

Reading is less dangerous for Lequinio than oratory because readers have time to reflect, and he develops three metaphors to catch the essence of demagoguery. First, seduction: the democratic audience resembles a girl yearning to be seduced, impervious to any speaker who confines himself to the cold voice of reason. Second, with echoes of the Garden of Eden, is the serpent whose poison spreads slowly through the veins. And for his third image he turns to the mountebank, the quack doctor hawking snake-oil as a cure for every illness. Though reason looks dry and dull by comparison, Lequinio believes optimistically that truth can ultimately become a passion.[61]

Lequinio describes the evils which human passions have introduced into the elected assembly, a body constituted on fine principles that has become a chaos of interruptions with no-one ever listening. He lists types of orator including the garrulous drunkard, the man of bile who cannot spit his words out, the self-satisfied bore, the pseudo-intellectual and the handsome charmer. The clerk and minute-taker has power to determine what has or has not been decided, while the President from his chair manipulates events by determining who speaks and whom to admit as a petitioner.[62] The presence of individuals and groups petitioning from the floor of the House added to the theatrical flavour of the Assembly, as it pursued its ideal of democratic openness.[63] Writing before the Jacobins to the left of the hall had separated themselves definitively from the Girondists on the right, Lequinio explains how secret procedural agreements created the reality of political parties. He extends his analysis to the clubs, which in theory allowed issues to be mulled upon thoughtfully, but in reality were hotbeds of intrigue, hypocrisy and flattery just like the Assembly. Things are no better in the public square, where street orators blow hot and cold before ignorant audiences. In his *School for Labourers* Lequinio imagined illiterate Bretons becoming politically engaged through listening to readings from newspapers in public places and debating them, but this is no longer possible because the Parisian press has lost its integrity.[64]

Lequinio moves on from character sketches to techniques, observing how easily the crowd is directed towards enemies of the public good, just as the needle of a compass is attracted by a magnet. In a fail-safe strategy of invoking 'the people', speakers tend to conflate the whole French nation with the 900 vocal Parisians gathered in the viewing galleries, and the orator can sometimes also pack the auditorium with stooges who applaud or boo on cue, or voice absurd counterarguments which make the speaker's advice seem sensible.[65] Lequinio's critique is driven by the spectre of a monster, the demagogue, that will emerge from its lair with shining eyes, fearsome face and stinking breath to devour its victims, but he is hard put to say how democracy might be made to function better. 'How to resist despotism in an assembly like this?', he wonders. 'Were it composed only of philosophers, there would no danger to fear; but what age could bring such things to pass?'[66] Yet all is not quite despair. With the 1789 'Declaration of the Rights of Man and of the Citizen' in mind, Lequinio ponders how it can be that 'in this hall soiled by passions, light shines forth; here are shaped, amid storms and tempests, at the heart of intrigue and inconsistency, august resolutions that will everywhere restore to men their rights, send tyrants to their death, and bring freedom to people'. A rational, enlightened politics seems to have sprung mysteriously from the hotbed of emotion that is the Assembly.

When Lequinio left Parisian politics to suppress counter-revolution in the Vendée, he was caught up in the operations of the Terror, ruling with absolute authority in the manner of Plato's philosopher-king.[67] When he quelled a prison riot by personally shooting the ringleader, and gave orders for 500 prisoners to be shot, he acted in the heat of the moment and used his powers of rationalization to vindicate himself retrospectively, explaining that this was a means to avoid greater bloodshed. While he was busying himself knocking down churches in the Vendée in a fervour of rationalist zeal, Robespierre and Saint-Just came to the conclusion that the French people could only be ruled though a surrogate religion, and objected to Lequinio's *Prejudices Destroyed* not for its political satire but for its atheism. Saint-Just wrote a memo to himself: 'Tell Lequinio that in a revolution philosophy must accord with politics, unless you wish to lose all by setting public opinion against you', and he duly chastised Lequinio for failing to see that 'religious opinions are those most resistant to force'.[68] To act on public opinion meant accepting the fundamental irrationality of human nature – something Lequinio refused to acknowledge.

Comte de Mirabeau: The Power of Passion

Honoré Gabriel Riqueti, Count of Mirabeau, made few claims to rationality or honesty, but in the first phase of the Revolution, until his death in April 1791, his was the dominant voice in the National Assembly.[69] He became a celebrity in 1782 when he defended himself in court, seeking to reclaim his wife whom he had abandoned in order to elope with the bride of an elderly Marquis. He was up against his own father, his wealthy in-laws and a battery of expensive lawyers, and as a penniless rebel defying and exposing the establishment he caught the public imagination, developing a persona that would serve him well in the Assembly. Like Hérault he combined the authority of an aristocrat with the romantic aura of a rebel, but where Hérault played the elegant charmer, Mirabeau played the clown, a physically distinctive figure with his large head, barrel torso, scarred face and a mass of tousled hair. When shortly before the Revolution he attended an aristocratic dinner-party, one observer commented on the colour and size of his buttons, and the enormity of his buckles:

> In short, you could see in every aspect of his dress a travesty of current fashion, quite out of keeping with courtly taste. His face was disfigured by the scars of smallpox. His gaze was dark, but his eyes full of fire. Trying to show himself polite, he exaggerated every nicety. He began with pretentious and distinctly vulgar compliments, and to be brief, he possessed neither the manners nor language of the society in which he found himself. Although

by birth the equal of his hosts, you could see at once from his manners that he lacked the ease of those accustomed to high society.

Once talk turned to politics, however:

> All that had at first seemed ridiculous in Mirabeau's appearance vanished in a trice. You saw only the breadth and depth of his thinking, and everyone was captivated by the brilliance and energy of his conversation.[70]

Whether Mirabeau was genuinely gauche and unpractised or set out to mock the absurdities of a society he had come to deplore remains ambiguous, but in either event his later success as a politician would lie in counterpointing against his comic exterior smouldering passions and an incisive intellect. His physical persona allowed him to create the double image of authority figure and common man of the people.

Mirabeau was able to play the victim in court in 1782 because he had just spent four years locked up in the Château de Vincennes. Here, in addition to developing his political case for tolerance, translating Latin love poetry and writing pornographic novels, he penned passionate love-letters to the young Marquise, mother of his child, who was now locked away in a convent. The challenge in these letters was to communicate through words his living presence, his beating heart, and the authenticity of his feeling, counteracting his beloved's anxiety that he was a mere rhetorician, and he honed a skill in seducing through words that would serve him well in the political arena. He complimented the Marquise on the pure simplicity of her style that allowed the expression of true feelings, but reassured her that writing can still allow *esprit* – wit or intelligence – even as it resists mere ornament. 'True eloquence consists in saying things that fit a given situation, and giving to each feeling, each thought, its equivalent colouring; in a word, to say everything just as it should be said. This is the whole secret of the orator's art, my Sophie, it is to be passionate. So – you are wiser than you thought.'[71] Perhaps, as one biographer suggests, when they wrote these letters the couple imagined themselves as the two protagonists in Rousseau's romantic novel *Julie*.[72] Desire soon faded, but there is no reason to insist that Mirabeau was being consciously insincere as he crafted his passionate Rousseauesque prose.

When he reflected upon the central problem that confronted the revolutionary government, how to educate the people for democracy, unlike Condorcet and Lequinio Mirabeau did not fall back on the utopian ideal of reason and science. In a speech to the National Assembly, he argued that human beings are not driven by principles but by 'imposing objects, striking images, fine spectacles, deep emotions':

> Man, I repeat, obeys his impressions rather than his reason. It is not enough to show him the truth; the key point is to make him passionate for truth. It is of little use to meet his material needs if you do not also take hold of his imagination. So it is less a matter of convincing him than of moving him; less about proving how excellent are the laws by which he is governed, than making him love those laws with feelings of deep affection which he cannot erase, try as he may, and which follow him always, for ever setting before him a cherished and reverential picture of the fatherland.

Mirabeau saw no role for Christianity because it cared only about heaven, but admired the festivals of antiquity tied to a religion which was connected to the earth.[73] Faced with the challenge to create an inclusive democracy capable of winning the hearts of the uneducated, he had no easy answer to the problem of affect. His reputation plummeted after his death when his secret communications and financial arrangement with the King and Queen came to light, and it is evident that he could not envisage any alternative to constitutional monarchy as a means to create the bonds of feeling that hold a society together.

Before these revelations, a fellow orator paid tribute to Mirabeau as a second Jupiter. The 'pomp' of Mirabeau's similes

> made reason more attractive, gave a magical colour to the driest discussion, and knew how to throw an alluring veil over gaps in a rhetoric sometimes overwhelmed by the ardour of its patriotism. It was in improvisation above all that his greatness seemed to exceed the measure of humanity. His speech began slow, his chest looked tight, he might have been labouring to forge thunderbolts. Soon his delivery came to life, lightning leapt from his eyes, and with a terrifying gesture his menacing hand weighed the doom in store for enemies of the nation, the vaults of the temple rang with his now piercing voice, he filled the rostrum with his majesty – he was its god.[74]

The tribute catches the physicality of Mirabeau's performance when he hammers out words as if they were objects, his eyes and hands inseparable adjuncts of language. Mirabeau evidently had huge lungs, related to his unusual physique, and these helped him command a large auditorium notorious for its bad acoustics and unruly listeners. Improvisation was a crucial skill because one never knew what interruptions were coming. Speeches in the Assembly were not formally delivered to the presiding chair, as in the House of Commons, but directly to the elected representatives, and in practice also to the galleries.[75] Mirabeau knew how to use embodied speech to build belief in his own overwhelming patriotic emotion, and when the Assembly is likened to a temple, the metaphor is no empty one because patriotism now substituted for the old religion.

Despite his apprenticeship in gaol as a writer, Mirabeau's greatest skill lay in acting, and he was fed material by a team of scriptwriters as he engaged in the workaday business of running government.[76] Camille Desmoulins once compared him to a Roman mime who performed with his flexible body while an unseen accomplice voiced the text behind the backdrop. The comparison was prompted by a speech penned by Mirabeau's assistant Jean-Joachim Pellenc which conceded the King's right to declare war when Mirabeau had just declared himself a committed republican, and it seems the orator had not read his text carefully enough in advance. The two functions of actor and politician fell apart, with text and performance at odds, and Mirabeau needed all his skills in spontaneous improvisation to extricate himself. He chose a musical metaphor to explain the disaster: his job was to play the organ, and Pellenc had failed to operate the bellows. A recent study dubs Mirabeau a 'performance artist' who 'understood the inherent theatrical nature of a revolutionary politician'.[77]

The actor François-René Molé was present in 1789 when Mirabeau delivered one of his most famous speeches warning the Assembly of national bankruptcy. According to Mirabeau's secretary and script-writer Etienne Dumont, Molé found himself overcome by admiration:

> "Ah! Monsieur le Comte," he said to him in tones of high emotion, "what a speech! what expression in your delivery! My god! how you have missed your vocation!" And he smiled to himself, recognising the singularity of his praises, but Mirabeau was most flattered.[78]

A later memoir embroiders this account, having Molé revere Mirabeau 'as an artist in words, a fine craftsman of sound, a sublime musician without notes, the Gluck of spoken language'. Molé is said to have been dumb-founded when Mirabeau in the manner of a tragedian conjured up the picture of a yawning gulf 'as one hand, rigid with terror, reached forward to reveal the depths of the abyss, while the other clung to the bar in the action of a man seizing a life-raft'.[79] Dumont saw that Molé's compliment was double-edged in its emphasis on technique rather than feeling, but knew for himself that the famously passionate orator always kept control of his emotions when addressing the Assembly.[80] When Molé triumphed as Fabre's Alceste a few months later, his observation of politicians like Mirabeau must have helped him find the right gestures and intonations to simulate Alceste's famous honesty. There was no way to succeed as a politician in the Assembly without being an artist in words, a craftsman of sound, a composer of grand operatic narratives, and above all, a painter of emotional conviction.

Maximilien Robespierre: The Quest for Sincerity

Following Mirabeau's death in 1791, revolutionary politics was increasingly dominated by Robespierre, and if Mirabeau had lived collision would have been inevitable. A spat in the Jacobin Club in December 1790 shines a light on the issues at stake. The old Jacobin monastery was a convenient place for like-minded representatives to gather in the early evening after the Assembly had finished its business. The Jacobin Club became a place where genuine deliberation was possible and real political business could be done.

A satirical engraving will help us picture the scene. It depicts a later fracas in 1792, when the club had moved from the smaller library to the abandoned monastery church (Figure 4.3).[81] The seated members are relatively well dressed because they had to pay to enter, and they display a variety of strong emotions. The general illumination would have been dimmer than the engraving suggests, with a light over the speaker's

Figure 4.3 Parodic representation of a meeting of the Jacobin Club in 1792.
Source: *Grande Séance aux Jacobins en janvier 1792*. Anonymous aquatint, Musée Carnavalet, Paris, G.25851.

podium directing attention to the speaker's face. The issue in 1792 was war, and in the centre of the hall between two stoves we see the Minister of War, dressed as an aristocrat and in a play upon his name bearing the tiny head of a linnet. On the left, four speakers have crowded onto the podium, shouting out conflicting views. On the right, the elected president vainly tries to keep order, his bell and hat resting on the table. A group of women have removed his britches to suggest that he is shitting himself with fear of fighting, and one of them holds up a poster, indicative of the way women had no political voice except through writing, and we see more women egging on the men from the balcony. Above the president, beside a bust of the King, the angel of death unveils his face. "The case is embarrassing", declares the beleaguered president, whom we could read as Robespierre since he led the minority opposing war. The bellicose Brissotin faction subsequently seceded from the club, leaving Robespierre to become the effective master of an increasingly influential organisation.[82] Two years later, war led to suspension of the constitution and imposition of the Terror by the Committee for Public Safety.

The confrontation in 1790 is described by Camille Desmoulins, a school-friend and supporter of Robespierre. The Assembly had just decreed that citizens falling below a property threshold would not be allowed to serve in the National Guard:

> I will analyse the decree no further. But impossible not to jump into the unholy row at the Jacobins that evening provoked by Robespierre's fine speech. The applause heaped on him, such a condemnation of the afternoon's ruling, evidently troubled Mirabeau who was presiding at the Club. He had the temerity to call Robespierre to order, saying it was forbidden for anyone to speak against a decree that had been passed. This intervention provoked uproar at the gathering, already shocked at the plan to strip 'non-active' citizens of the right to wear uniform. Could anything be more tyrannous than the silence which Mirabeau imposed on Robespierre, and the alleged excuse? You have only the right to demand we obey decrees, not the right to silence us. It is in your power to bind our wills, that is enough, but not to suppress our thoughts. See what a tyrant this president is, refusing to allow an orator to speak, when through their applause the members are insisting, he must go on.

Desmoulins now expatiates on Athenian democracy where citizens were free to challenge decrees:

> Not a peasant or market woman in Athens but they would have laughed in Mirabeau's face had he trotted it out, saying no they could not speak against some decree or other. So the hubbub went on for an hour and a half.

Mirabeau, realising the sound of his bell was inaudible and he could not make his voice heard, decided to address the eye, and catch them with some new action, so instead of donning his hat like the president of the National Assembly, he clambered onto his chair. "Let all my brothers stand by me!" he cried, as though it were a question of physically protecting the decree. At once some thirty honourable members came forward and surrounded Mirabeau. Facing him was Robespierre, always so pure and so incorruptible, and at this meeting so eloquent, surrounded by every true Jacobin, republicans to their souls, the elite amongst patriots. Mirabeau did not grasp that if idolatry be permitted in a free people, the idol must be virtue!

Desmoulins recalls how he once used to idolise Rousseau, later grasping that some principles cannot be reconciled with the fallibility of human nature, and then returns to his narrative:

> The silence which Mirabeau's bell and theatrical gesture had failed to win was successfully achieved by Charles Lameth, his arm in a sling. Lameth climbed onto the podium, where, whilst congratulating Robespierre for his love of the people and calling him his very dear friend, he gave him a sharp punch, insisting, like Monsieur le Président, that no one was allowed to question a decree, whether ratified or otherwise.

Another speaker then supplied a verbal fudge, maintaining that the Constitutional Committee had a different interpretation of what the decree actually meant. Robespierre continued his speech to further applause, but Desmoulins expresses his frustration at a messy outcome which reflected no credit on the Club. If other freedoms have been lost, he concludes wryly, at least there remains his own freedom as a journalist to publish the truth.[83]

This spat could have been the occasion when Mirabeau said of Robespierre: "That man will go far, for he believes everything he says."[84] Perhaps it was sarcasm, or perhaps he saw prophetically how the younger man's aura of sincerity would, over the next few years, trump his own method of working the crowd. Two different concepts of democracy were at stake. While Mirabeau believed in representative democracy, and insisted upon the authority of the elected Assembly, Robespierre believed in participatory democracy, and dreamed of a better assembly with 12,000 persons present.[85] The decree passed by the Assembly was a crucial one, denying to the poor, the so-called *sans-culottes*, the right to bear arms and serve in the National Guard. Robespierre insists on the right of the 'people' to intervene in the debate.[86] The desire for equality collided with fears about anarchy and the security of property, much as it did in Putney when Cromwell held out for suffrage based on a property qualification.

Desmoulins invoked Athens and Rome to support the republican principle that citizenship equates with the right and duty to fight for one's city, while Robespierre turned to Rousseau's Geneva, using religious language to support the citizen's 'sacred' right to fight for his country. As a southerner answerable to electors in Provence, Mirabeau could never be comfortable with the sacralization of a 'nation' centred on Paris, and it is easy to see why he was so disturbed when Robespierre built up to the claim: 'It is impossible that National Guardsmen could themselves become a danger to liberty, for it would be a contradiction to think the nation might seek to oppress itself.'[87] The *sans-culottes* were conspicuous by their absence from the Jacobin club, and everyone knew the threat they posed to law and order.

Robespierre's route to power lay through the Jacobins. At its outset, the Club was part of the bourgeois public sphere, modelled on literary clubs where intellectuals gathered to discuss ideas, and it had a valuable role as a forum where more deliberation was possible than in the Assembly, with the to-and-fro of ideas allowing scrutiny of issues that faced the Assembly as it sought to build a new social and political system. Mirabeau's theatrical skills were less crucial in the old monastic library than they were in the hall of the Assembly. Robespierre lacked the vocal virtuosity and expansive physical presence of Mirabeau, but was a master of the written word, and it was a carefully crafted speech that he read out to the Jacobins, with emotive catchphrases laid out in measured tones. Once his speech had been delivered, he had it printed and distributed to the thousand or more Jacobin clubs set up across the country, using the cheap technology of print just as the English Levellers had done to reach a wider *demos*. Mirabeau's oratory was always of its place and moment, and could not be replicated by another speaker, but Robespierre's speeches, reliant on familiar rhetorical tropes, could be read out to great effect by someone else whose main task was to display emotional commitment. The spat between Robespierre and Mirabeau is a symbolic moment when democratic debate broke down. Language no longer served to resolve conflict when Lameth gave Robespierre a punch with his available arm in a symbolic act of violence.

Desmoulins condemns Mirabeau's antic of climbing on a chair as a 'theatrical gesture', and Lameth no less theatrically flaunts his wounded arm, the consequence of putting his life on the line in a duel fought on behalf of his political principles. Robespierre could not afford to appear 'theatrical' when seeking to put his republican soul on display, so he developed a studied neutrality based on old-fashioned formal dress and limited modulation of the voice in order to divert attention away from the external body. A supporter of Robespierre claimed that the tears of emotion which he elicited in the Jacobin Club when unmasking members of the Assembly were proof of his virtue:

> Ah, yes, I need have no fear of being contradicted by true patriots when I say that he is the most eloquent man of the revolution, because he is the most virtuous. He is more eloquent than that mountebank, the comedian Mirabeau, who dazzled the soul with fine words and grand gestures but never touched it. Virtue alone is truly eloquent, because it draws its methods from nature – unlike drama [*l'intrigue*] which uses artifice to dazzle without convincing, or the mountebank who lacks those sublime movements of the soul which characterise the virtuous man, so unlike the cool calculated technique of the *comédien*.[88]

The claim that excellence in oratory equates with moral virtue is grounded in Cicero and Quintilian, but it was Demosthenes who established the principle that tears are the sign of authentic patriotism. Politics tends to be cyclic. Mirabeau appealed to the French public as a renegade, a breaker of social norms in his dress, manner and sexual mores, but when the old order had fallen and the new order seemed frighteningly insecure, the demand arose for truth and personal integrity. The attraction of Mirabeau, a man of the flesh, yielded to the lure of a man who was restrained, celibate, frail, spiritual and reputed 'the incorruptible'.

Robespierre was a devotee of Rousseau, whose critique of theatricality was connected to a cult of personal authenticity underpinned by the *Confessions*, a pioneering work of autobiography. In his oratory Robespierre pursued Rousseau's emotional sensitivity rather than the heroic style of Mirabeau because he wanted to be seen as the champion of ordinary people united by universal human feelings.[89] Rousseau's political theory of the 'General Will' envisaged consensus with no place for the *agon* of debate but it was, paradoxically, a manifestation of individualism through its rejection of parties and groupings, and its demand that individuals should reach into themselves to find what connects them to the community. For both Rousseau and Robespierre, class conflict was dissolved by a homogeneous 'nation' or 'people', and by the transcendental figure of the 'patriot'. In revolutionary France, war was the price paid for establishing a collective sense of nation, setting up an enemy in order to define what it was to be French, and it was war that led to suspension of due democratic process, leaving Robespierre to cast himself as privileged interpreter of the General Will. Robespierre followed Rousseau in recognising that human beings have spiritual needs, and his sense of the sacred put him at odds with the materialism of a Condorcet or a Lequinio. In the surrogate religion of the Revolution, Mirabeau echoed the Catholic fallen Adam, a self-acknowledged creature of sin, while Robespierre the tortured disciple of Rousseau replicated the Calvinist who sought to be identified by their faith and moral purity as a member of God's elect.

The key term that ties politics and theatre together in the French Revolution is 'representation'.[90] Mirabeau championed representative government, and himself *represented* the people of far-away Aix-en-Provence without being their mere delegate or mouthpiece. In private, he saw the monarchy as a symbolic representation of the nation, and the only feasible way to maintain civic order, and as an orator he delivered texts written for him by others, making no effort to hide the way he used vocal and gestural tools of representation to express deeply felt passions, constructing the figure of the good citizen in the minds of his listeners without himself embodying that impossible being. Performance skills of this kind were indispensable if the National Assembly was to function. Robespierre saw no place in politics for the mountebank or comedian, and tried to reject representation in favour of authenticity and transparency, but in practice he could not dispense with rhetoric, and declaiming speeches from the French tragic poets was one technique he used in private to develop his performance skills, cultivating the art of the tragic pause to lay bare the feeling that lay behind the words he declaimed.[91] The act of reading, emphasised by his prominent spectacles, positioned him as someone who did not look like an actor. Robespierre dreamed of an inclusive democracy that would embrace the poor, but in practice he fell back on Plato's ideal of the philosopher-king, the individual with enough wisdom, virtue and fellow-feeling to legislate for the common good. He spoke passionately on behalf of the poor in the Jacobin Club, but the poor could not afford the entrance fee to listen to him. The flamboyant rhetoric of Danton did a better job of reaching out to the *sans-culottes*, but Danton lacked the moral purity that Robespierre demanded.

On the road to the scaffold Fabre is said to have shouted at Robespierre's window: 'You vile Tartuffe!'[92] He knew that Robespierre was ultimately an actor, but had never succeeded in unmasking him. The emotional truth of the actor has been a mystery ever since the Greek actor Polos carried the ashes of his dead son onto the stage in order to give an authentic rendering of Electra's grief. The catch in this philosophical teaser is that Electra only simulates grief for her brother in order to deceive their mother.[93] We face the same conundrum when we ask: Was Robespierre ultimately a version of honest Alceste, or was he Tartuffe the hypocrite?

In the public arena, Robespierre had no way to be true to himself without performing a role derived from heroes like Rousseau or Cato. Republican virtue could not be imagined without reference to models, and when condemning his friends Desmoulins and Danton to the guillotine Robespierre modelled himself on Roman heroes like Brutus, painted by the artist Jacques-Louis David in the act of condemning his own son to death.[94] The quest for an authenticity that transcends representation led Robespierre to the verge of mental breakdown when he tried in 1794 to unmask all those false patriots who refused to speak their minds:

> It is so much easier to put on the mask of patriotism and debase the sublime drama of the revolution with a coarse parody, compromising the cause of liberty by turning into a hypocritical moderate or calculating extremist ... Not every heart has changed, but look how many faces now wear masks!... You try to stop the plotting? you'll be reminded of the clemency of Caesar; you seek to rescue patriots from persecution? they say, model yourself on the rigour of Brutus. They're beyond imagining, the lengths they go to, these counter-revolutionaries, bent on wrecking the cause of revolution.[95]

There was no hero's role left for Robespierre to fall back on in the 'sublime drama' that he sought to play out.

***

When these six tragic and in some ways heroic lives are placed side by side, they confirm the proposition of Gorgias that without rhetoric there can be no democracy. Hobbes seems to have been right to insist that without the theatrical mask there can be no social order. While Fabre, Hérault and Mirabeau all understood the need for any democratic politician to be a species of actor, Condorcet and Lequinio held out for an impossible ideal, dispensing with political theatre in hopes of running a rational and empathetic government on behalf of the poor. Robespierre saw the need for theatrical events like the Festival of Unity, but could not find his personal route to becoming an actor. Thanks to the Catholic tradition, the necessity of rhetoric and/or theatre was more readily accepted by would-be democrats in France than it was by their contemporaries in Protestant America.

CHAPTER 5

American Democracy
From the Founders to Feminism

Alexis de Tocqueville's *Democracy in America*, based on a visit in 1830, remains an indispensable guide to early American democracy, using the term 'democracy' to embrace both a constitutional structure and a way of life.[1] Rescuing the word from its connotations of mob rule, De Tocqueville used it to describe a system that he believed would become the global norm. He saw how American democracy was grounded in the puritanism of the founding fathers, and showed how it was tied both to individualism, a concept he distinguished from egotism, and to commerce, anticipating Max Weber's argument in *The Protestant Ethic and the Spirit of Capitalism*.[2] Seeing America through the lens of the centralised French Revolution allowed De Tocqueville to explain what was gained and lost by Jefferson's philosophy of localism, and in the second volume of his book he established connections between literature, language, public speaking and theatre which indicate why it is still important today to think about art and politics as an ensemble.

De Tocqueville saw the theatre as an important barometer of public opinion. Despite municipal censorship, it was becoming an American institution, and De Tocqueville argued that 'democratic' audiences, having little desire to study texts, preferred plays to be addressed to their hearts and ears rather than their minds. These new democratic Americans wanted to see their own ordinary lives reflected and celebrated on stage, and were not interested in the exotic otherness of history. American audiences, he wrote, 'enjoy seeing on the stage that muddle of classes, feelings and ideas encountered before their eyes every day. The theatre becomes more striking, more vulgar and more true.'[3] Put another way, American theatre thrived on melodramatic emotion, making no attempt to elevate audience taste, and the word 'true' anticipates a distinctive twentieth-century American taste for 'naturalism'.[4] De Tocqueville expresses regret at the lack of public interest in antiquity, so unlike France, and we might therefore be surprised to learn that the great hit in New York at the time of his visit was a play about the slave rebellion of Spartacus.[5] In actuality, *Gladiator* had no serious interest in history, and was a symbolic vehicle for the heroism and pathos of an isolated working-class hero.

John Adams

With her husband John, later to become second president of the new USA, Abigail Adams visited England and France in 1784–1786, and her reactions are representative of American bourgeois attitudes to European values. In London, she was shocked by the prospect of the famous actress Sarah Siddons performing while pregnant, relieved by Siddons' choice of costume, pleased by Siddons' reputation for moral rectitude (enhanced by performing opposite a brother not a lover), worried that Siddons might be morally contaminated by playing the evil Lady Macbeth, and aware of her own prejudice when repelled by seeing Siddons as Desdemona touch a man made up to look African.[6] In Paris, Abigail complained about the behaviour of French women of all social classes: 'Habituated to frequent the theatres from the earliest age, they become perfect mistresses of the art of insinuation and the powers of persuasion. Intelligence is communicated to every feature of the face, and to every limb of the body; so that it may with truth be said, every man of this nation is an actor, and every woman an actress.' At the ballet, Abigail was initially enchanted by the beauty of the dancers, but upon seeing transparent costumes and exposed underwear 'I felt my delicacy wounded, and I was ashamed to be seen to look at them'. However, she soon had to confess to her sister 'that repeatedly seeing these dances has worn off that disgust, which I at first felt, and that I see them now with pleasure', while reassuring herself that 'neither my reason nor judgement has accompanied my sensibility', and she was no less enchanted by the 'soft, persuasive power' of French music. The opera house, she concluded, was a temple of Venus where the shield of Athena was needed 'to screen youth from the arrows which assail them on every side'. French Catholicism was part of the problem because actresses were denied church burial and therefore saw no need for moral restraint.[7]

The significance of Catholicism becomes clearer when we turn back a decade to see what John Adams told Abigail about his life in Philadelphia. He was bored by democratic speech in the new Continental Congress because, as he wrote ironically: 'Every man in it is a great man – an orator, a critic, a statesman, and therefore every man upon every question must show his oratory, his criticism and his political abilities.' Equally unimpressed by the local Presbyterian preachers, he confessed that curiosity had led him into the Catholic Church:

> This afternoon's entertainment was to me, most awful and affecting. The poor wretches ... bowing to the name of Jesus, wherever they hear it ... The dress of the Priest was rich with lace –his pulpit was velvet and gold ... But how shall I describe the picture of our Saviour in a frame of marble over the altar at full length upon the cross, in the agonies, and the blood dropping and streaming from his wounds. The music consisting of an organ, and a choir of singers, went all the afternoon, excepting sermon time, and the assembly chanted – most sweetly and exquisitely. Here is everything which can lay hold of the eye, ear, and imagination. Everything which can charm and bewitch the simple and ignorant. I wonder how Luther ever broke the spell.

Though he hated submissiveness, Adams could not prevent his own surrender to the sensuous appeal of the choral music, the fabrics and the graphic image of the crucifixion, and his ambivalence mirrors that of Abigail at the theatre.[8] Later in life he recalled ascending the *via crucis* on Mont Calvaire near Paris to discover for himself 'the theatrical machinery of Popery', and realise: 'Human nature cannot stand against this imposing pomp, splendour and magnificence, profoundly studied to touch and overbear the finest feelings of the heart. The gratitude, the tenderness, the compassion, the sympathy.' He returned often, but recalled how it drove him mad. Self-censorship may explain why he seems to have told Abigail nothing of this encounter.[9]

These powerful responses to theatre and to Catholicism help us understand the roots of America's Puritan democracy because they mirror debates about public speech, where the sensuous power of words was felt to overwhelm rationality and self-censorship in the listener. Adams was bored in the Congress because there was a cultural pressure to be boring. Puritanism taught people to open up to God alone, and not let their emotions be aroused by the persuasive techniques of actors or priests. Honesty was the thing that mattered. Thomas Jefferson told King George III before the Declaration of Independence that '[t]he whole art of government consists in the art of being honest', and he refused to offer the King flattery because 'it is not an American art'.[10] Judith Shklar offers insight into the conundrum of American honesty when she argues that what matters is cruelty, and the 'ordinary vices' of hypocrisy, snobbery and misanthropy are inescapable, forgivable concomitants of human coexistence.[11] In the first part of this chapter, I focus on the figure of John Adams who was much maligned for these ordinary vices, his reputation overshadowed by Thomas Jefferson, the man who succeeded him as president.[12] In two crucial instances, Jefferson closed his eyes to cruelty in a way that Adams refused to do, living off slave labour and excusing the French Jacobins for imposing the Terror.[13]

Jefferson declared that he wrote to the English king 'with that freedom of language and sentiment which becomes a free people, claiming their rights as derived from the laws of nature'.[14] Adams never signed up to this doctrine of 'nature' grounded in Locke and Rousseau, preferring to view social life through the lens of theatrical performance. While Jefferson created his personal Garden of Eden at Monticello, staging a vision of utopia that was actually built on the proceeds of slave labour and debt, Adams drew from the Protestant tradition a sense that humans bear individual responsibility for the sin of Adam without any conviction that he himself was one of God's elect, and this sense of self fused with a performative conception of the world derived from classical antiquity. His understanding of life as theatre was first articulated in a letter to a Harvard classmate when he was settling on the idea of a career in the law:

> Upon the stage of life, we have each of us a part, a laborious and difficult part, to act, but we are all capable of acting our parts, however difficult, to the best advantage. Upon common theatres indeed the applause of the audience is of more importance to the actors than their own approbation. But upon the stage of life, while conscience claps, let the world hiss! On the contrary if conscience disapproves, the loudest applauses of the world are of little value.

The Stoicism of Horace reinforced the Christian sense of duty that pointed Adams to a career in the law:

> We have indeed the liberty of choosing what character we shall sustain in this great and important drama. But to choose rightly, we should consider in what character we can do the most service to our fellow men, as well as to ourselves.[15]

Adams retained his theatrical conception of the world into old age, and in 1805 he told his friend Benjamin Rush that he was thinking of writing a book called *The Scenery of the Business*, explaining how the business of politics was too often shaped by stage effects rather than the important components of character and plot.[16] Quoting the adage that 'Louis XIV, if not the greatest king, was the best actor of majesty that ever wore a crown', Adams told Rush that in the old days the same aristocratic art of acting sustained Protestant America. Public funerals and celebrations commemorating the landing on Plymouth Rock showed how the first citizens of Massachusetts were in fact great masters of the theatrical exhibitions of politics ... Washington understood this art very well, and we may say of him, if he was not the greatest president he was the best actor of presidency we have ever had. His address to the States when he left the army; his solemn leave taken of Congress when he resigned his commission; his farewell address to the people when he resigned his presidency. These were all in a strain of Shakespearean and Garrickal excellence in dramatic exhibitions.

After likening the hero famed for never telling a lie, George Washington, to the great Shakespearean actor David Garrick, Adams added resentfully that 'we Whigs attempted something of the kind. The Declaration of Independence I always considered as a theatrical show. Jefferson ran away with all the stage effect of that: i.e. all the glory of it.' The refusal of an English general to pardon rebel ringleaders also acted on public opinion to create a pair of modern saints. 'This however was not their contrivance nor any device of our party. It was an incident in the play that was not prepared by the author or actors.' Adams worries at the end of his letter that banking may one day replace theatre as the best way to exercise power.[17]

Adams' political point of reference was the Roman Republic, and in 1790 he wondered if there had 'ever been a nation who understood the human heart better than the Romans, or made a better use of the passion for consideration, congratulation, and distinction?' Antiquity and personal observation alike showed him that human beings yearn for marks of distinction that will elevate them over others, with money merely a means to this end. The Romans knew that

> [r]eason holds the helm, but passions are the gales. And as the direct road to these is through the senses, the language of signs was employed by Roman wisdom to excite the emulation and activate virtue of the citizens.

Examples of such symbols include the laticlave (the purple stripe on a senator's toga), and the parading of conquered rulers through the streets where it is 'easy to see how such a scene must operate on the hearts of the nation'. In Adams' view citizens are even more status-obsessed in modern republics than they are in monarchies, and so need new ways to stage their social positions in order to satisfy 'that desire of the attention, consideration, and congratulations of our fellow men, which is the great spring of social activity'.[18] While Jefferson, like the Levellers who faced up to Cromwell, harked back to an Anglo-Saxon utopia where a natural order prevailed, Adams looked to Greece and Rome where no social order ever survived for long.[19]

Adams' concern for distinction and ceremony was not always well judged, and he made mistakes when serving as Washington's vice-president: over-dressing, powdering his wig, demanding a carriage, and seeking a quasi-royal title for the presidential office.[20] It took him time to grasp that Americans were different from Europeans and did not respond well to visible status symbols but demanded more subtle signs of distinction. As a committed republican Adams believed that self-sufficient citizens should be free from aristocratic rule, but he was no democrat or Jacobin trusting in the *demos*, and believed '[t]here never was a democracy yet that did not commit suicide'.[21] His study of antiquity taught him that the essential business of politics was balance, and middle-class rule was the best way to prevent civic violence.[22] Here again, he did not grasp that America was different from Europe. Geographic dispersion combined with ethnic and religious diversity meant there could be no emergence of a *sans culottes* or homogeneous working class. Adams was a Federalist whose thinking was predicated on rule from the centre, from a capital city which would allow the inspiration of leaders in the Assembly to ripple out to the periphery, and this misunderstanding of America helps explain why Jefferson swept Adams from power in the election of 1800.

Rhetoric in America

Adams' lifelong role-model was Cicero whose picture of Rome, he thought, allows us to 'see the true character of the times, and the passions of all the actors on the stage'.[23] Cicero battled with his weapon of the spoken word to save the Roman Republic from demagogues and warlords, and ultimately died for his beliefs. Oratory stood at the centre of Roman life, and Adams knew how his own political speeches had built up the will to fight England. Before becoming sixth president of the United States, his son John Quincy was Professor of Rhetoric at Harvard, and set out the shared ideals of father and son for the benefit of an aspiring undergraduate:

> Let him catch from the relics of ancient oratory those unresisting powers, which mould the mind of man to the will of the speaker, and yield the guidance of a nation to the dominion of the voice. Under governments purely republican, where every citizen has a deep interest in the affairs of the nation ... the voice of eloquence will not be heard in vain.[24]

John Quincy took it for granted that the Harvard-educated elite would provide the voice of eloquence needed to mould the new Republic, and his concern was not equity but liberty. 'Eloquence is the child of liberty', he insisted, 'and can descend from no other stock'.[25] In his vision of a free society, John Quincy ignored the risk of enslavement to the art of the demagogue, and assumed that education must equate with wisdom.

American Democracy: From the Founders to Feminism

As Benjamin Constant argued in the wake of the French Revolution, the liberty of the ancients did not easily match onto the individualistic world of the moderns,[26] and although it is easy to see the Adamses as dinosaurs in their harking back to ancient Rome, their core insight that a democratic public is swayed by rhetoric rather than logic has lost none of its force. For the Adamses, people are by nature neither rational nor virtuous, and it is their emotions that have to be addressed. Jefferson was a better writer, but John Adams was a more effective speaker, and understood that people respond more instinctively to the spoken word than the written.[27] While listening tends to be a social activity, radio demonstrates the capacity of the voice in a pre-television age to connect individuals to the personhood and emotions of a speaker. As Roland Barthes put it, the grain of the voice 'has us hear a body'.[28] With the decline of newspapers and rise of ear-buds in the twenty-first century, speech is regaining something of its old place in the sensory hierarchy.[29]

When John Adams was training as a lawyer, he loved to read Cicero aloud: 'The sweetness and grandeur of his sounds, the harmony of his numbers give pleasure enough to reward the reading if one understands none of his meaning. Besides I find it, a noble exercise. It exercises my lungs, raises my spirits, opens my pores, quickens the circulations, and so contributes much to health.'[30] He knew that a lawyer needed the 'talent, and art of moving the passions' in order to sway a jury – a sentiment that is heresy to a modern British barrister, but less so to their US counterpart.[31] John Adams declaimed Cicero because he enjoyed the sounds and rhythms he heard in the Latin:

> [A]s a musician, to get the skill of moving the passions, must study the connection between sounds and passions, so should an orator . . . An orator to gain the art of moving the passions, must attend to nature, must observe the sounds in which all sorts of people express the passions and sentiments of their hearts, and must learn to adapt his own voice, to the passion he would move. The easiest way to this will be to possess his own mind strongly, with the passion he would raise, and then his voice will conform itself of course. Thus if you will raise in a jury a resentment of some great crime, resent it strongly yourself, and then the boldest thoughts and words will occur to your mind, and utter themselves with the most natural tone of voice, expression of countenance and gesture of your body.[32]

The lawyer in court has therefore to become an actor, combining observation with imagination, living his role so that words, voice, face and gesture combine to convince the jury of the speaker's real indignation, offering no clue to the rational mind or learnt script that lurks unseen. These

Ciceronian principles demand much of the performer,[33] and after becoming a Senator, John Quincy confessed in his diary how difficult it was for his mind to keep pace with the words tumbling from his mouth. Only 'in the ardor of debate, when my feelings are wound up to a high tone, elocution pours itself along with unusual rapidity, and I have passages which would not shame a good speaker'.[34] Theory was one thing, the practice of speaking persuasively another.

Within the person of John Adams, the classicist and the Christian collided. Adams conceived the political world in terms of theatre, but was also committed to moral integrity. Machiavelli fascinated him because he could not decide whether the famous playwright, champion of republicanism and critic of the Catholic Church 'was in jest or in earnest. I cannot discern one trace of sincerity in all his writings'. Machiavelli reminded him of Garrick, because you knew that at any time he might simply be 'acting a part', which led him to wonder whether critics of Machiavelli were in fact any more sincere. And then again: 'Was Tom Paine more sincere than either? I know he was not.'[35] When Benjamin Rush urged him to set down for posterity an account of his political and moral values, Adams knew he could not deliver because although his conscience was 'clear as a crystal glass', anything he wrote about alcohol, marital fidelity or paper money would be regarded as proofs of his hypocrisy. While Washington and Franklin had gone down in history as disinterested patriots, posterity would take it for granted that Adams 'never had anything in view but his private interest, from his birth to his death', and he needed a skilled writer like Jefferson to create the appropriate persona for him. After all, Washington had successfully employed others to write his speeches and 'borrowed eloquence if it contains good stuff, is as good as own eloquence'.[36] What mattered for Adams the politician-orator was speech in the here and now, but part of him could not let go of the Christian idea that it is wrong to be an actor, and more importantly, he knew that others judged him on the basis of his supposed inner being. The ideals of Ciceronian oratory were incompatible with a society that became fixated on private motives and personal morality.

This tension explains the distinction which emerged in early nineteenth-century America between the two separate arts of oratory and public speaking.[37] An early historian of American oratory, echoing De Tocqueville, saw no scope for magnetic oratory in Congress because elected representatives care only about their constituents back home, and at election time 'do not oratorize, they build platforms'. Consolation lay in the thought that good public speaking 'will long be universal with

Americans' because democratic life offers so many opportunities.[38] Countless public speakers in community meetings found their Bible in Hugh Blair's *Lectures on Rhetoric and Belles Lettres* first published in 1783, which showed how it was possible to reconcile the dangerous classical tradition with a puritan sensibility. Blair was a well-connected Presbyterian minister in Edinburgh, and he positioned rhetoric as the means to acquire 'taste', a euphemism for membership of an anti-aristocratic social elite. His lectures glide smoothly from public speaking to literary composition, and steer clear of addressing the bodily challenge of standing up before a crowd. Blair skirts cautiously round Cicero's principle that the speaker has to feel for himself the emotions he wants to impart, and warns against the idea that students can learn from arguing both sides of a case irrespective of what they personally believe. A speaker, rather, should be 'in earnest, and uttering his own sentiments'.[39] Blair irons out signs of social disparity by insisting on correctness of pronunciation, while observing wistfully that the intense passions of Demosthenes cannot be accommodated by a politer and more enlightened age. The energetic gestures advocated by Cicero, he warns, would nowadays 'be reckoned extravagant anywhere except upon the stage. Modern eloquence is much more cool and temperate'.[40] Blair taught prosperous Americans how to reconcile the two opposed ideals of decorum and personal authenticity as they reached for a homogeneous public language. When John Adams urged Congress in 1780 to create an equivalent to the French Académie Française in order 'to have a public standard for all persons in every part of the continent to appeal to, both for the signification and pronunciation of the language',[41] he had the same goal in mind – equality, but only amongst the educated.

In London the 'elocutionary' movement was initially driven by the Irish actor Thomas Sheridan, who worked to establish a standard and expressive English in order to reanimate public life. The movement was political because it eliminated regional differences (Sheridan was Irish, Blair was a Scot) in favour of a consistent middle-class voice capable of wielding authority over the aristocracy. Elocution was a philosophical project of the Enlightenment because it assumed that language is a transparent medium giving access to the scientific reality that lies behind the word. It resists the old principle of Rhetoric that words are material productions of the body deployed less to express truth than to act upon others.[42] Although Sheridan was interested in sound values, and the Scottish Calvinist James Burgh had some impact on America with work on gesture, Blair's elocution won the day because he eliminated the body in order to place speaking as an extension of writing.[43] Words for Blair were a vehicle for revealing truth, and as a good Protestant he was committed to truth, so the goal of his teaching was to coat truth with an elegant layer of 'style'. De Tocqueville noticed how everyday speech was pulling away from the standard written idiom of democratic America, but as a Francophone he did not consider how that normative language associated with the written word was a tool of power, vesting an aura of natural authority in the educated classes.[44] In the light of Blair's project to establish a 'proper' way of speaking, we need to ask, who in the new America was in a position to speak? I shall focus in the second part of this chapter on three alternative voices that soon clamoured to be heard: the working-class Irish voice, the black voice, the female voice.

The Astor Place Riot

Like Cromwell, John Adams assumed that only men of property deserved the right to vote, and extending the suffrage to all adult white males was a piecemeal process,[45] complete by the time Europe was riven by working-class revolutions in 1848–1849. The nearest the American *demos* came to revolution was in 1849 in the seething industrial city of New York, in front of a new opera house built in the architectural manner of a Greek temple. The Astor Place riot was triggered by rivalry between two actors, the American Edwin Forrest and William Charles Macready on tour from England. When the National Guard opened fire, they left twenty-two dead (Figure 5.1).[46] Theatre riots were frequent in the early nineteenth century, the most notorious of all being the protest in Paris against Victor Hugo's *Hernani* a year before De Tocqueville's tour of the USA, and De Tocqueville concluded that such riots were part of the process that led to the embedding of democratic ideas. He saw the theatre as a democratizing force because of the way the lower classes audibly and visibly expressed their views: 'It is in the theatre that men of learning and letters have always had most difficulty getting their own taste to prevail over that of the people, and in preventing themselves from being swept up by theirs. The pit has often laid down laws for the boxes.'[47] In De Tocqueville's conception theatre was both a precursor and paradigm of democracy, providing a formal structure that left everyone free to have their voices heard.

In Philadelphia in 1848, protests against the actor from England retained a certain ritual quality:

> After he had withdrawn, some one in the pit proposed "three cheers for Macready," which were heartily given – with "three more," and "three

Figure 5.1 Outside the Astor Place opera house, the National Guard fire at the crowd.
Source: *Astor Place Opera-House riots.* The Miriam and Ira D. Wallach Division of Art, Prints and Photographs: The New York Public Library. The New York Public Library Digital Collections. Anonymous print from the *Illustrated London News,* 2 June 1849.

more." Another one in the pit proposed "three cheers for Ned Forrest," which were given with considerable strength, but not equal to those just given for Macready. "Three more cheers" were given for Macready; after which affairs settled down'.[48]

In New York in 1849, however, disorder slid into uncontained violence. The new opera house erected by a property tycoon in Astor Place was a symbol of class exclusiveness, and democratically minded working men were outraged at seeing a rich elite behave like high European aristocracy. For men who worked with their hands, the white kid gloves worn by these opera-goers was a special affront. One of the leaders of the *demos*, a printer and migrant from Cork named Mike Walsh, articulated a different philosophy in his newspaper: 'Demagogues tell you that you are freemen. They lie – you are slaves, and none are better aware of the fact than the heathenish dogs who call you freemen.'[49] To put this another way, the prevailing rhetoric of democratic freedom was the hypocritical posturing of a capitalist ruling class, and Walsh's Irish ring is caught in his phrase 'heathenish dogs'. Walsh challenged the elected leaders of the new so-called 'Democratic' party, arguing for the native intelligence of the working man: 'We understand Democracy – that is pure and unadulterated Democracy, as well as these gentlemen do. It is plain, simple and beautiful in its naked simplicity.'[50]

In the aftermath of the riot, it was not trigger-happy guardsmen but the rioters who came under scrutiny. When ringleaders were put on trial, Judge Daly pronounced that 'under institutions like ours, where every man is an integral part of the government, and has a voice in the creation of its laws, where the remedy for redressing grievances and reforming abuses is both certain and speedy, an unauthorised appeal to physical force is wholly without apology.'[51] Many rioters felt with Walsh that in democratic America they had no such voice or remedy. The problem was that in New York, unlike Paris and London, no single proletarian voice had the ability to unify the masses. The city at this time was controlled by rival gangs and bosses with a vested interest in gaining control of the Town Hall. Walsh's following of 'Bowery B'hoys' whose fire-engines gave them freedom of the streets were Irish Protestants, but many new immigrants in the wake of the potato famine were Catholic Irish, and hostility to England was a unifying force.

Edwin Forrest developed a persona on the stage that allowed him to capture and express the anger and frustration of white working men, dissolving diversity of religion, ethnicity and occupation within a single heroic figure.[52] The Bowery Theatre where Forrest reigned supreme sat in a working-class area, unlike the opera house. His most celebrated roles were tragic rebels, like the white-skinned Thracian slave Spartacus, Shakespeare's medieval Jack Cade or the 'redskin' leader Metamora who embodied the ideal of the uncontaminated natural savage. Forrest took pains to develop a muscular body that expressed the masculine aspirations of working-class men.[53] As a young actor on the circuit, the three books that he carried around with him were the Bible, Shakespeare and the elocutionist John Walker's *Critical Pronouncing Dictionary*.[54] These were the foundations of a universal stage idiom, a set of speech rhythms which unlike Blair's touched the hearts of ordinary white Americans of whatever extraction. Forrest considered going into politics and in 1838 addressed a crowd of thousands on behalf of the Democratic party, but his speech lacked the fire and single-mindedness which he imparted to dramatic roles.[55] On the theatrical stage Forrest was always visibly himself Edwin Forrest, but on the political podium Edwin Forrest found himself playing the alien role of an orator.[56]

Forrest's authorised biographer explained why, when characterising Forrest 'by the epithet American, it is necessary that we should understand what is meant by the word in such a connection. We mean that he was an intense ingrained democrat. Democracy asserts the superiority of man to his accidents.'[57] Forrest was the archetypal self-made man who overcame the random circumstances of his birth. Formerly a friend of Macready, he whipped up a public feud because it served his persona as an energetic and virile American quite opposite to the aloof, book-bound British actor whom the elite welcomed into the sanctity of their opera house. Forrest mounted his own performances of *Macbeth* to coincide with those of Macready, and his Macbeth was a straightforward rebel against royal authority, lacking the guilt and introspection of Macready's version (Figure 5.2).[58] When he displayed the power of his voice and muscles, Forrest offered up his performances as the fruits of his physical training, notably in boxing. He tapped into the romantic ideal of the natural savage, a man free in both his body and his emotions, allowing the *New York Herald* to declare: 'As Americans, we prefer the unsophisticated energy of the child of nature to the polish of the artificial European. Some prefer the toga, some the tomahawk.' The toga symbolises a classical education, the tomahawk Metamora.[59] Macready by contrast showed what a man could do by developing his mind, believing that 'to fathom the depths of character, to trace its latent motives, to feel its finest quiverings of emotion, to comprehend the thoughts that are hidden under words, and thus possess oneself of the actual mind of the individual man, is the highest reach of the player's art',[60] and a delivery broken by pauses helped communicate this inner world of the character. Because Forrest preferred unbroken passion, Macready described him as 'only an actor for the less intelligent of the Americans',[61] complaining that 'the democrat party' came in crowds to support Forrest, and that 'the papers speak of him in the same admiration and respect that they would of a real artist and a real gentleman!'[62]

When supporters of Forrest infiltrated the opera house, the scene that ensued was a form of direct democratic politics. The player of Malcolm, who in Shakespeare's play ousts Macbeth from power, was cheered as a hero, while Macready displayed extraordinary sang-froid under a hail of chairs, eggs, coins and rotten potatoes, to the sound of breaking windows. Through his self-possession under fire, Macready proclaimed his loyalty to wealthy patrons, but also the superiority of education over brawn, lacking the body of a boxer but possessing the same courage. While Walsh highlighted the intelligence of the working man, Macready pointed to superior qualities of the soul available to an educated elite. Through championing cosmopolitan over local American values, he also seized control of cultural capital. According to De Tocqueville, almost every pioneer's cabin contained 'a few odd volumes of Shakespeare',[63] but

Figure 5.2 Edwin Forrest as Macbeth.
Source: National Portrait Gallery, Smithsonian Institution; gift of the Edwin Forrest Home for Retired Actors. Photo by Mathew B. Brady, c. 1861.

Macready showed how the Shakespearean text conceals an inner world open only to cognoscenti. The riots have been seen as a turning point when high culture diverged from popular culture and took sole possession of the Bard.[64] The working Irishman could still go to the theatre to vociferate, but the theatre would no longer be a place where he could address himself to power.

For the protesters Macready represented the values of English gentility, but Macready himself was no aristocratic sympathiser, and in hindsight looks more like the embodiment of Whig values and bourgeois taste.[65] The introspective nature of his performance recalls De Tocqueville's theory of individualism. Democracy, De Tocqueville believed, 'never ceases to return man to himself alone, with the ultimate threat to imprison him completely in the solitude of his own heart.'[66] In Europe as in New York, theatre ceased to be an arena for political display of a kind that can be regarded as a form of direct democracy, and when the stage was lit first by gas then electricity, and the lights were dimmed in the auditorium, the theatre morphed into a place where individuals in the privacy of their seats perceived actors not as creators of collective feeling but as celebrities defined by unique personalities.[67] In the short term, the power of the gun triumphed in 1849 and order quickly returned to the streets of New York, but a political point was made and the opera house soon closed. In order to retain their power within an electoral democratic system, the rich had to learn to perform their social ordinariness, to play the role of individuals who lacked any collective identity as a ruling class.

Frederick Douglass

'Three cheers for Macready, Nigger Douglass, and Pete Williams!' was one of the mocking cries from rioters inside the theatre.[68] The responding cheers linked the actor from England to two prominent black Americans in order to place all three as outsiders, and many of the rioters moved on next day to target abolitionists.[69] Many working-class New Yorkers thought the liberalism of white campaigners a symptom of elite values, and there was a widespread fear that liberated slaves would lower factory wages. The fault line between a group descended from poor European immigrants and a group descended from slaves continues to bedevil America, creating an uncomfortable relationship between liberalism and democracy. In the first half of the nineteenth century, Celts were not identified with Anglo-Saxons and it was a slow process whereby the Catholic Irish became 'white'.[70]

Frederick Douglass has become an iconic figure because of his success in constructing a voice audible to the American elite, not least to Abraham Lincoln. As a self-educated escapee from slavery, Douglass achieved the remarkable feat of speaking the language of the educated, winning for black American males, at least provisionally, the right to vote. In the story that he tells about himself, a decisive moment came when, after persuading his master's wife to teach him to read, he purchased at the age of twelve a battered copy of Caleb Bingham's *The Columbian Orator*, an anthology of texts for declamation in schools. In this collection, a dialogue between master and slave demolishing the moral case for slavery is followed by an Irish political speech calling for Catholic emancipation.[71] From the first of these, Douglass began to learn how to argue, and from the second how to orate on behalf of human rights. There is no reason to doubt that reading aloud from this volume was the basis of his political education. Douglass explains how the 'these speeches added much to my limited stock of language, and enabled me to give tongue to many interesting thoughts, which had frequently flashed through my soul, and died away for want of utterance'. When he began his career as a public speaker, he was so familiar with the book that it 'whirled into the ranks of my speech with the aptitude of well-trained soldiers going through the drill'.[72]

Caleb Bingham is a very different figure from Hugh Blair. With personal experience of teaching both girls and Native Americans, Bingham was committed to mass education,[73] and he published *The Columbian Orator* in 1797 in the wake of the French Revolution at a time when it was possible to envisage radical social change. In the introduction, he refrains from moralising, leaving the extracts to speak for themselves, and offers his reader a lesson in how to perform culled from the teachings of antiquity. Cicero and Demosthenes reveal that the most important thing for the budding orator to master is not argument but 'action',[74] the key aspects of which are firstly posture and face, notably the eyes, and secondly voice, with special emphasis on varying tone and rhythm. Each emotion has its own way of being voiced and signalled, but Bingham like Cicero refrains from any codification which might imply that the body is just an instrument of the analytic mind. For Blair, oratory was a branch of literature, but for Bingham it was a performance art similar to but distinct from stage acting. While Bingham shows no interest in the social graces, Blair focuses upon the words the orator uses, preoccupied with taste and propriety, and he passes over Cicero's favourite topic of rhythm and cadence which doubtless smacked to him of manipulation. Both Blair and Bingham are concerned with emotion, but Bingham admires big political passions while Blair emphasises 'sympathy', the mark of a civilised individual. Blair pushes for a normative language that characterises educated people, while Bingham's volume offers his reader the chance to develop a multiplicity of voices to serve different occasions. Macready possessed an annotated copy of Blair,[75] for the book was consistent with his theatrical mission to prioritise what is said over the act of saying. Douglass, however, wanted to conjure up in the here and now the physical horrors of the external world that he had witnessed and endured. People remembered Douglass for his lips 'from which have fallen such golden eloquence, eyes from which have flashed such radiance, heart with such great throbs of sympathy for all God's downtrodden ones, hands which were always open and outstretched towards the wretched'.[76] These external signs of emotion connected Douglass' words to his body, so his whole person reached out to the listening other (Figure 5.3).

Thanks to Bingham, Douglass was in a position to master republican oratory, a tradition which a generation earlier was second nature to orators like Mirabeau, Hérault, and John Adams. His genius lay in fusing this republican tradition with a second voice that he developed over his years as a preacher, a career which began at the African Methodist Episcopal Zion Church of New Bedford when he was 21.[77] Here Douglass developed a different set of techniques based on rhythms and cadences shaped to elicit an immediate vocal response from the listeners. The emphasis here was not on the Bible but on the spiritual quality of the speaker called by God, and in the story Douglass tells about his childhood his first spiritual mentor was semi-illiterate: 'I could teach him "the letter" but he could teach me "the spirit"'.[78] The Methodist tradition was grounded in singing, and Douglass recalled how slave songs 'told a tale which was then altogether beyond my feeble comprehension; they were tones, loud, long and deep, breathing the prayer and complaint of souls boiling over with the bitterest anguish'. Religious truth was found not in verses of the Bible but in the sound of the speaker's voice as it penetrated the soul, and Douglass believed that no man with a heart could fail to respond once he allows himself to 'analyze the sounds that shall pass through the chambers of his soul'.[79] This was a form of piety that derived in some greater or lesser measure from West African cults of possession, and saw nothing irreligious in humour and anecdote.

A description of Douglass' oratory in his early days as a campaigner picks up on these qualities. Like Forrest, Douglass' powerful voice is connected to a masculine body as he fights for the dignity of a scorned class, and prowess in boxing was part of both men's personal mythology:[80]

> He was more than six feet in height; and his majestic form, as he rose to speak, straight as an arrow, muscular, yet lithe and graceful, his flashing eye, and more than all, his voice, that rivalled Webster's in its richness, and in the depth and sonorousness of its cadences, made up such an ideal of an orator as the listeners never forgot.

Daniel Webster was a famous Whig orator in Congress. When Douglass described life as a slave

> his eyes would now flash with defiance, and now grow dim with emotions he could not control; and the roll of his splendid voice, as he hurled his

FREDERICK DOUGLASS, THE ESCAPED SLAVE, ON AN ENGLISH PLATFORM, DENOUNCING SLAVEHOLDERS AND THEIR RELIGIOUS ABETTORS.

Figure 5.3   Frederick Douglass speaking from a London stage: "The man who wields the blood-clotted cow's-hide during the week fills the pulpit on Sunday."
Source: Schomburg Center for Research in Black Culture, Manuscripts, Archives and Rare Books Division: The New York Public Library. New York Public Library Digital Collections. From *The Uncle Tom's Cabin Almanack, or, Abolitionist Memento*. London: J. Cassell, 1852.

denunciations against the infamous system, would pass to the minor key, whose notes trembled on his tongue. Then, with inimitable mimicry, he would give a droll recital of some ludicrous scene in his experience as a slave, or with bitter sarcasm he would tell a tale of insult...[81]

The challenge for Douglass was to combine these honed performance skills with evidence that he was sincere, so as to convince the unwilling listener that he was something more than a mere stage actor, and the issue came to a head once he became a campaigner. He recalled how John Collins, secretary to the Massachusetts Anti-Slavery Society, introduced him as a 'graduate from the peculiar institution ... with my diploma written on my back!',[82] Douglass refused to display the scars on his back and objectify his body, since this would have imprinted him on the gaze as one who would somehow always be a slave.

> 'Be yourself,' said Collins, 'and tell your story.' It was said to me, 'Better have a *little* of the plantation manner of speech than not; 'tis not best that you seem too learned.' These excellent friends were actuated by the best of motives, and were not altogether wrong in their advice; and still I must speak just the word that seemed to *me* the word to be spoken *by* me. At last the apprehended trouble came. People doubted if I had ever been a slave. They said I did not talk like a slave, look like a slave, nor act like a slave ... Thus, I was in a pretty fair way to be denounced as an impostor.[83]

Through his insistence on maintaining agency and speaking the words that he himself wanted to speak, Douglass ended up being charged with hypocrisy. The seductive invitation to 'be yourself!' is so often given and so often problematic, particularly for politicians. Collins proffered the advice in order to elicit a performance, seeking to shoehorn Douglass' self into a mould.

Racism taught Douglass to become an expert in hypocrisy. When his master Thomas Auld underwent a conversion experience via the religious movement known as the Great Awakening, Douglass crept forward from the area assigned to blacks in order to watch:

> Standing where I did, I could see his every movement. I watched narrowly while he remained in the little pen; and although I saw that his face was extremely red, and his hair disheveled, and though I heard him groan, and saw a stray tear halting on his cheek, as if inquiring 'which way shall I go?' – I could not wholly confide in the genuineness of his conversion. The hesitating behavior of that tear-drop and its loneliness, distressed me, and cast a doubt upon the whole transaction, of which it was a part. But people said, '*Capt. Auld had come through* ...' Master Thomas seemed to be aware of my hopes and expectations concerning him. I have thought, before now, that he looked at me in answer to my glances, as much as to say, 'I will teach you, young man, that, though I have parted with my sins, I have not parted with my sense. I shall hold my slaves, and go to heaven too.'[84]

Since true inner emotion can all too easily be simulated by men like Auld, Douglass proceeded differently, acting upon the world in order to change it and never inviting anyone to peer into his hidden psyche. The power of his voice and gaze when he worked an audience did much to ward off the charge of hypocrisy, for his listeners became an active part of the performance, not critical bystanders.

The black British novelist Zadie Smith responded to the election of Barack Obama in 2008 with a lecture in New York entitled 'Speaking in Tongues'. Despite the fact that like Obama and Douglass she was born to a white father, Smith acknowledges the label black as a cultural given. Her lecture began with a discussion of how she lost her North London working-class voice when she acquired the fresh voice of a Cambridge undergraduate:

> This voice I picked up along the way is no longer an exotic garment I put on like a college gown whenever I choose – now it is my only voice, whether I want it or not. I regret it; I should have kept both voices alive in my mouth. They were both part of me. But how the culture warns against it! ... Voice adaptation is still the original British sin ... We feel that our voices are who we are, and that to have more than one, or to use different versions of a voice for different occasions, represents, at best, a Janus-faced duplicity, and at worst, the loss of our very souls.

Smith goes on to praise Obama's gift of holding many voices in his ear, and to declare that like Obama she too was born in 'Dream City' where 'everything is doubled, everything is various. You have no choice but to cross borders and speak in tongues. That's how you get from your mother to your father, from talking to one set of folks who think you're not black enough to another who figure you insufficiently white'. She praises Obama's skill in 'tailoring his intonations to suit the sensibility of his listeners', a skill which provoked suspicion in the black community where people asked: 'How *can* the man who passes between culturally black and white voices with such flexibility, with such ease, be an honest man? ... Why won't he speak with a clear and unified voice?'[85]

The cultural pressure to peg a single voice to a single identity leads Smith to the theatrical question: 'For reasons that are obscure to me, those qualities we cherish in our artists we condemn in our politicians. In our artists we look for the many-coloured voice, the multiple sensibility. The apogee of this is, of course, Shakespeare: even more than for his wordplay we cherish him for his lack of allegiance. Our Shakespeare sees always both sides of a thing; he is black and white, male and female – he is everyman.'[86] Smith puts her finger on a fundamental problem that troubles an Anglosphere shaped by anti-theatrical puritanism: to win election, the politician needs to speak in many voices in order to substitute 'I' with 'we' on diverse occasions, and yet to win approval as a human being judged 'honest' and 'authentic' they need a singular voice. One explanation for Douglass' success lies in the religious tradition of 'speaking in tongues' where God is not found within the self but descends from above in order to take possession of both soul and body.

Rights for Women

Adult black males were granted the formal right to vote by the 15th Amendment to the US Constitution of 1870, but women had to wait another fifty years. American girls seemed to De Tocqueville to be better educated and more independent than their French counterparts, but they submitted themselves more willingly to the authority of their husbands. Prostitution appeared a lesser evil than extramarital affairs. De Tocqueville saw one explanation in religion, another in the industrial logic that prescribed a division of labour. Although religion proclaimed that women were different in nature, the facts proved otherwise, and when De Tocqueville described how American men trusted their wives' rationality, he could have offered John and Abigail Adams as an example.[87] He saw gender as performance when explaining that 'American women who display a quite manly intelligence and energy generally maintain the most delicate of appearances, and always remain women through their manners even though through their hearts and minds they may show themselves to be men'. Americans, he continued, 'do not believe that men and women have the duty or right to do the same things, but they show the same regard for the roles of each, and they consider them as equal in worth though their destiny is different. They do not give a woman's courage the same form or *emploi* as a man; but they never doubt that courage.'[88] The term *emploi* is drawn from the theatre and refers to the role type that an actor was employed to undertake.

De Tocqueville admired this American approach to equality of the sexes, deploring the flirtatiousness characteristic of aristocratic French society while also rejecting the extreme view of some Europeans that women are not only the equals of men but also identical, and so should have the same roles in society.[89] A case in point might have been Fanny Wright, a Scottish philosopher, activist and admirer of Mary Wollstonecraft. Wright arrived in America in 1818 with starry eyes: 'Here there is no *mob*. An orator or a writer must make his way to the feelings of the American people through their reason. They must think with him before they will feel with him, but, when once they do both, there is nothing to prevent their acting with him.'[90] She found her public voice as a dramatist, and Jefferson admired her tragedy staged in New York. Believing that English theatre had degenerated into pantomime, she saw America as a place where a 'dramatist might breathe the sentiments of enlightened patriotism and republican liberty'.[91]

Wright stayed within socially acceptable bounds when confining herself to writing, in the manner of other radicals like Hannah More in England, Mercy Otis Warren in the USA, or Olympe de Gouges in Paris, but when she took to lecturing she broke the unwritten rules. Trained in elocution, she set out rationalistic arguments in measured tones, and her materialist premises led her to radical conclusions about the malign influence of religion, the evils of slavery and racism, the oppression of women, the value of birth control, and the unequal distribution of wealth, all of which she had come to see as problems in American society. Despite her calm delivery, Wright could not break the problem of theatricality, and the fact that she seemed to be flaunting herself as an actress by placing her body on a stage. In 1829 at the Park Theatre in New York, it was possible to pay twenty-five cents to stand in the pit to watch an Irish actress play Shakespeare's outspoken heroine Rosalind, and next night pay twenty-five cents to watch the Scottish radical deliver one of her lectures on knowledge. Often dressed in Grecian muslin to underline her demand for physical freedom, Wright could look dangerously like an opera singer.[92] Her rationalism was turned against her, adduced to prove that she was a calculating actress, and there was no way out of this bind: damned for not being rational, or damned for failing to exude passion. Wright was initially a celebrity, but the press repositioned her as the whore of Babylon and her name became a byword for depravity. Thanks in part to the French Revolution, the rationalism of the Enlightenment, exemplified by men like Adams and Jefferson, seemed a less and less viable way of explaining the world. The conversion of Douglass' master Thomas Auld is symptomatic of the religious fervour which gripped America in the mid 1800s, and for the remainder of the century any campaign for women's rights had to be set within the frame of Christianity.

The classical republican tradition was no more sympathetic to gender equality than Christianity. As Mary Beard has argued, in the ancient world 'public speaking and oratory were not merely things that ancient women didn't do: they were exclusive practices and skills that defined masculinity as a gender ... Public speech was a – if not *the* – defining attribute of maleness. A woman speaking in public was, in most circumstances, by definition not a woman.'[93] The French revolutionaries held firmly to this masculine tradition. In America the demand for gender equality rose up most strongly in the context of the Quaker campaign to abolish slavery. In Quakerism there was neither male priesthood nor promise of obedience in the wedding ceremony, and in theory if not in reality all were equal because everyone had the right to speak at meetings. When they took to the public podium, however, many Quaker women found their male peers less than sympathetic.

Angelina Grimke was one of the most eloquent campaigners for female rights. As the daughter of a plantation owner and a convert to Quakerism, Grimke had a personal story to tell in a way that Fanny Wright did not, and her southern voice lent authenticity to her tale of what she had witnessed. The Southern voice had and still has a relish for the musicality of words in contrast to the harsher tones of the puritan North, and so, like Douglass, Grimke proved persuasive thanks to the feelings generated by the sound of her words.[94] The persona she adopted was that of the prophetess, and the rhythms of the Old Testament can be heard in a typical opening: "I stand before you as a southerner, exiled from the land of my birth by the sound of the lash and the piteous cries of the slave. I stand before you as a repentant slaveholder . . ." Or again: "I will lift up my voice like a trumpet, and show this people their transgression . . ."[95] Justifying herself to male colleagues, she explained that 'Ministers of the Gospel are the successors of the *prophets*, not of the priests . . . As there were *prophetesses* as well as prophets, so there ought to be now *female* as well as male ministers.'[96] The inspired prophetess was a persona that Protestant Christianity knew how to accept. In the Putney debates there was no place for women at the table, but in the aftermath the one female voice that did shape events was that of the prophetess Elizabeth Poole, who denounced the idea of executing the King.[97]

Grimke complained of the way she was allowed to preach but not to 'lecture', contravening the 'human rights' she found in the Bible – and we hear something of her angry spoken voice in her italics: 'I will explain myself. Women are regarded as equal to men on the ground of *spiritual gifts*, *not* on the broad ground of *humanity*. Women may *preach*; this is a *gift*; but women must *not* make the discipline by which *she herself* is to be governed.' Grimkle understood the bind in which female campaigners were caught when male colleagues rejected their moral right to address public meetings: 'If we dare to stand upright & do our duty according to the dictates of *our own* consciences, why then we are compared to Fanny Wright . . .'[98] The persona of the prophetess was liberating but also a constraint, denying Grimke the right to participate in dialogue and debate.

Clothing was an important aspect of Grimke's predicament. Sarah, her sister and collaborator, lamented that dressing up like dolls for the sake of fashion was both an insult to the poor and contrary to the Bible, but she had little affection for the uniform dress of Quaker women and longed for something 'more commodious'.[99] Male costume, with its freedom of the arm and display of the leg, was tied up with the code of rhetorical gesture that allowed the male body to command large performance spaces. An early critic complained of how Angelina 'belabored the slaveholders, and beat the air like all possessed',[100] and when fellow Quakers grumbled that she was using too many gestures, Angelina responded: 'I am so absorbed in my subject I forget myself ... To stand motionless when the feeling is deeply excited is perfectly unnatural and I cannot admire or approve it.'[101] The austerity of Quaker costume was not easily reconciled with the emotional expressivity of a Southern prophetess.

Lucretia Mott was a hard-line northern Quaker who adopted the opposite technique when fighting for the abolition of slavery. Mott belonged to a branch of Quakerism that prioritised the 'inward light' of the speaker over strict adherence to the Bible,[102] and so for example when addressing a group of students she refused to begin with the expected hymn and declared that we should find 'singing and making melody in the heart, without a dependence upon measured lines or the music of the voice'.[103] Quakerism taught her to appreciate the power of silence, and her diminutive physique helped her words sound larger. She never spoke from a script but allowed her inward voice to seize the moment. While Grimke worked through sound and gesture, foregrounding her own physical presence, Mott asked the audience to focus on her inner world. She believed that the same inward light could be found in all religions, and the strength of this approach lay in its inclusivity.[104] The austerity of her Quaker outfit certified that this inner world was not tied to any sense of ego.

Elizabeth Cady Stanton collaborated with Mott at Seneca Falls in upstate New York in 1848 to set up a women's rights convention which called for female suffrage. This began the process of separating the cause of women from the cause of the enslaved.[105] The daughter of a judge, Stanton grew up as a surrogate for the lawyer son he never had, and before marrying a lawyer she received a near full legal training. The voice she contributed to the campaign for women's rights was a legal voice, skilled in marshalling arguments, always deflecting attention from her personal story towards shared experiences and shared aspirations. Stanton stands in a long line of lawyer-politicians that includes Demosthenes, Cicero, Prynne, Robespierre, Adams, Jefferson and Gandhi to name but a few. After a brief but traumatic conversion experience, her approach to religion was rationalistic, and she never played the preacher, renewing Wright's secular call for gender equality without the accompanying demand for wider reform. Stanton's voice became the voice of the future as she developed her creed based on the rights of the individual, theorising a liberal feminism that sat comfortably with established democratic principles.[106]

While republican democracy demands liberty for a group defined as citizens, and Jacobin democracy insists on equality for the *demos*, 'liberal democracy' focuses on the freedom of the individual. In old age Stanton summed up her position before a committee of Congress:

> The point I wish plainly to bring before you on this occasion is the individuality of each human soul; our Protestant idea, the right of individual conscience and judgment – our republican idea, individual citizenship. In discussing the rights of woman, we are to consider, first, what belongs to her as an individual, in a world of her own, the arbiter of her own destiny, an imaginary Robinson Crusoe with her woman Friday on a solitary island. Her rights under such circumstances are to use all her faculties for her own safety and happiness.[107]

Stanton understood how the historic convergence of Protestantism and republicanism had generated the thing which her generation had not yet learned to call 'liberal democracy'.[108] She was addressing an educated audience that would pick up on her reference to Defoe's classic novel, and the reference to 'woman Friday' is striking for its casual racism and assumption that the educated will always have a worker to assist them. Defoe's desert island serves as a metaphor for Stanton's new sense of self, and through the rest of this speech she develops her vision of the hermetic individual, ending up with memories of herself in an Atlantic storm or climbing above the treeline in the Alps which lead her to muse that 'there is a solitude, which each and every one of us has always carried with him, more inaccessible than the ice-cold mountains, more profound than the midnight sea; the solitude of self'.[109] Stanton's claim for gender equality grew out of the proposition that humans are individuals before they are social beings or manifestations of some divine plan. The secret and lonely choice of the voter in electoral democracy might be regarded as another metaphor for selfhood comparable to Stanton's mountaineer and shipwrecked mariner. Her tragic vision of human loneliness echoes De Tocqueville's perception that American democracy tends to imprison a man 'in the solitude of his own heart'.[110] She inhabited a godless world informed by romanticism where encounters with storm and mountain substituted for religious experience.[111]

Democracy, as I have argued throughout this book, turns upon two or more speakers seeking to impress a single audience. At school Stanton was nurtured on Blair's elocutionary principles,[112] and her secular, legalistic voice of privilege allowed her to claim a place on a podium long dominated by lawyers. The students whom John Quincy Adams taught at Harvard were destined to stand here, and the figure always missing is Man or Woman Friday. When arguing for the importance of education, Stanton declared in an unguarded moment that 'we prefer Bridget and Dinah at the ballot-box to Patrick and Sambo'.[113] As Douglass had done, Stanton found a way to speak the language of power, jostling for position. Zadie Smith argues for the importance of polyphony but it is one of the conundrums of democracy that debate breaks down when there is no common language.

John Adams exemplifies the vanished figure whom Richard Sennett labelled 'public man', not ashamed to be acting out a quasi-theatrical role in civic space. The love letters that passed between John and Abigail Adams are full of playful role-play rather than attempts to express deep personal emotion.[114] Sennett tracks back to puritanism the desire to authenticate one's self, endorsing the earlier idea that the world should be conceived as a stage. Since good people often do bad things, he argues, people in public life should be valued for the quality of their actions rather than their inherent characters.[115] This raises the question: Was Stanton just as much of a public performer as Adams? Was she ultimately performing her romantic solitude – in the Atlantic storm, gazing up at the snows above the boulder field, playing Robinson Crusoe – or were these authentic expressions of her selfhood?

In her autobiography Stanton explains how she brought her father round to her way of thinking about a point of law, painting for him a word-picture of an injustice external to herself:

> I began, with a dogged determination to give all the power I could to my manuscript, and not to be discouraged or turned from my purpose by any tender appeals or adverse criticisms. I described the widow in the first hours of her grief, subject to the intrusions of the coarse minions of the law, taking inventory of the household goods, of the old armchair in which her loved one had breathed his last, of the old clock in the corner that told the hour he passed away. I threw all the pathos I could into my voice and language at this point, and, to my intense satisfaction, I saw tears filling my father's eyes. I cannot express the exultation I felt, thinking that now he would see, with my eyes, the injustice women suffered under the laws he understood so well. Feeling that I had touched his heart I went on with

renewed confidence, and, when I had finished, I saw he was thoroughly magnetized. With beating heart I waited for him to break the silence.[116]

Like an actress, Stanton works from a script in order to build empathy, inflecting her voice with the appropriate emotion, and keeping a watchful eye on how she holds her audience. As a skilled performer, she knows that she needs to play the situation rather than bombard her audience with direct personal feeling. Stanton's solitary ego monitors the performance that her body is giving, a performance that is simultaneously calculated and truthful.

***

The rival stage actors Edwin Forrest and William Macready exemplify two broad approaches to political performance. A rhetorical tradition grounded in Cicero concentrates upon externals, crucially the voice, and is understood to be the art of working an audience. Like Forrest, John and John Quincy Adams, Douglass and Grimke were grounded in these principles. Against them I have set another performance tradition that seeks to deny its own theatricality, exemplified perfectly by the Quaker Lucretia Mott. As a fellow abolitionist recalled, a sermon by Mott 'was so born of all conviction, so surely out of the inner heart of the truth, and so radiant with the inward light for which she had been waiting, that he went home feeling as he supposed they must have felt in the old time who thought they had heard an angel.'[117] Twentieth-century American theatre, where the Puritan influence was inflected by Judaism's distaste for external signs, is famed for the idea that good acting starts from personal self-exploration and not from thinking about the audience. Teachers in the Stanislavskian tradition like Stella Adler, Sanford Meisner and Lee Strasberg developed these principles.[118]

Liberal democracy imposes heavy demands upon the performers who stand on its political stage and seek to renegotiate an inherited, ever shifting mix of equality and personal liberty. While republicanism (in the older sense of that word) has always cherished theatre, Puritanism has always condemned theatre, and modern democracy is a function of that collision. The consequences remain unresolved, in the theatre no less than in politics: how to reach out to others by adopting their voices, whilst also keeping the inward light aflame, the light of sincerity and personal authenticity? As Stanislavski famously demonstrated, there are technical skills involved in keeping that light aflame. Liberal democracy never fails to generate what Judith Shklar calls an 'interplay of hypocrisy and vocal anti-hypocrisy'. Seeing 'anti-hypocrisy' as a psychic weapon inherited from religious conflict, Shklar insists that liberal democracy can never do away with public pretence.[119] This was a truth that John Adams embraced, but it is a hard one for modern liberals to swallow when faced with 'populists' who succeed best when they lure their opponents into the diverting game of pulling off masks. There is no point in demonstrating that an actor is in fact an actor, but every point in persuading an audience to act collectively in the common good.

CHAPTER 6

Democracy as a Universal Good
Gandhi, Tagore and the New India

The English democratic impulse was grounded in Puritanism, a creed which in its many manifestations was committed to the authenticity and inner life of the individual, and was challenged by theatre's capacity to simulate. The Jacobin revolution, nourished by its vision of antiquity and a secular faith in reason, put more value on the externalities of public life, but struggled to find the right public way to perform truthfulness. In America, where the anti-theatrical Puritan tradition was a substrate of Enlightenment rationalism, it proved impossible to define the collective *demos* that rules in a *demo*cracy, and liberal calls for personal freedom and self-expression collided with the egalitarian demand for inclusiveness. India was caught up in these contradictions when seeking its own postcolonial path. The word democracy was a rallying cry, but neither Europe nor America could provide any coherent account of what the word meant.

Gandhi's Authenticity

Rejecting claims that India was as yet unfit for democracy, Gandhi pronounced in 1934 that Western democracy was itself on trial: 'May it not be reserved to India to evolve the true science of democracy by giving a visible demonstration of this fitness? Corruption and hypocrisy ought not to be the inevitable products of democracy as they undoubtedly are today'.[1] In the context of the war against Hitler, fought in the name of democracy, he grew more forceful, declaring that Western democracy was 'merely a cloak to hide the Nazi and Fascist tendencies of imperialism … It was not through democratic methods that Britain bagged India', he went on, and the USA was scarcely better because of the way it 'treated the Negro'. India, he declared, was seeking to escape such hypocrisy and 'evolve true democracy'.[2] Raising fundamental questions about the nature of democracy, Gandhi suggests that Asia may have answers to contradictions in the Euro-American tradition. From one perspective Gandhi represents Asian otherness, but it is equally possible to place him in the line of puritans like Prynne and disciples of Rousseau such as Robespierre who laid similar claim to freedom from hypocrisy. Like Prynne and Robespierre, Gandhi offered up his body and austere lifestyle as testament to the authenticity of his soul, making truth-claims that turned on the assumption that he was not a performer. In this chapter, I shall pass from Gandhi to his most important interlocutor, Rabindranath Tagore, who as a poet and man of the theatre viewed the political world through the lens of performance.

In his 2005 essay 'The Argumentative Indian', responding to claims that democracy was a gift from the West, the Indian economist and political philosopher Amartya Sen places public argument at the centre of an indigenous political tradition. Sen's premise that 'public reasoning is closely related to the roots of democracy across the globe' helps him explain why independent India took so quickly to electoral democracy.[3] Gandhi started from a different premise when, differentiating himself from the 'intelligentsia' of the National Congress, he portrayed himself in 1934 as 'a born democrat', a claim he justified on the grounds that 'a complete identification with the poorest of mankind, an intense longing to live no better than they ... can entitle one to make it.' He was responding to complaints that 'instead of remaining the most democratic and representative institution in the country, the Congress had degenerated into an organisation dominated by my one personality and that in it there was no free play of reason.'[4] Gandhi's relationship with Congress grew no easier when the Congress party finally governed India, and he did not share Sen's faith in public reasoning. 'Reason, as a rule, follows in the footsteps of feeling', he argued. 'But we have not sufficiently penetrated the hearts of the intelligentsia to convince their reason.'[5] Like Aristotle, Hume, Haidt and many others, Gandhi understood that the heart, or whatever is symbolised by that organ, is always the main driver of human behaviour.

Sen argues that democracy is a 'universal value', and for him there can be no question of separate 'Asian values'. Countries do not become 'fit for democracy', but rather democracy is what makes them fit. The problem with this stance lies in the lack of any satisfactory definition of what democracy is.[6] A helpful perspective is offered by the 'WEIRD' hypothesis formulated in 2010 by the Canadian anthropologist Joseph Henrich. Henrich argues that the convergence of five categories – Western, Educated, Industrialised, Rich and Democratic – represents a cultural configuration, driven initially by the medieval Church, that now dominates much of the world. He associates electoral democracy with an 'individualism complex' which from the global perspective of an anthropologist looks distinctly 'weird'.[7] Western electoral democracy put Gandhi in a dilemma. Having witnessed the British parliamentary system at close hand he initially rejected it, but then in the 1920s he came to recognise that national independence would require 'parliamentary *swaraj*', before the failure of the Congress party to bridge communal divides sent him back to the ideal of the *panchayat*, the assembly of village elders.[8] Gandhi's concept of *swaraj* – political 'self-rule' grounded in personal self-rule – might be seen as distinctively Asian, prompted by his reading of the *Bhagavad Gita* where Arjuna learns that what matters is not rights but duty, but we should remember that William Prynne would have endorsed similar principles of personal self-government and transcendent duty.

Imprisoned in Johannesburg in 1908, Gandhi read, alongside the *Gita* and Carlyle's account of French revolutionary violence, Plato's rendition of Socrates' speech before the Athenians when he faced the death penalty on a politically driven charge. Writing initially in Gujarati, Gandhi drafted his own shortened version entitled *Story of a Soldier of Truth*, declaring to his readership in South Africa and back home: 'We must learn to live and die like Socrates.'[9] His text begins:

> I cannot tell, O Athenians, how far you have been carried away by my accusers' words. For my own part, they nearly made me forget who I was, so plausible were they. But I say that their arguments are a lie. Among their falsehoods there was one which astonished me most. They asked you not to be misled by my eloquence. It is they who are rhetorical. I have no skill in the art of speaking. If by rhetoric they mean truth, I admit that I possess it. However, if they allow that I am a truthful person, I am not an orator in their sense of the word. For they have spoken with dazzling effect, but there is nothing of truth in their words. For my part, I shall place before you the whole truth and nothing but the truth. I have not come to you with a prepared speech. I am an old man. It is not for me to speak before you eloquently or in brilliant words. Do not be surprised, therefore, if I speak as simply as I am used to. I am now more than seventy years old, and this is my first experience of a law court.[10]

I set out in Chapter 1 Plato's argument that democracy entails rhetoric and rhetoric entails falsehood. Gandhi found in Socrates not merely a fellow exponent of *satyagraha* or non-violent resistance, a hero willing to die for his beliefs, but also a man capable of speaking truth stripped of rhetoric. Gandhi's short sentence structures work well as a rhetorical device to create the illusion of Socratic directness.

Gandhi found much to admire in Socrates' commitment to self-control, truth, and a personal conscience experienced as an inner voice, and in

Soldier of Truth his own voice merges with that of Socrates.[11] He had no opportunity to explore the Greek context, however, and unpick the paradox that Socrates was the victim of a democracy restored after the ejection of a ruling foreign power. Gandhi's sense of truth was not analytic but experiential. As Tagore put it in 1939, people generally preferred to overlook Gandhi's 'natural cleverness in manipulating recalcitrant facts. They have rather dwelt upon the truth which shines through his character in lucid simplicity.'[12] This internal, personal truth does not sit easily with Sen's ideal of the 'argumentative Indian'. Gandhi explained in 1926 why he found it so difficult to engage in debate with the learned, having found 'that I am always true from my point of view, and am often wrong from the point of view of my honest critics.' He cited the Jain parable of the seven blind men who each lay their hands on a different part of the elephant and offer correct but completely contradictory descriptions.[13] Since reason and the senses offer no path to ultimate truth, people need to trust in a different kind of knowledge.

In 1909 Gandhi published his manifesto *Hind Swaraj*, recommending Socrates' speech as follow-up reading,[14] and Plato may have inspired the dialogue form which dresses up his fiery rhetoric in the garb of deliberation. *Hind Swaraj* attacked the English parliamentary system, amongst other aspects of so-called civilisation, claiming that 'the Mother of Parliaments is like a sterile woman and a prostitute', sterile because unproductive, and a prostitute because buffeted about by a sequence of different men. British parliamentarians are hypocrites, Gandhi went on, voting blindly according to party, asleep in the chamber and subject to lobbying, and the electorate swing like a pendulum except in their patriotism.[15] Gandhi was no less scathing about his own profession of the law, another species of prostitution, understanding that the British legal system underpinned imperial rule.[16] Drawing on Thomas Huxley, he attacked the ideal of a liberal, academic education designed to produce intellect as 'a clear, cold, logic engine with all its parts of equal strength and in smooth working order'.[17] Character building rather than academic education had to be the foundation of *swaraj*, a ruling of self that he considered the only viable basis for political self-rule and the restoration of Indian civilisation. For all its limitations, a western education had at least taught Gandhi 'that action is much better than speech; that it is our duty to say exactly what we think and face the consequences and that it will be only then that we shall be able to impress anybody with our speech'.[18] This was the road that he himself would follow, inviting reprisals from the British and from now on using actions rather than eloquent words to sway the masses.

Gandhi himself was a poor public speaker, which probably explains why he failed to develop a career in the Bombay High Court.[19] When he first arrived in London, the study of elocution was one of the vanities he abandoned along with dandified clothes.[20] At the bar his tone was monotonous, he made no use of gesture and a slight speech defect resulted in a characteristic hiss. His first biographer explained in 1909 that 'Gandhi is not an impassioned speaker. His speech is calm and slow, appealing chiefly to the intellect. But with this quiet way, he has the gift of placing a subject in the clearest light, simply, and with great force. The tones of his voice, which are not greatly varied, bear the note of sincerity'.[21] Many years later a member of Gandhi's audience in Lancashire in 1931 recalled 'the sober statement of fact which he recounted to us of the conditions in the villages out there, the social life of India, and his own relationship to it. He spoke without gesture and in well-modulated tones. The only feeling he displayed was in the inflection of the voice. I got the impression that this man really believes he is the chosen vessel of God.'[22]

Gandhi tells us in his *Autobiography* that: 'As a student I had heard that the lawyer's profession was a liar's profession. But this did not influence me, as I had no intention of earning either position or money by lying', and for this reason he claims he never took on what he considered a false case. For the young law student in London the task of delivering an after-dinner speech to the Vegetarian Society was traumatic, but looking back he turned his youthful failures into a virtue:

> I must say that, beyond occasionally exposing me to laughter, my constitutional shyness has been no disadvantage whatever ... My hesitancy in speech, which was once an annoyance, is now a pleasure. Its greatest benefit has been that it has taught me the economy of words ... Experience has taught me that silence is part of the spiritual discipline of a votary of truth. Proneness to exaggerate, to suppress or modify the truth, wittingly or unwittingly, is a natural weakness of man, and silence is necessary in order to surmount it ... My shyness has been in reality my shield and buckler. It has allowed me to grow. It has helped me in my discernment of truth.[23]

In *Hind Swaraj* Gandhi describes the pain of a barrister who cannot use his mother tongue in court, and language was a factor in his preference for action over speech.[24] The English language was inseparable from British ethical values, and key terms like *swaraj* and *satyagraha* have no direct equivalence. Although in *Hind Swaraj* Gandhi argued for Hindi as a common language,[25] as a political activist seeking to reach across communal divides he soon discovered that a universal language of the body was his most potent tool.

One of Gandhi's most famous acts of protest, described by the viceroy Lord Irwin as a 'theatrical march', was a procession to the sea to collect natural salt in defiance of a new tax, and Gandhi's distinctive stride led an eyewitness to describe him as a 'consummate artist-realist'.[26] When Gandhi went to Irwin to negotiate about the salt tax, dressed in his loincloth and shawl, squatting on the floor at lunchtime for his dates and goat's milk, Winston Churchill was outraged and declared it was 'nauseating to see Mr. Gandhi, a seditious Middle Temple Lawyer, now posing as a fakir of a type well-known in the East, striding half-naked up the steps of the Viceregal palace ... to parley on equal terms with the representative of the King-Emperor'.[27] Irwin himself took a more subtle approach, after warnings from an Indian adviser that Gandhi needed to be 'wooed like a capricious woman' because his dominant quality was 'vanity, unconscious, but not less real':[28]

> I kept asking myself all the time 'Was the man completely sincere?' I think that as our conversation went on I came to feel about this in rather double fashion. I came to have no doubt whatever that, if Mr Gandhi gave me his word on any point, that word was absolutely secure, and that I could trust it implicitly. On the other hand, I found what had always been my impression being confirmed, namely, that though intentionally he was completely sincere, yet in some matters he was the victim of unconscious self-delusion.[29]

Though Churchill was right in the sense that Gandhi had chosen to change his image, abandoning the lawyer in suit and tie to adopt the physical persona of an Indian saint, Gandhi clearly experienced the suit-and-tie lawyer as a spurious role he needed to cast off. Irwin puts his finger on the central paradox of acting, that actors learn how to get themselves into a certain state of mind so their body will respond in accordance with unconscious processes.[30] While hypocrisy can be calculated, as in the case of Tartuffe, the postulate of an unconscious mind makes any judgement about total sincerity problematic.

Fasting was Gandhi's ultimate proof of personal sincerity, showing there was no gap between what he thought and what he did. As an American visitor said of Gandhi's fast in 1948, 'we think of it as a political manoeuvre, a strike, a gesture. But here ... was a 79 year old man deliberately killing himself in the most difficult and excruciating way.'[31] During an earlier wartime fast, when Churchill tried to persuade himself that Gandhi was secretly taking glucose, the new viceroy agreed that he had 'long known Gandhi as the world's most successful humbug', but could offer Churchill no evidence of fraud. This did not prevent Churchill in his war memoirs from pronouncing it as certain that Gandhi took glucose whenever he drank water, and that his health was never seriously affected.[32] When Gandhi was asked about the danger of others imitating him because of his fame, he responded that because few have the willpower, 'fasting is its own safeguard against abuse'. He was less sanguine about the 'inner voice' that ordered him to fast and acknowledged that 'unfortunately, there is no remedy against hypocrisy. Virtue must not be suppressed because many will feign it'. In a circular argument, he concludes that penitential fasting is worth imitating because it makes it easier to hear the inner voice.[33]

Gandhi's most famous attribute, his regular stage property so to speak, was the *charkha* or spinning wheel. It was a symbol which took hold of Gandhi's imagination before he had ever seen one, an improvement on the manual loom proposed in the *Hind Swaraj*.[34] The wheel represented the dignity of labour, gender equality, the rejection of mechanisation, and the importance of wearing homegrown cloth. The loom resonated because the British had destroyed the Bengali weaving industry to set up industrial production in Lancashire, but the wheel was portable and served as a mystical symbol of eternal regeneration. It was at the same time a material object which demanded bodily labour, and, long before Castro and Mao, Gandhi wanted the intelligentsia to escape the world of pure intellect. When he visited England armed with his wheel, he explained its purpose in a newspaper article:

> I have read many varying descriptions of myself. Some call me a saint. Others call me a rogue. I am neither the one nor the other. All that I aspire to be – and I hope I have in some measure succeeded in being – is an honest, godfearing man. But the things I read about myself do not annoy me. Why should they? I have my own philosophy and my work. Every day I spin for a time. While I spin I think. I think of many things. But always from those thoughts I try to keep out bitterness. Study this spinning-wheel of mine. It would teach you a great deal more than I can – patience, industry, simplicity. This spinning-wheel is for India's starving millions the symbol of salvation.[35]

Gandhi explains the *charkha* as a sign of simplicity, a vehicle for mental transformation, a quasi-religious symbol, and a means to impress his values on others.

Rabindranath Tagore was unimpressed by the cult of the wheel. In one conversation, when he queried why Gandhi allowed his followers to use the saintly title of 'Mahatma', Gandhi responded that 'Indians by nature have always been worshippers of symbols, of images', and for this reason urged the poet to take up spinning. For Tagore, the poet and intellectual, this was no way to be honest with the people. '"Poems I can spin, Gandhiji," I said, "songs and plays I can spin, but of your precious cotton what a mess I would make."'[36] When Gandhi insisted that intellectuals needed to spin 'in order to represent in a living way, their sympathy with the poor', Tagore declared himself fearful of the blind faith in the *charkha* that Gandhi's forceful personality was creating. 'I am strongly of opinion that all intense pressure of persuasion brought upon the crowd psychology is unhealthy for it. Some strong and widespread intoxication of belief among a vast number of men can suddenly produce a convenient uniformity of purpose, immense and powerful. It seems for the moment a miracle of a wholesale conversion ...' Nevertheless, warned Tagore, if you stun the rational mind and raise false hopes, 'the rebound is sure to follow'.[37] Tagore shared all Gandhi's objections to 'the tyranny of the machine', but insisted, 'we must refuse to accept as our ally the illusion-haunted magic-ridden slave mentality that is at the root of all the poverty and insult under which our country groans.'[38] Tagore was happy to be a spinner of songs and plays which declared their own artistry, but rejected the magic of the demagogue. As an artist, he understood the artistry deployed by the Mahatma. To the dismay of many he was unwilling to dirty his hands by engaging in politics because the contradictions were intolerable to him.

Gandhi's cult of the spinning wheel was tied to a demand that everyone should wear *khadi*, homespun or 'sacred' cloth as he called it when interviewed by the *Manchester Guardian*.[39] Wearing this coarse fabric was a road to self-sufficiency, with no money passing to the rich or to Britain, and the salt-marchers used it to create solidarity. In the short term, however, *khadi* proved more expensive than imported industrial cloth, and this was one reason that led him to adopt his famous loincloth. He worried that people might think him mad, and that his impulse to dress in this extraordinary way was 'tinged with egotism', an anxiety we might paraphrase as fear of becoming a performer, but he went ahead as a means to 'hearten the people', and what started as a temporary gesture became a way of life.[40] Gandhi conceived the loincloth as the dress of a poor agriculturist, but increasingly it came to be seen as the dress of a saint. This was the culmination of a process that began when he shaved his head in a South African prison, exchanged his jacket and tie for traditional rural dress upon return to India, then adopted white *khadi*, and set a fashion for his plain white 'Gandhi cap' that eliminated signs of caste and religious difference.[41] It was something of a coup when Gandhi came to England in 1931 and in breach of protocol was allowed to wear his loincloth to speak with King George V in Buckingham Palace.[42]

For this English visit, Gandhi based himself in London's working-class East End, where he had an encounter with Charlie Chaplin. Although he had no interest in cinema, Gandhi agreed to meet Chaplin because he heard that Chaplin 'came from the people and lived for the people' and reached out to millions. The pair had a long discussion of mechanisation, which helped inspire Chaplin's *Modern Times*. After the meeting, Gandhi's secretary commented that 'Chaplin struck me to be a genial, unassuming gentleman and nothing like we find him on the film. But perhaps in concealing himself lies his skill.'[43] Chaplin was struck by a similar mismatch in a fellow celebrity, feeling that Gandhi's 'legendary significance evaporated in the London scene, and his religious display fell short of impressiveness. In the cold dank climate of England, wearing his traditional loincloth which he gathered about him in disorderly fashion, he seemed incongruous ... One's impressiveness is greater at a distance.' In the course of the conversation, however, he was impressed by a 'virile-minded visionary', and when the conversation was over he sat on a sofa watching Gandhi and his entourage squat down to pray: 'What a paradox, I thought, as I watched this extremely realistic man, with his astute legal mind and his profound sense of political reality, all of which seem to vanish in a sing-song chant.'[44] In his *Autobiography*, Chaplin explained how he discovered his own character of the tramp by donning the relevant shoes, clothes and painted moustache. 'I had no idea of the character. But the moment I was dressed, the clothes and the make-up made me feel the person he was. I began to know him, and by the time I walked on the stage he was fully born ... As the clothes had imbued me with the character, I then and there decided I would keep to this costume whatever happened.'[45] Gandhi's loincloth probably worked in a similar way, a costume decision that created an instant persona. We should not reach the reductive conclusion that just as behind Chaplin's tramp lay the gentleman, so behind the saint lay the calculating politician, for what Chaplin describes is a kind of possession that creates reciprocity between actor and role. Chaplin himself was at ease shedding his mask or persona in order to separate Charles from Charlie. It may be that Gandhi engaged in ever more extreme behaviour in order to prove to himself that he was different, and that, although he protested against the label, the true Gandhi was inseparable from the saintly 'Mahatma'.[46]

It was no mark of disrespect when Chaplin positioned Gandhi the politician as a fellow performer. When Gandhi was still a suit-and-tie barrister in South Africa in 1909, his Baptist friend Joseph Doke sought permission to write his biography:

'My friend,' I began, 'I want to ask you a strange question – how far are you prepared to make a martyr of yourself for the good of the cause ?' ... 'Well,' said he ... 'I am willing to die at any time, or to do anything for the cause.' 'Take care,' I rejoined, 'perhaps I shall ask something too great ... You know very well that, with us Europeans, character and personality are of the first importance. It is so here, and it must be so at home ... Your position as leader makes your personality of great importance to the cause. It has occurred to me that if I could write a short book – bright, graphic, and reliable – making your personality real to the people of England, it might do something to help the cause in the great struggle that is to come.' The emphatic nods became appreciably weaker, but they did not altogether cease, so I went on ... 'You must tell me about your childhood and youth, allow me to picture your personality, and depict your character, and if I know anything of you, to submit to this will be the severest kind of martyrdom that you can suffer.' 'Ah,' he said, as my purpose dawned upon him, 'you have caught me completely.'[47]

Gandhi grasped the political necessity of constructing a character for himself, and in the first instance it was a form of psychological martyrdom. The character constructed by Doke was at once the truth of who he was and a falsification. Gandhi's concerns about the inauthenticity of Western character construction were still there twelve years later when he responded to his secretary Mahadev who wanted to keep a diary: 'You merely wish to imitate the West. If I always keep someone with me merely in order that a record of my activities may be kept, I myself would come to behave unnaturally ... Extensive notes of Johnson's talks were taken but I do not see they have conferred on the world any great benefit that I know of.'[48] Admired by Thomas Carlyle as a modern prophet, Samuel Johnson was, Gandhi implies, transformed into a wit or 'character' by the memoirs of his young disciple James Boswell. Again Gandhi compromised for the sake of the cause, accepting the egotism that is an inescapable feature of self-consciousness.

Tagore's Challenge to 'Representation'

In the dominant tradition of Western theatre, the actor represents a 'character' whose actions reveal the sort of person he or she really is, and Tagore's plays have not been easy for Western readers and audiences to assimilate because they resist this principle first established by Aristotle. As a modernist, but also as an Indian, Tagore preferred the ideal of expression to that of representation. He was repelled when he saw Henry Irving perform in London in 1890, insisting that acting 'has the responsibility of drawing

Democracy as a Universal Good: Gandhi/Tagore/New India 155

apart the curtain of naturalism' in order to 'reveal the inner reality of things. If there is too much emphasis on imitative naturalism the inner view becomes clouded.'[49] Tagore's concept of 'inner reality' was not tied to a Christian realm of the soul or a Freudian realm of the psyche but embraced human connections with the social, natural and spiritual realms, and his theatrical project offers a vantage point from which to consider the political question of 'representation'. In the Western political tradition, the actor on the podium represents the voter, and is obliged to construct a character that connects with whatever the voter takes to be their own identity. If voters first and foremost identify as individuals, which the secrecy of the ballot box tells them should be the case, then a representative of those voters should correspondingly appear to be an individual, a character defined by unique features. Even though constituency boundaries may group individuals on the basis of geography, and party politics has a tradition of grouping individuals on the basis of class, the principle or enabling fiction stands that each individual votes according to their private conscience. In the Indian context, the western idea that the politician stands up to represent aggregated individuals became unsustainable.

As India moved towards parliamentary democracy, Gandhi fought against the idea that representation should be based on communal identities, crucially the identities of the Moslem and of the 'untouchable' Dalit (or Harijan) caste. His campaign for all to wear *khadi* was tied to the notion that all men and women are politically equal, but he clung at the same time to tradition and was reluctant to obliterate caste and gender roles that seemed part of the social fabric. He adopted for himself a character that many believed to represent the essence of the Indian nation, stripping away social distinction as far as he could to expose the universal human body. The figure of the 'Mahatma' remained, however, a representation that left many feeling unrepresented. Moslem culture does not happily endorse bare bodies, and the poorest Hindus forced to live on the brink of starvation did not necessarily identify with voluntary starvation. Gandhi's act of representation did not seem to everyone to reveal 'the inner reality of things'.

As an artist rather than activist, Tagore probed the nature of selfhood in a way that Gandhi could not. In a speech to the Indian Philosophical Society in 1925, he described a formative theatrical experience in rural Bengal, where an opera handed down by tradition was performed to a largely Moslem peasant audience:

> Then came a dialogue during the course of which was related the incident of a person who wanted to make a journey to *Brindaban*, the Garden of

Bliss, but was prevented by a watchman who startled him with an accusation of theft. The thieving was proved when it was shown that inside his clothes he was secretly trying to smuggle into the garden the self, which only finds its fulfilment by its surrender. The culprit was caught with the incriminating bundle in his possession which barred for him his passage to the supreme goal. Under a tattered canopy supported on bamboo poles and lighted by a few smoking kerosene lamps, the village crowd, occasionally interrupted by howls of jackals in the neighbouring paddy fields, attended with untired interest, till the small hours of the morning, the performance of drama, that discussed the ultimate meaning of all things in a seemingly incongruous setting of dance, music and humorous dialogue.

It is implicit in Tagore's account that the mode of performance, with its unseen animal chorus, darkness, smell, obliteration of clock time, power of rhythm and the infectiousness of laughter, supported a surrender of the individual self. This performance sat at an opposite extreme to the imported naturalist style of theatre which used an elaborate set to support its claim to represent material reality.

Tagore went on to draw the political moral, arguing that the fisherman on the Ganges is potentially freer than the millionaire because he refuses to be atomised in a hermetic selfhood. Although one might imagine that only 'an individual who succeeds in dissociating himself from his fellows attains real freedom, inasmuch as all ties of relationship imply obligation to others', it is a paradoxical truth 'that in the human world only a perfect arrangement of interdependence gives rise to freedom.'[50] Tagore's challenge to Western concepts of representation in the theatre is inseparable from his challenge to received notions of nation, self and democratic representation. Rejecting the romantic cult of solitude articulated by figures like Elizabeth Cady Stanton, Tagore embraces a different language of freedom which from a republican perspective looks like capitulation, and from a materialist perspective looks like sentimentality. It is easy enough to condemn him as the voice of privilege.

As an activist on the coalface of politics, Gandhi clung to the instrumental value of the word 'democracy', but insisted that democracy could be distinguished from what he called 'mobocracy' by a dividing line which was 'often thin but rigid and stronger than steel'.[51] He repeatedly challenged the elitism of the elected Indian National Congress while many members challenged his own populism, and his relationship to Congress was never easy. As independence loomed, Gandhi reached the desolate conclusion that 'the social order of our dreams cannot come through the Congress of today', and that 'anybody who goes into politics gets contaminated.'⁵² Tagore was at one with Gandhi in seeing a link between colonialism and materialism and in concluding that a new bottom-up politics had to begin with the unit of the village. Their key difference lay in Gandhi's embrace of an Indian 'nation', while Tagore shunned the nationalist impulse, and saw no way to disengage the ideal of democracy from the imported idea of the nation-state.

As a man whose life was dedicated to the arts, Tagore distinguished the cultural entity described as a *samaj* or society from the political entity of the nation-state, and as a poet his feelings about being a Bengali were stronger than his feelings about being an Indian. He set out his argument in a lecture in Calcutta in 1904 in response to British plans to partition Bengal, a plan that became reality in 1947. He contrasted the overarching power of the European state, which in England took responsibility for welfare, education and religion, with a pre-colonial India which gave central government a limited remit because the social fabric was maintained by bonds of *dharma* or personal obligation. In the Bengali context, he questioned the value of setting up a Provincial Conference as a Western-style talking shop where it was sure to be dominated by the English-speaking elite and absentee landlords. As a musician and man of the theatre, he had a different proposal based on the principle that the heart of India lies in its villages:

> Think how we must proceed if the Conference is to make a strong impression on the country. Instead of a meeting in the English way, we shall have a huge fair in the Indian way. A grand festival of folk-plays and songs will draw people from all over the land, prizes to be awarded to the best singers, dramatic groups and orators. The country's agricultural products will be exhibited and rules of hygiene graphically explained with the aid of such things as lantern slides. Above all, whatever we have to say on questions of national interest will be discussed in simple Bengali by the highborn and the humble alike.

He envisaged that a band of entertainers would take collections to support their singing and *kathak* dance-dramas, for 'it has to be remembered that our people have immemorially enjoyed literature and absorbed religion through the medium of festivities', and he argued that in this festive ambience people's hearts would be opened to talk freely about their material needs. Tagore insisted that political bonds had to be underpinned by interpersonal human bonds, and although the Indian National Congress may have had a 'westernised exterior', he saw beneath it an 'Indian heart' expressed through convivial 'hospitality'. The British might have robbed India of its wealth, he argued, but they must not be allowed also to rob it of its soul.

From this bucolic ideal, Tagore moved to the pragmatic issue of casting off colonial oppression.

> If the community is to protect itself, it must take its stand on united strength. The best way would be to invest a strong personality with leadership and rally round him as our representative; to submit to his rule would mean no loss of self-respect, for he would be a symbol of freedom itself. Such a leader of society may sometimes be good, sometimes evil, but if society is alive and alert, no leader can do any permanent harm ... If society recognizes its unity as symbolized in a particular person, it will become undefeatable.[53]

Tagore was an obvious figure with the charisma and patrician credentials to take on the mantle of Bengali leadership, but, after briefly using festive bracelets to link the hands of individual Hindus and Moslems on the streets, he retreated from active politics, shocked by the speed at which protest turned into violence.[54] In the years that followed, when Gandhi became just this kind of strong but symbolic leader, Tagore was uncomfortable with the consequences, describing Gandhi in a private letter as a 'moral tyrant'.[55] It is only a small step from Tagore's theory of symbolic leadership to Thomas Hobbes, and in the aftermath of civil war Hobbes lacked Tagore's trust in the natural virtues of the *demos*.

Unlike Gandhi Tagore was a cosmopolitan who delighted in Western art, which lends added weight to his critique of Western democracy. Warning an audience in Japan about the dangers of nationalism in 1924, Tagore declared:

> Often have my western friends almost sneeringly said to me, that we in the East have no faith in Democracy, and thereupon have asserted the superiority of their own mind over ours. Not being combative, I did not want to argue the matter and contradict them in their deep-rooted illusion that they were democratic.

There seemed no way to reconcile British claims to moral superiority with British racism:

> Today, they are almost openly ready to drop their pretensions to moral culture; but nevertheless they cling to their two illusions, the one of the Nordic race, and the other of Democracy. We, who do not profess democracy, acknowledge our human obligations and have faith in our code of honour. But are you also going to allow yourselves to be tempted by the contagion of this belief in your own hungry right of inborn superiority, bearing the false name of democracy? ... Do you not see how this malady of imitation is rapidly spreading from shore to shore, from nation to nation? It has the same monotony of features, in its offices, barracks, dress and

manners, its attitude of mind. Every people in this world is vying with its neighbour to copy it, because being non-living it is easy to copy indefinitely. It is a mask that can be precisely similar in its multiplication, not a face which has spontaneous variety of self-expression.[56]

As a man of the theatre, Tagore saw democracy as a masquerade, a uniform way of pretending to be Western and living the life-style. As a creative artist his aim was to shed Western ideas of art as imitation or mimesis in order to build a form of theatre that was socially interactive and expressive of inner realities. He was not seeking sincerity in the spot-lit human face so much as spontaneity in the whole human body.

Addressing Bengalis in 1924, Tagore explained in more practical terms that in democracy 'the organs of information and expression, through which opinions are manufactured, together with the machinery of administration, are all openly or secretly manipulated by those prosperous few', likening democracy to 'an elephant whose one purpose in life is to give joy rides to the clever and the rich'.[57] He saw no way to extend a culture of public argument to the masses. While Gandhi was a poor public speaker, preferring the multilingual possibilities of the printing press, Tagore was a fine stage actor and relished the interaction that his lectures provided, but he had no faith in the Western culture of debate, understanding that no amount of verbal combat was capable of troubling British illusions about their innate superiority. In Tagore's holistic understanding, human beings are not simple functions of cognition, and his plays, though often addressing political themes, are not structured round debate according to the Greek principle of the *agon*. His trajectory as a dramatist led him in the opposite direction, towards dance-drama where speech fused with music and movement. As he explained to the French dramatist Romain Rolland in 1926, 'theatre has to be a kind of dance, the rhythm of which will go hand in hand with the rhythm of the poetic text. There is nothing more ridiculous than the Western style of reciting poetry along with gross realistic imitation of everyday gestures and postures'.[58]

The high Western tradition of acting, informed by Greco-Roman antiquity, is broadly speaking rhetorical: actors use hands, face and intonation to support the word as they deliver a text penned by a dramatist or librettist, and emotional language is a vehicle for persuasive argument.[59] The Indian classical tradition centres upon the body of actor, and the dominant interest of its theoreticians lies not in the act of imitation but in the quality of expression and interaction. The key word in Greco-Roman aesthetics is *mimesis*, implying use of the stage to mirror the world of the audience in what has to be a moral project, while the key word in classical

Indian theory is *rasa*, a joyous aesthetic response, and in the *Natya Sastra*, the foundational work of Sanskrit dramatic theory, the sage likens the eight basic *rasas* to flavours of food.[60] The tenth-century commentator on the *Natya Sastra*, Abhinavagupta, spells out the corollary that theatrical experience is collective, bound up with the surrender of ego, and works towards a unity of consciousness.[61] In the broadest terms, the Greco-Roman tradition turns upon division, giving centre stage to one or more isolated egos, whilst the Indian tradition rejects the moral void of tragedy in favour of harmony. Tagore traced the outlines of this distinction in a comparison of two classic texts from East and West, *Shakuntala* and *The Tempest*.[62]

Tagore believed that thought, exemplified by his own creative process as a poet, was always tied to bodily movement, at its minimum a wrinkling of the brow, and he saw how children expressed their thoughts and feelings with the whole body before they were constrained by education. He believed that Western-style actors were effectively surrogates in face of loss, people whom we 'pay . . . to cultivate their natural gifts, and to give us the chance of experiencing the joys we crave, but can no longer achieve through the repression of our bodies.' He told Leonard Elmhirst of his admiration for Japanese actors trained from childhood to use 'every muscle in the body' in order to 'give our inner sentiments their own perfection of expression.'[63] Reversing the Western trope that acting is a form of fakery, Tagore saw theatre as a space of truth because mind and body reconnect, the key to this connection being rhythm. While the West privileges the spoken word in order to establish the ego that is the unseen source of those words, in Tagore's vision of Indian theatre the integration of word, body and movement connects the body-mind of the actor to the rhythms of the social group and of the physical environment. This conception of theatrical truth has no room for the democratic performer standing in front of a microphone. Nazi orators knew how to use the microphone to create a common rhythm, but they had no interest in reciprocity or the natural world. Because Tagore's dance-drama centred on female performers, it calls into question the masculinity associated since Quintilian with the authority claims of performers who seek to command the democratic podium. His festive model implies a different starting point.

Oratory and Truth

Gandhi expressed fear of oratory when he faced the reality of violent demonstrations in the summer of 1920: 'A good speaker arrests the attention of the audience and there is order such that you can hear a pin

Figure 6.1 Muhammad Ali Jinnah and Mohandas Gandhi photographed in 1944.
Source: British Library. Photo 429 (17). Photographer unknown.

drop. All the same this is mobocracy. You are at the mercy of the mob. So long as there is sympathy between you and the mob, everything goes well. Immediately that cord is broken, there is horror.' Though it might be organised by thoughtful individuals, Gandhi considered that Congress too was but a form of 'mob-demonstration'.[64] In order to create a more binding democratic discipline than any mere orator could achieve, Gandhi developed non-verbal strategies which Tagore saw as a call for blind obedience. Tagore himself loved the spoken word, and he considered paradox, metaphor and oral expression as the road to truth. Though he was indebted to the Western literary tradition, especially the romantic and modernist poets, the orality of Indian culture shaped his conviction that Indians should stop replicating the rituals of Western politics.

Gandhi's political nemesis Muhammad Ali Jinnah, the founding father of Pakistan, was unlike Gandhi a fine orator whose command of voice, gesture and timing allowed him to grip an audience (Figure 6.1). When he was training as a barrister in London Gandhi consorted with mystics in vegetarian restaurants, but Jinnah in the same situation joined a company of Shakespearean actors, and asked his parents' permission to change career, knowing of course that they would refuse. In his sister's version of events, Jinnah left the stage because he wanted to be 'a hero on a much bigger platform'.[65] Gandhi and Tagore were both horrified by the House of Commons, but Jinnah became a regular visitor and studied proceedings with interest, imagining himself a participant.[66] Gandhi empathised with the Indian poor to the point of living a life of extreme poverty, but Jinnah succeeded in becoming the leader of India's diverse and schismatic Moslems precisely because of the distance which he maintained between actor and role, speaking on behalf of his supporters as their advocate rather than their physical incarnation. His uniform was not any form of Moslem dress but an English three-piece suit accompanied by monocle and cigarette holder, and he preferred to conduct politics through the English language. His strategy was to play the game by English rules. At a crucial meeting of Congress in the autumn of 1920, he faced down a hostile crowd, insisted on referring in parliamentary language to Mr Gandhi rather than Mahatma Gandhi, and argued for negotiation rather than non-cooperation. Afterwards he told a Hindu journalist: 'I will have nothing to do with the pseudo-religious approach to politics. I part company with the Congress and Gandhi'.[67]

The divide between these two political styles was never healed. Jinnah was at one with Tagore in perceiving the nationhood of India as a construct of the British, but by the 1940s he saw no way to separate culture from government. Gandhi's insistence on the spiritual dimension of politics had made such separation impossible, leaving Jinnah to make his fateful claim that India's Moslems constituted a 'nation'.[68] Although Gandhi made desperate efforts to win Moslem support for a united Congress, he was the victim of his own political strategy. His naked flesh was less appealing to Moslem sensibilities than an English suit, and the sight of fervent Hindus seeking *darshan* of their living idol offered no reassurance that a united India would ever be other than a Hindu India. The progressive and tragic political rift that built up between Gandhi and Jinnah cannot be separated from their different approaches to performance. From Gandhi's perspective, Jinnah looked like a man of borrowed English words, an actor driven by his need to win acclamation from his audience, but from Jinnah's perspective Gandhi looked like Churchill's 'fakir', a man who used his religious persona to manipulate the masses. Tagore's sartorial style was different again, weaving together Hindu and Moslem elements in an all-embracing robe that offered no glimpse of any supposedly real Tagore beneath.[69]

Gandhi's other political nemesis was the leader of the Dalits or 'Untouchables', B. S. Ambedkar, who in an angry lecture of 1943 denounced both Jinnah and Gandhi for their egotism, claiming: 'Both have developed a wonderful stagecraft and arrange things in such a way that they are always in the limelight wherever they go.' Ambedkar complained that like the Pope both these lovers of the limelight believed in their own infallibility.[70] He had in the past been furious when Gandhi went on hunger strike to defend the principle that because all Indians had to be treated alike Dalits must not receive voting rights as a community. Since Gandhi, whatever his stagecraft, could not be condemned as insincere when offering up his life, Ambedkar turned to Carlyle to resolve the conundrum. In Carlyle's romantic account, true heroes from Mohammet the prophet to Samuel Johnson the rationalist are characterised by 'heart-sincerity': 'Not the sincerity that calls itself sincere: ah no, that is a very poor matter indeed; - a shallow braggart conscious sincerity; oftenest self-conceit mainly. The Great Man's sincerity is of the kind he cannot speak of, is not conscious of: nay, I suppose, he is conscious rather of *insincerity*; for what man can walk accurately by the law of truth for one day?'[71] Ambedkar's English intellectual training allowed him to condemn Gandhi as a man who protested his sincerity too much, but it did not offer him a way to resolve the paradox that Gandhi was simultaneously sincere and a master of stagecraft, which forced him back to the old democratic trope: I am a man of truth, you are a hypocrite. This trope calls for resolution through public argument, in a forum where the audience arbitrate between truth and hypocrisy. Having retreated from the law-court, Gandhi had little faith in fora of this kind.

Tagore had a different approach to the problem of truth: 'After sixty years of self-experience, I have found that out and out hypocrisy is an almost impossible achievement, so that the pure hypocrite is a rarity indeed. The fact is, that the character of man has always more or less of duality in it. But our logical faculty, the trap-door of our mind, is unable to admit opposites together.'[72] With his metaphor of the trap-door, derived from years acting on a stage, Tagore turns the ideals of the European Enlightenment back to front, so it is now reason that equates with subterranean darkness. In respect of politics, Tagore believed that India had to find a non-Western model that did not polarise but embraced opposites. In the American Revolution, English colonies broke away from their single 'parent', and in the French Revolution class divisions were eliminated 'to bring emancipation to a homogeneous people', but India, he thought, was different because 'in no other country under the sun has such a juxtaposition of races, ideas and religions occurred'. Since the rationalistic thinking of the Enlightenment had failed to resolve the problem of race, the only possible answer lay in 'steady and purposeful education', not 'blind revolution'.[73]

Escaping the Weirdness of Individualism

Amartya Sen quotes Tagore's most famous poem *Gitanjali 35* in order to enlist him as a fellow advocate of 'the clear stream of reason' and a 'heaven of freedom'. He presents Tagore as Gandhi's opponent 'pressing for more room for reasoning, and for a less traditionalist view, a greater interest in the rest of the world, and more respect for science and for objectivity', and he concludes: 'It is in the sovereignty of reasoning – fearless reasoning in freedom – that we can find Rabindranath Tagore's lasting voice.'[74] Martha Nussbaum turned to the same poem in order link Tagore to the educational principles of John Dewey and argue for critical thinking as the foundation for democratic citizenship.[75] These readings pass over Tagore's insistence on the limitations of rationality that follow from his premise that true freedom is freedom of the soul. Tagore's hostility to the idea of a political nation makes it hard to frame him as a champion of liberal democracy. Because individualism is the critical issue, Tagore's way of seeing the world is more easily aligned with Henrich's *The WEIRDest People in the World: How the West Became Psychologically Peculiar and Particularly Prosperous*. While Henrich traces his story back from Protestantism to early Catholic kinship rules, Tagore draws on the *Upanishads* for his vision of a universal soul. Throughout his career Tagore negotiated a tension between the social and creative freedom of the individual (opposing Gandhi's insistence on rigid discipline) and (now echoing Gandhi) the spiritual need for a surrender of self. In a typical metaphor, he likened the individual to a river enclosed by banks yet open to the sea.[76] Henrich's five headings will help me sum up the world Tagore tried to engage with:

Western. This is a fundamental construct for Tagore.[77] In his 1917 essay on Nationalism, fearing that China and Japan would be poisoned by the soulless apparatus of Nation, he appealed to 'You, the people of the West, who have manufactured this abnormality'.[78] In the arts, he believed that Western artists contemplate the soul of man but Oriental artists look into the soul of the universe,[79] and in the case of theatre, since Europeans cannot do without the truth of material fact, the actor's art can only be set free for spectators 'untutored by European puerility'.[80] I follow Rustom Bharucha in maintaining that we should not dismiss such sentiments with the postcolonial claim that they are 'essentialising' and 'orientalising' strategies, a claim which takes its own secular premises to be unquestionable.[81] I have argued in this book that the roots of Western democratic practice lie in spiritual experience.

Educated. Tagore became an educational guru rather than a political activist because he believed this was the way to build a better society, and he deplored Gandhi's cult of 'non-education'.[82] As he explained to children in China, Western education attended to the intellect rather than feelings except in one regard: 'The one desire produced in the heart of the students has been an ambition to win wealth and power, — not to reach some inner standard of perfection, not to obtain self-emancipation. Such an ideal is not worthy of human beings.' He qualified this critique by adding that 'we must accept truth when it comes from the West and not hesitate to render it our tribute of admiration... Moreover, the Western people also need our help, for our destinies are now intertwined'.[83] The colonial education system, Tagore argued, turned out performers wearing ideas as if they were body-paint, 'so we go strutting about, our bodies smeared with an alien English learning which has hardly any connection with the inner reality of our life. We swagger about with a few cheap, flashy English words... unable even to see ourselves as unwitting actors in an absurd farce'.[84] Western universities fail because they 'have not yet truly recognized that fullness of expression is fullness of life',[85] and in his own school he aspired to educate the feelings and bodily senses, with the performance of dance-dramas a medium for collaborative and experiential learning.[86]

Industrialised. Though Tagore was not like Gandhi an opponent of technology in principle, the artist in him resisted the notion that 'man's salvation depends upon his disciplining himself into a perfection of the dead rhythm of wheels and counterwheels'. Weaving exemplified the central problem of rhythm: 'In the products of the hand loom the magic of man's living fingers finds its expression, and its hum harmonizes with the music of life. But the power loom is relentlessly lifeless and accurate and monotonous in its production.'[87] He was interested in the expressivity of the Bengali weaver's art, not the uniformity of Gandhi's thread. Stage technology exemplified the 'cumbrous and bloated' nature of Western theatre, and Tagore preferred performances in the open air that engaged with the rhythms of nature.[88] Gandhi hated the railways, but he also needed them to build an Indian *demos*, in a contradiction which Tagore did his best to avoid.

Rich. Tagore was no ascetic like Gandhi, but he resisted the individualistic motivation of greed which had led to British imperialism, and he was careful to distinguish simplicity from poverty.

Democratic. Henrich draws on Weber's account of Protestantism to help explain the WEIRD psychology which allows individuals to acquiesce in remote collective decisions because they have had some notional voice. Henrich recognises the diversity of cultural psychologies, but steers clear of the moral issues raised by Amartya Sen's contention that democracy is a universal value.[89] Highlighting the connection between democracy and the nation-state, Tagore did not endear himself to nationalists when he bracketed commerce and politics as twin aspects of the machine called 'Nation'.[90] On his way to Japan from China, where students had given him a rough reception, he reported that 'China was really living in those of her people, who had never been to Harvard; had never seen skyscrapers; had never used the word Democracy'.[91] Sailing perilously close to the language of populism when he sets the 'people' against the formal institutions of democracy, Tagore's enduring point concerns the gap between theoretical political structures and organic human bonds. Democracy for Tagore depends upon the establishment of social relationships.

Were he in a position to contemplate India in the twenty-first century, Tagore would be observing the same democratic elephant giving joy rides to the clever and rich. Partition and the election of a Hindu nationalist government would have reaffirmed his conviction that the borrowed idea of Nation cannot be reconciled with the social and cultural relationships of *samaj*. In his lifetime Tagore rejected Gandhi's essentially Jacobin conception of democracy, which sought to assimilate all Indians into a single General Will. For Gandhi, the only song needed by the hungry millions was food, and he dreamed of converting theatres and cinemas into spinning halls,[92] but for Tagore human beings need mental alongside physical sustenance. It has indeed been shown that because humans need mental as well as physical sustenance, many in extreme poverty prefer to go hungry in order to purchase a television.[93] Gandhi made space for a theatre in his model *panchayat*, but he saw it only as a vehicle for tradition and stability.[94] Tagore believed in the principle of change, not Gandhi's repetitious wheel.

We need to track back to Athens to pin down Tagore's difficulty with the very idea of democracy. The Greek model is a 'tragic' one: two lonely persons stand on a stage and articulate two incompatible moral goods, leaving the chorus to make an impossible but necessary collective choice. Irreconcilable moral principles are articulated through the spoken word which is supported by the gestures and intonations of the actor.

Democracy as a Universal Good: Gandhi/Tagore/New India   167

Everything in Tagore's cultural and philosophical background pushed him towards another model, that of harmony in its cosmic, social and individual dimensions, steering him away from the combative public *agon*, and the personal *agon* of head versus body. Speech, song, dance and music converge in Tagore's mature theatre practice, and the spoken word is not a vehicle for the ideas of the playwright but a 'melody of the body'.[95] Text is central to the West's dramatic tradition, as the score is central to its musical tradition, and a concert or dramatic performance is an act of representation, a procedure for representing a pre-existent work that sits on paper. In the Indian performance tradition, *rasa* and beauty are created in the moment, and art is never representational in the same sense. Tagore criticised Western theatre for its reproductive naturalism within a production system that required actors to repeat themselves night after night, and he preferred the idea that the audience's imagination should be engaged in creating a unique performance event.[96] The musicologist Matthew Pritchard observes that Tagore's songs rarely work well in a standard concert setting or in recordings, and describes their power for Bengalis when one hears them 'sung impromptu and unaccompanied ... next to an open doorway ... the tune whispering softly of the longing in the night breeze'.[97] Tagore's plays likewise resist being transformed into 'works' by a famous writer.

Tagore has no magic recipe for twenty-first-century politics, where his ideal of separating *swaraj* from the modern nation-state seems to have become an impossibility. Tagore matters nevertheless as a reminder that 'democracy', a term with no equivalent in the Bengali language, is not a global given but an ideal that needs continuous redefinition. I share Bharucha's view that Tagore matters because 'he makes life difficult for us. He makes it harder for us to think by denying us easy alternatives and glib solutions', and he does so because he 'defies dominant categories'. I have focused on Tagore in this chapter because he was a playwright who knew that anything purporting to be real 'democracy' had to be a kind of performance, while having no patience with the 'marionette show of politicians, soldiers, manufacturers and bureaucrats, pulled by wire arrangements of wonderful efficiency' which he observed mutilating humanity in World War One.[98]

Gandhi did all in his power to demonstrate his personal sincerity and freedom from hypocrisy, but this did not prevent others from seeing him as a stage ham. Starting from his different premise that performance is part of life, Tagore tried to step outside the Western dialectic of truth and hypocrisy, of reality and representation, categories that ensnare theatre and democracy alike. He shows us that mere 'representation' can never be enough. As a political ideal, representation in India ran up against an unsolvable problem: Whom does the political actor represent? Individuals or communities? Tagore tried to escape the trap of representation, recognising that any politics capable of bringing experiential freedom to the people, the non-elite, must be built on relationships that traverse the boundary line symbolised by footlights and microphone. He valued human connections forged in a particular place and time, where 'place' implies a relationship to the natural environment, and 'time' a relationship to lifecycles rather than electoral cycles.

CHAPTER 7

Theatre and Theatrocracy in Democratic Athens

Democracy is and always has been a form of theatre. It is akin to tragedy in the way it likes to pit two moral goods against each other, usually in the form of fairness or equality versus liberty. In the theatre of democracy, relationships of power are negotiated through verbal warfare to save bloodletting, and the performers on stage compete to tell the most winning stories and play best upon the emotions of the spectators. The idea that reason and sincerity will suffice to shape the behaviour of a *demos* is an illusion which tends paradoxically to open the door to demagogues with a better understanding of human behaviour. Reason can never be unhitched from emotion, though calm reasoning may often be the best way to create the *feeling* in your listener that you are the right leader for this particular moment.

To be a democratic politician is to be an actor or *hypokrites*, and it is a common ploy to dismiss your opponent as a 'hypocrite' because it is the mark of a bad performance to be seen to be acting. The Greek word *hypokrites* means 'answerer', and Greek theatre seems to have begun when an actor emerged from the choral dance to have a dialogue with the chorus. Sincere convictions are a block to dialogue because this means that you know exactly what you believe and are not open to persuasion. When I criticise 'sincerity', I'm not defending political corruption, far from it. My point is that corrupt practices all too often stem from a lack of scrutiny and open debate. Nor do I want to belittle principled leadership. Democracies need leaders just as a troupe of actors, however collaborative its company ethos, needs a director with a coherent artistic vision.

When politicians change their minds, they are often charged with being hypocrites rather than people who have learnt and adjusted to circumstance. Sincerity means a conviction you are right, and history holds up few timeless heroes proved right by time. Gandhi was and for many Indians remains a hero, but in retrospect it may be that his disdain for traditional democratic debate did much to precipitate partition and the associated death of millions.[1] Jefferson the libertarian was Jefferson the slave owner, though the contradiction was invisible to most Anglo-Saxons at the time. The English Cromwell was not the Irish Cromwell. Pericles was a hero for Thucydides, but to citizens of Mytilene he must have looked a lethal imperialist. Sophocles' *Oedipus* tells the story of yesterday's hero who becomes today's villain because he has brought the plague to Thebes, and for Sophocles' audience there must have been clear echoes of Pericles whose patriotic policies led to urban overcrowding and a crippling plague.[2] Moral judgements can only ever be provisional because the world is a changing place, and perspectives never stand still.

Leaving aside figures like Angelina Grimke and Frederick Douglass who held no political office, I have not succeeded in excavating any democratic heroes in the course of writing this book, and when failings both personal and political emerge at every turn, it is tempting to echo Plato's despair at democracy itself. Among the educated young in Europe and America, as I suggested in my introduction, individual self-determination often now has a stronger emotional pull than collective self-determination. We need democracy, I suggest, because like theatre it is an essential tool for reciprocal listening. In the theatre characters batting dialogue to and fro are only a trigger for the important act of collective listening when audiences respond to actors and actors to audiences in a feedback loop. Any good actor has a clear conception of the role they are playing, and must if they are to hold the attention of the audience, but their performance will fail if they do not keep making micro-adjustments in the moment. The *hypokrites* is an 'answerer', and living theatre must be distinguished from what Brook called 'deadly' theatre because it seeks an inert response.[3] Since democracy is a form of theatre that entails constant readjustment by the listener, it is inherently adaptive, a biological principle geared to survival.

Reading Greek Tragedy in the Twentieth Century

In this final chapter, I will not push my narrative on towards an ever more confusing and disputed present, but will rather turn my argument around and pass from democracy *as* theatre to the place of theatre *in* democracy. I have taken Athens in this book not as a point of origin, not as a seed from which modern democracy has grown, but rather as a reference point that allows democracy to be rethought. Since democracy and theatre were twin Athenian institutions which emerged and thrived together, I shall explore that symbiosis in order to ask where our own democracy in the future might go. Because the past can only be viewed from the perspective of the present, I shall track back to antiquity via 'political' theatre as we have come to know it in our own times. I will take as my point of reference a 1999 essay by the playwright John McGrath entitled 'Theatre and Democracy', which typifies the way late twentieth-century theatre makers viewed the proper relationship of theatre to the democratic process, within the frame of an influential socialist tradition.[4]

McGrath begins and ends his essay with a homage to the father-figure of modern European political theatre, Bertolt Brecht, whose Marxist assumptions meant that 'democracy' in its familiar form could not be on the agenda for discussion. McGrath resurrected the ideal of democracy by turning back to Athens. The modern Greek philosopher Cornelius Castoriadis pointed him towards a 'Golden Age of Pericles' just before 'democracy came unravelled' when there was a 'fragile equilibrium' between individuality and popular power and the great tragedians were at the height of their powers.[5] McGrath draws from Castoriadis a picture of tragedy as a reminder of self-limitation and mortality, and a demonstration of how conflicting rights can coexist, an ideal form of theatre which scrutinises the values of the *demos*, gives voice to the excluded and keeps questioning the borders of freedom. Underlying McGrath's essay is an assumption characteristic of his era that the pre-eminent figure is the playwright whose ideas are the focus of the audience's attention, and behind him lay a canon of late twentieth-century British 'political' playwrights like Arden, Bond, Brenton, Edgar, and Hare. Ahead lay a twenty-first-century change of emphasis, with ensembles coming to the fore in a process that mirrored the transformation of academic departments of 'drama' centred on texts into departments of 'theatre' centred on bodies.[6] Though McGrath is most famous for the plays he took to the urban and rural poor in Scotland,[7] his essay paid little attention to the social institution of theatre, and he passed over Castoriadis' account of tragedy as a competitive *agon*.[8] For the Brechtian tradition grounded in Marxism, the job of the playwright was to unmask the real workings of bourgeois society by turning upon it a critical scientific gaze.[9] In the twenty-first century that faith in an underlying real has evaporated, and McGrath's political certainties seem the product of a bygone age. His concept of a Greek Golden Age recalls the seventeenth-century Levellers who dreamed of a lost Eden, and whose optimistic hopes for the future rested on their construction of a pre-Norman utopia.

Many theatre scholars have been frustrated by the spell of Aristotle's *Poetics*, a canonical presentation of drama as a branch of literature. Edith Hall in 1993, for example, read the *Poetics* historically as tragedy's 'petition for divorce from the Athenian democratic *polis*.'[10] Aristotle, in other words, was reframing a political institution as an artistic institution. A collection of 1990 entitled *Nothing To Do With Dionysos? Athenian Drama in its Social Context* was influential in shifting the academic paradigm from 'plays' to 'theatre'.[11] Institutions like the *choregia* (the funding of choruses by rich citizens), the *theorikon* (money allowing the poor to buy theatre seats), and the awarding of public honours (like Demosthenes' crown) were foregrounded to show how the performance of tragedy was embedded in Athenian democracy. Simon Goldhill's contribution entitled 'The Great Dionysia and civic ideology' proved particularly influential, and in 2000 Goldhill claimed as 'mainstream' his view that 'the festival is a performance integral to democracy in action ... Any analysis that simply treats tragedy as literature ... is nowhere less persuasive than with fifth-century Athenian drama'.[12]

Goldhill pinned his analysis to the term 'ideology', still widely used as a critical key in arts academia, and amongst classicists debate worried away at a paradox summed up by Chris Pelling: 'Part of civic ideology ... was to feel worried about civic ideology'.[13] Propositions about civic or democratic 'ideology' carry the unspoken implication that the thinking liberal subject (typified by an undergraduate sitting in a seminar) can somehow see through or beyond this mental thing called 'ideology', but it has never been clear which cognitive functions 'ideology' relates to, and the word has no Greek or Latin equivalence.[14] When Plato argued that the domain of the 'idea' could be separated from that of the body, he flew in the face of prevailing Greek assumptions. Learning to be a citizen, like learning to be an actor, depended on habituated bodily action. After dancing in procession and eating together, the Athenian theatre audience laughed and wept together, while the chorus danced together, and Athenian democracy entailed rowing or fighting side-by-side after the collective raising of hands in the Assembly to vote for war. The concept of ideology fails to capture the physicality of group behaviours and mind–body connections upon which democratic life rested.

In *Democracy: A Life* (2016), Paul Cartledge described the evolution of civic institutions, but as a historian he preferred to leave theatre on the sidelines, merely observing that the function of tragedy was 'to question the city's fundamental tenets and ideals'.[15] His book raises the question: Is it possible to separate art from from political praxis, and 'the city' from flesh-and-blood citizens? Is democracy ultimately a system of government, or a manifestation of *homo democraticus*, the type of human being who creates and is created by democracy? In *Nothing to do with Dionysos?*, Josiah Ober and Barry Strauss initiated a new approach through turning their attention to rhetoric. Oratory, they explain, 'drew on the audience's experience of theater; drama drew on the audience's experience of political and legal speeches. By doing so, each genre implicitly taught its audience that ... there was no compartmentalized division between esthetics and politics. Athenian political culture was created in part in the theater of Dionysos, theatrical culture on the Pnyx'.[16] In his account of Athenian democratic life published in 1989, Ober suggested that the theatre provided a kind of 'training' for jurors and assemblyman. This crucial insight was limited by Ober's dated assumption that theatrical spectatorship entails 'suspension of disbelief', a formulation that ignores the brain's ability to multifunction.[17] Chris Pelling took the conversation further by pointing to the transactional nature of rhetoric, observing that it 'takes at least two to make a performance, a speaker and an audience, and performance is duly a two-way thing.'[18]

Euripides' *Trojan Women* represents women taken into slavery after the fall of Troy, and is a useful case study to show how the modern era came to read the politics of Greek tragedy. Through his 1905 translation staged at the Royal Court Theatre, the classical scholar Gilbert Murray alerted the London public that Euripides could have been responding to the massacre of all adult males on the small island of Melos, when women and children were sent off to be slaves as the island became an Athenian colony. The production was mounted in the context of public opposition to the Boer War and the excesses of English imperialism, and it was revived in the USA at the start of the First World War as a plea for non-engagement. The anti-war message continued with Jean-Paul Sartre's adaptation, which responded to French imperialist atrocities in Algeria.[19] Euripides as reconstructed in the twentieth century became a liberal democratic dissident who used theatre as a vehicle for freedom of speech and anti-government polemic.[20]

The liberal twentieth century relished the anti-colonial sentiment of *Trojan Women*, but judged the play a flawed masterpiece. Richmond Lattimore's introduction to his much-reprinted Chicago translation offers an example of mid-century assumptions.

> The effect of current events and policies on *The Trojan Women* is, I think, so obvious that it scarcely needs further elaboration ... The play-long presence of Hecuba on the stage necessitates padding, which is supplied by elaborate rhetorical debates ... Out-of-character generalizations bespeak the inspirations of Euripides rather than of his dramatis personae. The trial scene of Helen is a bitter little comedy-within-tragedy, but its juridical refinements defeat themselves and turn preposterous, halting for a time the emotional force of the play. In candor, one can hardly call *The Trojan Women* a good piece of work, but it seems nevertheless to be a great tragedy.[21]

Plays for Lattimore need 'characters', and it is the emotions of these characters that give a play its force, while 'rhetorical' debate gets in the way of the play's proper task which is to show how the victims of war feel. The dramaturgy must be flawed because so many productions turn the play into a repetitive litany of suffering, which they do when they focus on the twentieth-century question: What does it feel like to be a slave? Liberal democracy is posited on the autonomy of the individual human subject, and theatre has done much to reinforce that premise.

Back in 1954 Amy Marjorie Dale was a pioneering critic who challenged the received assumption that the job of dramatic characters is to express themselves, and argued that the tragic dramatist resembles a professional speechwriter 'who promises to do his best for each of his clients in turn as the situations change and succeed each other'.[22] When the prophetess Cassandra seeks to persuade her mother that the defeated Trojans are better off than the victors, developing what in formal terms is a dispassionate argument, she exemplifies the 'out-of-character' digressions which Lattimore complains of. Andromache likewise tries to console a bereaved mother with the reasoned argument that it is even worse to be a sex slave than to be dead. And, in a mock trial scene, Helen seeks to exonerate herself from guilt for causing the war while Hecuba's case for the prosecution is riddled with flaws. In all these speeches, the context forces the audience to weigh arguments and through doing so guess at the feelings behind them. Most twentieth- and twenty-first-century audiences have little occasion to hear extended speeches, and little education in how to construct them, but for Athenian spectators evaluating speakers and arguments was the stuff of life.

Theatre and Rhetoric

The drift of Helen's speech in *Trojan Women* mirrors a surviving speech by Gorgias, and we cannot be certain which was written first. While the words of Euripides were offered free to the masses, Gorgias would have performed his version to wealthy paying customers.[23] With a delightful sense of paradox Gorgias seeks to persuade his audience that Helen should not be blamed for eloping with Paris because the seductive power of speech is irresistible so blame can only lie with the persuader. His Helen argues that speech is like a drug, like witchcraft or like rape in the way it works physical as much as mental change upon the listener. Gorgias' choice of the beautiful Helen was not random, for he taught his students to speak beautifully and beauty is persuasive, as Euripides' Helen demonstrates through the way she charms her estranged husband Menelaus. Euripides invites his audience simultaneously to be persuaded and to perceive the artistry of Helen's crafted rhetoric. In a male political environment, the paradoxical figure of the female orator served both the playwright and the rhetorician because it shone a light on the seductive artistry of public speech.

In Athens democracy relied exclusively upon speech, and writing was a tool to support an oral culture. In recent centuries the power of the printing press has supplemented the spoken word, and in our own era screened images have added another layer of complication. In Athens, writing was perceived as a challenge to democracy because rich speakers were in a position to hire a good speechwriter. As Gorgias' Helen puts it, 'when a verbal *agon* takes place, the crowd can be charmed and won over in any particular speech by the artistry of its writing rather than by any truth spoken'. Truth, Helen continues, is in any case useless because people can never accurately recall the past, perceive the present or foretell the future.[24] There is nothing new in modern anxieties about manipulation and 'post-truth', and the face-to-face culture of Athens was no golden age of authenticity. Like digital media, writing was once a new technology used in order to falsify.

Murray and his contemporaries were haunted by Thucydides' vivid picture of the massacre at Melos. The success and energy of democratic Athens led to a desire to expand, colonise and allow economic self-interest to overshadow religious and ethical considerations. Though democracy would seem to offer no path here to global justice, a close reading of Thucydides reveals a more nuanced story. Melos was a former Spartan colony, and the ruling oligarchs refused to let Athenian diplomats use their powers of rhetoric on the Melian *demos* to explain why the city should surrender to force majeure. Thucydides gives us a snapshot of the argument that ran behind closed doors, and makes it clear that the oligarchs said no to Athens because of an irrational devotion to honour.[25] A democratic Melos open to oratory would most likely have prioritised self-preservation, and there would have been no massacre. The Athenians could have used democratic rhetoric to touch the emotions of the crowd, but when confined to reasoning with a small elite group they had no means to shift entrenched convictions. Most modern productions of *Trojan Women* seek to create empathy with the victim and thereby moral outrage, but Euripides like Thucydides was more interested in uncovering the way rhetoric shapes human behaviour, knowing how speeches moved Athenian crowds to make life-and-death decisions.

Sophocles' *Oedipus the King* was canonised in Aristotle's *Poetics* as a masterpiece of dramatic form, and Freud went on to fix it for the twentieth century as a timeless account of deep human nature.[26] The *Poetics* however, also shaped Hannah Arendt's theory that 'action' is different from mere activity,[27] and we should not leap too quickly to the conclusion that in the age of Demosthenes Aristotle depoliticised Greek tragedy. Picturing an Athens where 'speech and action were considered to be coeval and coequal', Arendt celebrated political speech as a form of action that offered an alternative to violence,[28] and her reading of Aristotle points us to an Oedipus who uses words as political 'actions'. Aristotle defined tragedy as the imitation of three things: action, character and 'thought' (*dianoia*).[29] Though the storyline should arouse emotion, Aristotle never asks the playwright to represent emotion directly, and the use of language and gesture to arouse pity, fear and anger is in fact a manifestation of *dianoia*, a calculated ploy designed to work on a susceptible listener.[30] While modern theatre practitioners including Brecht have admired Aristotle for insisting that character is subordinate to action,[31] the category overlooked in modern discussions of theatre is '*dianoia*'.

Dianoia or 'thought' is defined in the *Poetics* as:

> the ability to set out facts and circumstances, being the task of speech in politics and rhetoric. The ancients [i.e. the generation of Sophocles] made people speak *politically*, the moderns *rhetorically*. Character is that which reveals choice, through the kind of things chosen or avoided, and thus character is missing in speeches where there is no such revelation, or where choice and avoidance are entirely absent. Thought is where the speaker demonstrates that something either is or is not so, or fits a general principle.[32]

Aristotle distinguishes what he sees as genuine 'political' speech from mere 'rhetoric', with the implication that political speech addresses actual choices. Elsewhere he cites Antigone's choice of an irreplaceable brother in preference to a replaceable husband as an example of speech that reveals choice and therefore character, and is not mere verbiage of the kind favoured by rhetoricians.[33] Many modern critics have followed Goethe in lamenting or excising these lines of Antigone because they seem inconsistent with her passionate character.[34] For such critics, a play must be an imitation of character first and last, and never an imitation of mere thought. The category of 'thought' ceased to be valued in European theatre once romanticism and modernity separated reason from emotion, and turned the 'self' or 'me' into something unique, private and special. The personal domain proper to the arts was bracketed off from the rhetorical domain proper to politics, and *dianoia* could no longer be understood as an expression of the authentic human subject. Within modernity, the purpose of 'political' drama, in plays like those of Ibsen, Miller or Hare, was to dig as it were beneath the surface and explore the hidden subjectivities of individuals caught up in the externality of public events.

It is instructive to set Sophocles alongside his contemporary Antiphon, a teacher and legal adviser who charged for his services. Antiphon's 'tetralogies' are four-part scripts for fictional murder trials where plaintiff and defendant each deliver two balanced speeches, and as in *Oedipus* the religious pollution that arises from killing provides an emotional context.[35] Antiphon's speeches were teaching aids addressing the complications of arguing from probability, and a play like *Oedipus* might be viewed as an equivalent teaching aid for the wider community, helping spectators evaluate emotive arguments as they reach for the most probable account: Is it probable, for example, that Oedipus could have unknowingly killed his father? Antiphon was known as the author of a controversial book about *Truth*, and when tried for plotting against democracy in 411 BCE he claimed it was highly 'improbable' that he, a master of writing speeches for others, would plot against a political system that relied on public speaking.

Both Sophocles and Antiphon wrote words for other men to perform, and Athenian audiences had to evaluate probability not just on the basis of a script but on how that script was delivered. Antiphon's prosecutor tried to pre-empt the power the defendant's tears would surely have as Antiphon for once stood on the rostrum to plead his own case.[36] Those tears failed to secure an acquittal, and one reason may be that the jurors were used to watching plays by Sophocles and Euripides. Characters in tragedy work on each other's emotions in an attempt to change them, and their speeches work at the same time upon the audience, who learn to develop a double vision, simultaneously moved and aware they are watching a rhetorical strategy. As a training in rhetoric offered free of charge to the Athenian poor, tragedy did much to build a democratic culture where it was possible for ordinary citizens to see through the art of trained rhetoricians like Antiphon.

Theatre as Public Contest

Greek tragedy was an *agon*, the leading actors were called 'protagonists', and an *agon* implies competition, a winner and a loser. Today, because we frame tragedy as art, we tend to see the competitive basis of tragedy as an incidental detail, but for democratic Athenians this was tragedy's raison d'être. Competition was a feature of Greek performance culture, and it was adapted by Athenian democracy to consolidate tribal identities. Tribes were the artificial building blocks of the system, and served as in the case of public funerals to bring citizens of different localities and economic means into face-to-face relationships.[37] Prior to the performance of tragedies at the Dionysian festival, a day was given over to 'dithyrambs', dances in honour of Dionysus performed by each of the ten tribes, with fifty boys and fifty men representing each tribe. Dancing in a circle built cohesion, and allowed many if not most citizens to experience what it was like to perform to a theatre audience. Playwrights worked in partnership with a *choregos*, a rich citizen responsible for recruiting and training the chorus and other production expenses, motivated by his desire to gain honour from victory.[38]

One judge from each tribe was selected by lot, and it appears that the prize was awarded not on the basis of all ten verdicts but on perhaps five chosen at random, according to rules that must have changed over time. In the theatre the ten tribal representatives swore an oath of impartiality, but could scarcely help but be swayed this by the noisy reactions of the audience. Plato described the courage needed by an educated judge to resist popular opinion:

> When he reaches his decision, a true judge should not take orders from the auditorium, doubly overwhelmed by the *thorubos* of the crowd and his own feeling of incompetence; nor should he, if he is an expert, yield to cowardice and fear, delivering a lie from the very mouth that swore an undertaking to the gods so he may come up with the easy verdict. Rightly and properly a judge sits not as pupil but as teacher of the audience, resisting spectators who stupidly and wrongly surrender to pleasure. This used to be possible under ancient Hellenic law, quite unlike the present regime in Sicily and Italy where decisions are made by the whole auditorium and the prize is awarded by a show of hands. This procedure corrupts playwrights, who supply their jury with base pleasures, letting poets take lessons from spectators. And it corrupts also the pleasures of those spectators, who should be receiving a higher class of pleasure from listening to men of higher morality than themselves, so unlike current practice.[39]

Theatre created a tricky democratic problem. The assembly worked by a show of the right hand because it needed to maximise consensus, while the law-court worked by secret ballot to ensure no reprisals.[40] Recognising that judgement by acclaim would have lowered the ability of playwrights to teach and challenge, the Athenians evolved a system that echoes modern jury service, with a small panel of ordinary citizens voting on behalf of the community at large. The Italian system would never have worked in Athens where citizens were mixed up with non-citizens, and some watched from outside the boundary of the auditorium. Part of the decision in Athens was left to chance, or the gods, because what ultimately mattered was the competitive striving.

No Athenian judge could have found himself unmoved by the reactions of the auditorium at large.[41] The small group of tribal representatives seated prominently in the auditorium functioned as a sort of collective moral conscience, torn between succumbing to the emotional impact of what they had just witnessed and following a more considered sense of rightness. Partisanship was fierce, and Plutarch describes the moment when Sophocles challenged Aeschylus' older conception of tragedy, which meant that the regular judges no longer had sufficient authority, and the ten generals elected from the tribes had to replace them.[42] When jurors pondered whether it was right to crown Demosthenes in the theatre, Aeschines asked them to apply the same integrity as that enforced in the theatre: 'With judges at the Dionysia, if someone judges the dithyramb illegally, they're fined; but you who sit in judgement not over dithyrambs but over the law and political standards, are you going to hand out your prizes, not according to the rules, not to the few who deserve them, but to the mere opportunist?'[43]

Euripides' poor track record in winning first prize testifies to a widespread feeling that there was something morally outrageous about the pleasure that he gave to audiences.[44] Aristophanes' comedy *The Frogs* lets us glimpse the criteria that led judges to make their decisions. In a contest between Aeschylus and Euripides, the god Dionysus goes through a long process of decision-making, and both contestants seem agreed on the criterion spelt out by 'Euripides': we applaud a poet 'for getting it right and getting it through, so he makes people better citizens.'[45] They disagree of course about what good citizenship means. Dionysus begins his task as judge by thinking about the character of the human beings set before him in the play, then turns to technical questions of style including diction and rhythm, before arriving at the playwright's role as political teacher and the enigmatic nature of any overt advice. He makes his final decision on what seems like a whim, quoting Euripides' famous line "My tongue it was that swore" to justify the fact that gut moral instinct has turned him against the playwright he once loved and praised.[46] Beneath the comedy lies a plausible picture of human decision making. Against the background of a sophisticated grasp of technique, Dionysus as judge resists his initial sense of gratification, and rationalises as best he can to support an instinctive judgement about what is at once morally and aesthetically 'right'.

The prize awarded to the best playwright was at the same time a prize awarded to the chorus, because for the judges there was no way of separating the quality of a choral lyric from choreography devised and overseen by the playwright. A separate prize for the best actor was introduced after playwrights had stopped taking the leading acting role, as the young Sophocles did when he first vanquished Aeschylus.[47] The awarding of a prize for best actor implies a crucial ability in the listener to separate out the quality of a text from the vocal and physical skills that help the actor touch the emotions of his audience. To distinguish the element of 'acting' or *hypokrisis* from the language and argument of a speech was a key democratic skill. In an Athenian law-court the plaintiff or defendant was free to employ a Gorgias or an Antiphon and learn his text verbatim, but he needed acting skills if he was to convince the audience that his words came from the heart. To fail was to be exposed as a hypocrite, spouting words that did not chime with his thoughts. The task of the jury was to search out such hypocrisy.

Plato on Theatrocracy

Political armageddon at the end of the great war against Sparta convinced many Athenians that they needed to rebuild democracy better, but it persuaded Plato that the democratic project was fundamentally unworkable. His critique bracketed rhetoric, tragedy and democracy together, and his reluctance to separate culture from politics makes more sense in the 2020s, an era dominated by so-called culture wars, than it did in the late twentieth century in the shadow of a Marxist and free-market assumption that economics must trump culture as a driver of human behaviour. In his *Republic* Plato envisaged benevolent dictatorship as the best path to human happiness, but later experiences in Sicily seem to have convinced him that autocrats are always corrupted by their position.[48] This explains why, late in life, he conceived in *Laws* a new utopia where citizens conditioned by education would be locked into a stable pattern of behaviour by intricate laws and regulations, though he conceded that a benevolent dictator would be needed to set the wheels of this system in motion.

In one regulation, Plato's spokesman stipulates that itinerant tragedians must be banned from visiting this new model society. Note that the Greek word 'poet' means literally a 'maker', and a tragedy could have a heroic rather than a doleful ending. He tells would-be performers:

> We ourselves are the poets of a tragedy, making it as noble and beautiful as we can. Our whole city-state constitutes the representation of a noble and

beautiful life, which we claim is the truest form of tragedy. You are poets, and we too are poets making the same thing, rivalling you in skill and performance [*agon*] to create the finest drama, which can be realised only by the rule of truth.[49]

For Plato life was a kind of dramatic performance, where humans are but imperfect imitations of their true selves. He understood that the lawmaker distributed roles and wrote the script for citizens to act out, ever hopeful that the actors would not deviate too far from the envisaged performance.

Before setting out his revised proposals for an ideal society, Plato provides a historical overview, contrasting the perils of monarchy with those of democracy. He looks back to a better Athens when a united democratic city led the Greek fight against Persia, and claims that in this period 'the *demos* was in a sense a voluntary slave to the laws'. By 'laws,' he explains that he means first and foremost conventions governing performance, and he praises the formal purity of an era when genres like the 'dithyramb' or 'paean' were codified. Tragedy was too fluid, yoking different genres together and constantly changing in a bid to please the public. In the past, Plato laments:

> There were men authorised to know the conventions and to award prizes on the basis of that knowledge, penalising those who dissented. There was no whistling and ignorant shouting out by the masses like today, nor stamping and clapping to show approval. It was expected that those with a responsibility to educate would listen through to the end in silence, while the threat of a stick kept order among children, their [slave] tutors and the assembled crowd. The mass of citizens were willing to be managed in this orderly way, and did not dare pass judgement through a *thorubos*. Afterwards, as time went by, poets led the way in artistic rule-breaking, possessed with a natural sense of the poetic but no grasp of the conventions and all that is laid down by the Muses, surrendering to bacchanalian pleasure, mixing lament with jubilation and Apollo's songs with those of Dionysus, performing on strings music composed for the pipes, joining everything to everything, driven by aesthetic ignorance into the false doctrine that there are no absolute artistic standards, so the joy of gratification allows anyone, good or bad as they may be, to pass judgement.[50]

Plato spells out the political consequences of artistic rule-breaking by writers of tragedy, the hotch-potch genre that keeps changing and is so distinctively Athenian:

> The auditorium, once silent, acquired a voice, as if qualified to discern artistic excellence, and in lieu of aristocracy there arose here a vile 'theatrocracy'. Now if a democracy of free men had gone no further,

nothing terrible would have happened. But what started in our case with the arts was a belief that everyone was clever enough to know all about everything and break every rule, and what ensued was liberty. They had no fear of ignorance, and fearless meant shameless. Their refusal to be intimidated by the views of their betters turns into coarse disrespect, such is the wild bravado that comes with freedom ... The next liberty is saying no to serving under officers; after that, rejecting your duty to support or take advice from fathers, mothers and the elderly; as the end approaches, doing what you can to block your ears to the rule of law; and at the last, letting all oaths, loyalties and religion be abandoned ...[51]

Tragedy from Plato's perspective is not a mere scrutiny of democratic politics but an active force that creates political change. It cannot be pigeonholed as a source of democratic 'ideology' because Plato's utopian society is a dance culture grounded in the body and he understood tragedy as a corrupted form of choral dance. He saw that tragedy was not a simulation, in his terms a third order of reality, but was a competitive *agon* that formed a crucial part of democratic living. It was a chance for the *demos* to have a voice, and exercise its freedoms.

Plato's coinage of 'theatrocracy' as a synonym for democracy implies not rule by actors but rule by the audience. Greek actors like demagogues tried to manage their audiences, but at the end of the day the audience had to pass judgement and a decisive vote took place. Plato advocated choral dancing in *Laws* because he knew that this mode of performance created social bonding, as it did in Sparta, and he was hostile to tragedy because it involved the masses in making judgements, in a process where thought could not be disentangled from emotion. Tragedy confounded Plato's philosophical project of separating the thinking head from the lower body, and of separating those who know from those who are told what to do. For *homo democraticus*, on the other hand, tragedy was a tool for self-knowledge and Plato's resistance testifies to its potency. Gathered in daylight in an enveloping auditorium, the Athenian *demos* eyed itself and heard itself as a collective organism endowed with thought and feeling, and as it made its journey through the emotional highs and lows, the cognitive shocks and surprises of a programme of tragedies, the democratic audience got to know itself better. To understand how you are being persuaded results ultimately in better decisions, better because more sophisticated and self-aware.

***

Plato was right to insist that accepting democracy means accepting 'theatrocracy'. In the seventeenth and eighteenth centuries theatre had a more prominent place than now in shaping public opinion within what we call the 'public sphere',[52] and modern theatre is a poor guide to what he meant by theatrocracy. I have traced in these chapters the story of many individuals who wrestled with Plato's dilemma, trying to envisage a democracy free of theatricality, stripped bare of all rhetoric so truth may appear in some naked and authentic form. The Athenians had a profound understanding of the problem. Today rhetoric with all its corporeal tricks of the trade continues to dominate the political environment that we inhabit, though it has of course taken on new forms in new media.

The argument of this book leads me back in the end to education. Plato, Mirabeau, Condorcet, Lequinio and Tagore all saw education as the way to build a better society, while the authoritarian Hobbes traced back to the universities the dangerous impulse to rebel.[53] A democratic education has to include a theatrical education, and more specifically a rhetorical education, teaching the young how to perform and how to evaluate spoken performances. While lip-service is always paid to the idea that minds are connected to bodies, in practice the target of education has become the disembodied mind, today's repackaging of what used to be called the soul. As this book goes to press, I am comforted to hear the leader of a resurgent Labour Party argue for the importance of teaching 'oracy' in British schools, alongside 'all the attributes ... that make us human, that distinguish us from learning machines.'[54]

But what does it mean to be human? Modern liberalism is increasingly ill at ease with the idea that human beings play roles in life because this calls into question the stability of the mind/soul/self, the imagined site of agency and free will. For this reason liberalism shares with puritanism a discomfort with the underlying idea of democracy, since democracy is posited on the idea that people can be coaxed into shifting from one role or identity into another. And that's what changing your mind means. There is ample reason for discomfort. Democracy has been responsible for many terrible things, repeatedly allowing wrong decisions to be made, and we live in dangerous times. Samuel Beckett knew about making theatre, and his mantra seems to me the only possible approach to the democratic project: 'Ever tried. Ever failed. No matter. Try again. Fail again. Fail better.'[55]

Notes

Introduction

1 Plato *Laws* 3.700.
2 Roy (2009) 2.
3 Plutarch *Solon* 29; Diogenes Laertius 1.59. Rosenfeld (2019) investigates political truth.
4 In the carnival of Dunkirk, the mayor throws kippers (now plastic wrapped) to the crowd. On the fish, see for example, Brueghel's *Battle between Carnival and Lent*. On Johnson's skills, see Senior, Stewart, Bucy and Lee (2021).
5 Applebaum (2019).
6 Lind (2020) has a helpful perspective on 'the new class war'.
7 Aristotle *Poetics* 6.2.
8 Hume [1739] (1888) 469–70.
9 Haidt (2012) 57.
10 Haidt (2012) 58–9. Mercier and Sperber (2017) extend and qualify Haidt's argument.
11 Sharot (2017) 24.
12 Lakoff (2008) 43–4.
13 Bennett Institute for Public Policy: 'Global Satisfaction with Democracy'. Cambridge. January 2020. For trust in UK politicians as measured in 2012, https://yougov.co.uk/topics/politics/articles-reports/2012/11/13/problem-trust and the related discussion in Wallis and Skrzypek-Claasens (2014). On the sense of crisis, see Grayling (2017).
14 Onward (2022) 19. Onward is a think tank aligned with the centrist wing of the British Conservative party.
15 https://api.parliament.uk/historic-hansard/commons/1947/nov/11/parliament-bill.
16 On the equivocation, see Dunn (2010) 109. On populism and the idea of the 'people', see Müller (2017) 22–3.
17 Flinders (2020) 22–3.
18 Adichie (2022).
19 Stock (2021). Richard Adams, education correspondent, described events in *The Guardian* 28 October 2021, 3 November 2021.

20 Adichie (2022). For a representative critique, referencing the topical 'trans' issue, see Owolade (2022).
21 On language as violence, see O'Connor (1995). Rosenfeld (2019) 155–64 offers a good account of the dilemma.
22 Rosenfeld (2019) 176.
23 Sennett (1977).
24 Ridout (2008). Ridout also draws on Hallward (2006).
25 D'Ancona (2021) catches the dilemmas of the age in which I am writing. Fukuyama (2018) offers a more historically grounded analysis.
26 Arendt (2003) 43.
27 Fukuyama (1989).
28 'What is Freedom?': Arendt (2003) 447.
29 *On Revolution* [1963]: Arendt (2003) 274.
30 Arendt (2003) 566–7.
31 *Between Past and Future* [1967]: Arendt (2003) 549–50, 558–60.
32 Aristotle *Poetics* 2.1, 6.5.
33 Mouffe (2000) 2. O'Donnell (1998) positions republicanism as a third stream alongside democracy and liberalism. For Mouffe's impact on theatre studies, see Nicholson (2014) 25–9, 32–3; Fisher and Katsouraki (2017); Harrop (2018).
34 Mouffe (2000).
35 On the second usage, see e.g. Lloyd (1992) 1–3.
36 See Euben (1993), Ober (2017).
37 Plato *Republic* 8.568c. For the sake of simplicity I have assumed that Plato's own views are voiced by the figure of Socrates.
38 See for example Pickard-Cambridge (1968) 58; Buckley (1996) 89–91.
39 Bosher (2012); Stewart (2017) 120–38.
40 Aristotle *Rhetoric* 2.1.8.1378a. On rationality and political choice, see for example Lakoff (2008), Sharot (2017).
41 Aristotle *Rhetoric* 3.1.4.1403b.
42 Aristotle *Politics* 4.1292a.
43 Churchill [1897] 2016. He draws on Cicero *De Oratore* 2.189–94.
44 Plutarch *Moralia* 15D, 348C.
45 See for example Garsten (2011).
46 Plato's school was called 'The Academy'.
47 On deliberative democracy, see for example Chambers (2003); Urbinati (2014) 230; on Habermas, Olson (2014); on deliberation in Greek tragedy, Sokolon (2019); on Ireland, https://www.citizensassembly.ie.
48 Parkinson (2014) 24.
49 Mouffe (1999).
50 Finlayson (2014a) 28. My summary draws principally on Finlayson's inaugural lecture (2014b) and also his methodological paper: Finlayson (2007). See also Condor, Tileaga and Billig (2013). For rhetoric and political theory, see Finlayson and Martin (2014).
51 The term is borrowed from Colin Crouch: Crouch (2004).

52 See for example Abell (2014); Anand, Pattanaik and Puppe (2009).
53 See for example Converse [1964] (2006); Achen and Bartels (2017).
54 Haidt (2012) 221.
55 Churchill (2016).
56 Reported of Boris Johnson by Simon Jenkins in *The Guardian* 27 July 2019.
57 Collins (2017) 3–4, 99.
58 Anthony (2022).
59 Glover (2011) and Leith (2011) have the same exclusive emphasis on the written word. See likewise Collins' website: https://www.thedraftwriters.com. On the attention to performance in Media Studies, see Craig (2016). Finlayson (2021) identifies the need to go further. Finlayson is associated with the University of Birmingham 'Network for Oratory and Politics'. Their 2023 project 'Speech! Speech! Dramatising rhetorical citizenship' involves a collaboration with actors: www.birmingham.ac.uk/research/networkfororatoryandpolitics/speech-speech.
60 Wiles (2020).
61 The core point of reference is Stanislavski (2008). Useful perspectives include Hornby (1995); Krasner (2000); Carnicke (2009).
62 Powell (2004) xlv.
63 Wiles (2011) 111–47.
64 On theatrical representation, see Derrida (1978); Shepherd and Wallis (2004) 225–35.
65 'Performance Studies' arose as an alternative to 'Theatre Studies' partly because of this crisis of representation. On Performance Studies, see Jackson (2004) 8–15; Davis (2008); Schechner (2019). Carlson (2017) places more emphasis on theatrical aesthetics. The 'dramaturgical' conception of society developed in Goffman (1956) and Berger (1963) has fallen out of favour as definitions of 'drama' have loosened. A broad notion of performativity lies behind the interdisciplinary work of Rai and Reinelt (2014); Rai, Gluhovic, Jestrovic, and Saward (2021).
66 Ankersmit (2002) 108–12.
67 Ankersmit (2002) borrows his citation from Manin (1997) 110. I have cited the text from the 2009 *Documentary History of the Ratification of the Constitution*: https://archive.csac.history.wisc.edu/Brutus_III(1).pdf.
68 See Saward (2010). For a historical sketch, Waskiewicz (2020).
69 Cotlar (2013) 13.
70 *On Revolution* [1963]: Arendt (2003) 274.
71 Shklar (1984) 51, 78.
72 Runciman (2018 [2008]) 7–9, 38–9. On political masks, see also Markowits (2008), who draws on Judith Butler alongside Arendt and Plato.
73 Runciman (2018) 212.
74 Runciman (2018) 228, 232.
75 See Grant (1997) 65ff. On hypocrisy and acting, see Wikander (2002). On Rousseau and theatre, Wiles (2011) 110–47. On democracy, truth and post-truth, Rosenfeld (2019).

Chapter 1

1. Osborne (1995).
2. 'The Old Oligarch' 11–12. This text was written sometime between 446 and 424 BCE.
3. See Gould (1980); Blundell (1998); Roselli (2011) 158–94.
4. Andreski (1983) 145–6.
5. Thucydides 3.82–3.
6. Thucydides 2.35–46; Loraux (1981) 179–83.
7. Thucydides 2.40.
8. Thucydides 1.22.
9. Thucydides 2.37, 2.40. On the historiography of this speech, see Grethlein (2011) 155–60.
10. Thucydides 2.43.4. The term translated as courage means more literally 'fineness of spirit'. Berlin (1969) 118–72 is the classic account of 'negative liberty'. Ober (2000) argues that a liberal strand of negative liberty was entailed by the realities of Athenian democratic inclusiveness.
11. Thucydides 2.40.5.
12. Thucydides 2.38, 41.
13. A recurrent theme in Pelling (2000).
14. Plutarch *Pericles* 9.1.
15. Aristotle *Rhetoric* 1.7.34.
16. Plutarch *Pericles* 8, and 4–5.
17. Thucydides 2.65.
18. Cartledge (2016) 61–75.
19. Pickard-Cambridge (1968) 130–1; Scullion (2002); Aristotle *Poetics* 4.
20. Csapo (2004) 240–44; Csapo and Wilson (2020b) 435–6.
21. Csapo and Wilson (2020a) 17.
22. Jurors, Ober (1989) 142; Assembly, Cartledge (2016) 112–13.
23. Roselli (2011) 64–6; Cartledge (2016) 224.
24. Roselli (2011) 67–9; Wiles (2017) 71–2.
25. Roselli (2011) 78–81.
26. Ober (1989) 155.
27. Ober (1989) 311.
28. Ober (1989) 153.
29. Aristotle *Rhetoric* 3.12.2.
30. Aristotle *Rhetoric* 1.2.
31. Bers (2009) 107.
32. Bers (2009) 145; Aristotle *Rhetoric* 3.7.10 (my translation).
33. Bers (2009) 46.
34. Bers (2013), challenging Hall (2006) 353–92.
35. Finley (1962) addressed the historiographic problem. See also Hall (2018).
36. Thucydides 3.37–8.
37. Thucydides 3.42–3.
38. Aristotle *Rhetoric* 2.1.8.

39 Aristotle *Rhetoric* 3.16.8.
40 Aristotle *Rhetoric* 1.2.3–5, 2.1.4.
41 *Nicomachean Ethics* 9.6.2.
42 See Blundell (1989) 26ff; Seaford (1994) xvii.
43 Thucydides 3.50.
44 Haidt (2012) 106.
45 Haidt (2012) 150, 107.
46 Plato *Phaedrus* 246–54; Haidt (2012) 58–9. Haidt builds on his 2006 study *The Happiness Hypothesis*. Mercier and Sperber (2017) extend and qualify Haidt's argument.
47 Aristotle *Nicomachean Ethics* 1.2.8.
48 Aristotle *Poetics* 14.2–3.
49 Aristotle *Rhetoric* 2.2.2.
50 Aristotle *Constitution of Athens* 28. The information about costume and gesture is confirmed in Aeschines 1.25.
51 Plutarch *Nicias* 8.
52 Aristophanes *Knights* 191–3. On the parody of Cleon's rhetoric, see Hall (2019).
53 Aristophanes *Knights* 137, 1023, 956; on shouting in general, 285–7, 311, 487 etc.
54 The 'knights' were defined under Solon's constitution by their property, and the use of their shrine at Colonus associates them with the events of 411: Thucydides 8.67.
55 Aristophanes *Knights* 396, 1119.
56 Aristophanes *Knights* 363, 475, 615, 722.
57 Aristophanes *Knights* 292; *Wasps* 1032, repeated in *Peace* 755.
58 Aristophanes *Knights* 231–2; Cratinus fragments 218, 228. In *Knights* and *Wasps* Aristophanes refers to attacking a monster and to sharp teeth. Cratinus' play may have inspired the name 'Paphlagon', where the word may evoke the sound of the channel guarded by the monster: frag.220.
59 Markle (1985) examines the relationship between the play and social reality.
60 Aristophanes *Wasps* 546–759.
61 Roisman (2004).
62 Aristophanes *Wasps* 725–32.
63 Henderson (1990) 298–9.
64 See Sommerstein (2004).
65 Justice Thurgood Marshall, cited in Lai (2019) 59.
66 Saxonhouse (2005).
67 Csapo and Slater (1995) 180–85; Phillips (2013) 124ff.
68 Henderson (1990), (2007).
69 On pay for jurors see Cartledge (2016) 117–18. Pay to attend the assembly was introduced in the next century. The question of payment for a seat in the theatre remains unresolved.
70 See Hall (2018), (2019).
71 On staging conventions, see for example Hughes (2012).

72 Justice Dikgang Moseneke, cited in Lai (2019) 11.
73 Plato *Apology* 18–19.
74 Plutarch *Pericles* 15.4, citing Plato *Phaedrus* 271c.
75 On Syracusan democracy, see Rutter (2002).
76 Robinson (2007); Bosher (2014).
77 Dodds (1959) 6–10; Consigny (2001).
78 Set at some unspecified date between 427 BCE and the defeat of Athens in 404: Dodds (1959) 17–18.
79 Plato *Gorgias* 452 d–e.
80 Plato *Gorgias* 466 b–c.
81 Plato *Gorgias* 462–5.
82 Plato *Gorgias* 467–73.
83 Dodds (1959) 12–15.
84 Plato *Gorgias* 503, 515–16.
85 Plato *Gorgias* 502.
86 This passage is the starting point for Carter (2011). Plato's *Laws* 817 also references a theatre audience that includes women, and since there is little other evidence for a substantive female presence in the Athenian Theatre of Dionysus, Plato probably has a wider context in mind. On Plato's familiarity with Syracusan theatre, see Csapo and Wilson (2020b) 376–8. There seems little doubt that boys and many foreign visitors attended the Dionysia in Athens.
87 Plato *Gorgias* 523–4.
88 Plato *Republic* 9.577. Cf. Monoson (2012) 159, 169. See also Pownall (2017).
89 Diodorus 13.92–3. On Sicilian theatre, see Csapo and Wilson (2015) 328–33.
90 Our principal source for this relationship is Plato *Letter VII*, commonly but not universally taken to be genuine.
91 Philistius in Plutarch *Life of Pelopidas* 34.1.
92 Diodorus 15.74.

Chapter 2

1 Bayliss (2011) 95–128.
2 The speeches are Aeschines 3 *Against Ctesiphon* and Demosthenes 18 *On the Crown*.
3 For Aeschines' biography, see Harris (1995) and Carey (2000); for Demosthenes, Worthington (2000; 2013). On the voice in Greek rhetoric, Porter (2009).
4 On roles and democracy, see Parkinson (2014) 21–5.
5 Cooper (2000).
6 Dionysius of Halicarnassus *On the Style of Demosthenes* 51–5.
7 Harding (2000); Norrie (2019).
8 Hume (1788) 92–9, 407. On Hume and political rhetoric, see Hanvelt (2012) 43–53.

9 Worthington (2013) 36.
10 Bayliss (2011) 31–4; Blanshard (2018).
11 Saint-Just (1908).
12 'Mitford's Greece' and 'Athenian Orators' in Macaulay (1841) 397–400, 410–11. On the English reception of Demosthenes, see Agnew (2016).
13 Grote (1875) 293.
14 Plutarch *Demosthenes* 28–9.
15 Plutarch *Demosthenes* 7. Cooper (2000), following Plutarch *Demosthenes* 11, attributes the tradition to Demetrius of Phaleron. While Plutarch refers to the actor Satyrus, another biography mentions Andronicus: Pseudo-Plutarch *Lives of the Orators* 845.
16 See Duncan (2006) 18–20 on the evidential value of anecdote.
17 Seraphim (2019) 350–1, n.12.
18 Plutarch *Precepts of Statecraft* 799.
19 Demosthenes 21 *Against Meidias*. This related to performance of a dithyramb, not tragedy. See Worthington (2012) 156–62.
20 This embassy was the focus of Demosthenes 19 *On the False Legation*, and its counterpart Aeschines 2. See Worthington (2012) 201–9.
21 Plutarch *Demosthenes* 11.
22 On this self-positioning, see Duncan (2006) 74–6.
23 For the complex political background, see Buckler (2000).
24 I follow the scenario outlined in Yunis (2001) 10–11. Worthington (2012) 295 floats other possibilities.
25 On the theatricality of the law-court see Hall (1995).
26 On the working of the 'People's Court' see Boegehold (1995); Hansen (1999) 178–224. See more broadly Todd (2005).
27 Yunis (2001) 11.
28 Blanshard (2014). The use of two stages was introduced in the later fourth century: Boegehold (1995) 201.
29 Aeschines 3.207. Documentation in Boegehold (1995) 192–4.
30 Aeschines 3.56.
31 Plato *Republic* 6.492.
32 Demosthenes *Exordia* Exordium 4.
33 Fundamental studies of *thorubos* are Bers (1985) and Wallace (2004).
34 Aristotle *Politics* 3.1281b. See Ober (1989) 164 with n.21.
35 Demosthenes 18.52.
36 Alcidamas *On the Sophists* 27–8, 11. A translation can be found in Gagarin and Woodruff (1995) 276–83.
37 Alcidamas *On the Sophists* 22–3.
38 Fischer-Lichte (2008) 38.
39 Aeschines 3.6. The speech is known as *Against Ctesiphon*.
40 Aristotle's *Constitution of Athens* 5ff. sets out Solon's reforms and places him as a foundational figure.
41 Aeschines 3.3–5.

42 Aeschines 1: *Against Timarchus*; Demosthenes 19: *On the False Legation*. On repetition, see for example Koch and Zerback (2013).
43 Aeschines 3.153–7.
44 Demosthenes 18.293.
45 Aeschines 3.55–7.
46 Demosthenes 18.11. The allusion is to ritual insults performed in the context of a Dionysiac procession.
47 *On the Style of Demosthenes* 53–6, 22. The reference is to Corybantic dances in honour of Cybele.
48 Demosthenes 19.206–8.
49 Demosthenes 18.280. On this passage, see Ober (1989) 167.
50 Aristotle *Constitution of Athens* 28.3. See Hesk (1999) 218–29 on deportment in oratory.
51 Aeschines 1.26.
52 Aeschines 1.189. On masculinity, see Roisman (2005).
53 Demosthenes 19.251–6, 314.
54 Aeschines 1.171, 2.166–70, etc.
55 Aeschines 3.255.
56 On identification, see Serafim (2017) ch. 2; Wohl (2009) 168.
57 Aeschines 3.251.
58 Demosthenes 18.272.
59 Aeschines 3.247.
60 McGann (2002) 8. On sincerity in the Athenian law-court, see Duncan (2006) 58–89; Seraphim (2019).
61 Hall (2000) 15. According to *quoteinvestigator.com*, the earliest identifiable source is the actress Celeste Holm in 1962.
62 Wiles (1991).
63 Aeschines 1.135ff.
64 The papyrus fragments of *Misoumenos* are translated in Arnott (1979) Vol.2, 247–370.
65 Demosthenes 18.259.
66 Punning on pederasty alongside Demosthenes' inability to sound his 'r' to pronounce *battaros* ('stutterer'): Yunis (2001) 211.
67 Demosthenes 18. 11, 122, 138, 180. On invective see Worman (2004).
68 Demosthenes 18.180, 242. Cf. Demosthenes 19.246–7.
69 Demosthenes 18.149.
70 Demosthenes 18. 283, 287.
71 Demosthenes 18. 291–2.
72 Demosthenes 18. 309, 298.
73 Aeschines 3.260; Demosthenes 18.127.
74 Aeschines 3.207, 209–10; also Aeschines 2. 156–7.
75 Aeschines 3.99.
76 Derrida (1978).
77 Aeschines 3.206.
78 Willett (1964) 8. Brecht's analogy is explored at length in Ruffini (2014).

Notes to pages 57–67

79 Stanislavski (1967) 123, 182. See Cicero *De Oratore* 3.221, with commentary in Wiles (2020) 52.
80 Willett (1964) 270. Brecht cites Horace *Ars Poetica* 102–3 by way of the eighteenth-century philosopher and dramatist J. C. Gottsched.
81 Aeschines 2.153.
82 Plutarch *Demosthenes* 11, 9.
83 *Rhetoric* 3.1.4.
84 Plutarch *Demosthenes* 24.
85 Plutarch *Phocion* 5. Plutarch *Demosthenes* 14 develops the comparison.
86 Aeschines 2.170, 184; Harris (1995) 37–9.
87 Reid (1953) 269–70. 'Fancy' was an aesthetic term explicated by Coleridge.
88 Gladstone (1968b) 127, 129, 148–50, 166; Gladstone (1968a) 79–81.
89 Reid (1953) 271.
90 Demosthenes 18.274.
91 Reid (1953) 267, 271.
92 Plutarch *Phocion* 7; Bayliss (2011) 68.
93 Aeschines 3.178–91.
94 Demosthenes 18.204.
95 Brook (1968) 9. For impersonation, see e.g. Bentley (1964) 150. On presence, Sauter (2021).
96 Wiles (2003) 241ff.
97 Easterling (1997) 215–23; Hall (2002) 12–19.
98 Mouffe (2013) 15.
99 Aeschines 1.49.
100 Gesture and the materiality of speech is a major theme of Wiles (2020).
101 See Wiles (2007) esp. 180ff.

Chapter 3

1 Weber (1948).
2 Schumpeter (1976) 265–7.
3 Schumpeter (1976) 269.
4 'Politics as a vocation' in Weber (2008) 155–208. On Weber's life see Radkau (2009).
5 Weber 183.
6 On charisma and presence see Goodall (2008) 17–18. Benedetti's 2008 translation of Stanislavski introduced 'charisma' as a theatrical concept (549–51); on charisma, see also Potts (2009).
7 'Of the life and times of Thucydides': Hobbes (1629) n.p.
8 *De Corpore Politico* XXI.6–7 [1640]: Hobbes (1994) 120.
9 *Behemoth* I: Hobbes (2010) 164; *Leviathan* XXIX: Hobbes (1962) 290.
10 Hobbes (2010) 135.
11 Hobbes (2010) 138.
12 Hobbes (2010) 139.

13 Hobbes (1629) n.p.
14 *De Corpore Politico* XXVII.14–15: Hobbes (1994) 171.
15 *Leviathan* XXV: Hobbes (1962) 242.
16 *Leviathan* VIII: Hobbes (1962) 107.
17 For the broad implications, see Sennett (1977).
18 *Leviathan* XVI: Hobbes (1962) 168.
19 Runciman (2018) 40.
20 *Leviathan* XVI, XIX: Hobbes (1962) 171, 188.
21 Gardiner (1877) 36.
22 Kirby (1931) 7–19.
23 Barish (1981) 94, 87. Freeman (2017) addresses this bias.
24 Prynne (1633) 'Epistle Dedicatory', 306, 794–5; Freeman (2017) 41.
25 Prynne (1633) 'Epistle to the Christian Reader'.
26 Prynne (1633) 5–6.
27 Prynne (1633) 156–7.
28 Prynne (1633) 302ff.
29 Prynne (1633) 374–5.
30 Prynne (1633) 352–3, 389–91.
31 Prynne (1633) 852. Prynne later accepted the allusion: Prynne (1649) 5–6.
32 Kirby (1931) 26–9, Kishlansky (2013).
33 *A briefe relation* (1637) 16–30; Cressy (1999); Kishlansky (2014) 345–51.
34 See as a representative example Rebecca Loukes' remarks in Zarrilli, Daboo and Loukes (2013) 238–40.
35 Baukol (2007) 173–9.
36 On the trial, see Forward (2012) 140–62.
37 Lamont (2004).
38 Prynne (1649) 5.
39 Prynne (1649) 3.
40 Bancroft (1663) 6–7. The sermon was recorded by Froissart, and the rhyme 'When Adam delved' by Holinshed: Knowles (1999) 307.
41 Prynne (1644) 6.
42 On the dual use of the legend of the Fall, see Hill (1968) 59.
43 Locke (1690) was probably written a decade earlier. He treats gender equality in section 83. Filmer's *Patriarcha* (1680) was written during the reign of Charles I. On Locke, see Simmons (2013).
44 For the custom, see Clopper, Mills and Baldwin (2007) 1.329–30.
45 Weber (1958) esp. 206.
46 Mills (1992) 7–8. The text of the play is on 26–48.
47 In Norwich, coats, hose and wigs for Adam and Eve and the Serpent (along with a tail for the Serpent) were inventoried by the Guild of Grocers, also three painted cloths for the hangings. Tydeman (2001) 219.
48 Cressy (1999) 227–9. On the broad transformation, see Mills (1991).
49 Shakespeare *Henry VI Part Two* 4.2.113–25.
50 Shakespeare *Henry VI Part Two* 4.8.11–64.
51 Shakespeare *Henry VI Part Two* 4.10; Wright and Buck (2007).

52 On the enclosure controversy, see for example Quarmby (2015).
53 *The Free-man's Freedom Vindicated*: Woodhouse (1986) 317.
54 Woodhouse (1986) 6–7.
55 *The Creation and Fall of Man* (1649) 128, 30: cited in Stephens (1658) 98, 20. Copies of the original do not appear to be extant.
56 Everard (1652) 4–5, 14.
57 Harrison (1684).
58 Wolfe (1933).
59 Jenkins (1998).
60 Milton *Paradise Lost* ix. 665–78.
61 Smilansky (2012), Miles (2013) 216. For the modern debate initiated by Peter Strawson, see McKenna and Russell (2008).
62 Aristotle addresses the problem in the first five chapters of his *Nicomachean Ethics* Book III.
63 The value of the dramaturgical model for breaking the freedom/determinism binary is set out in Berger (1963) ch. 6.
64 Kishlansky (1979); Harrison (1987); Gentles (2012). On the officers, Gentles (1997).
65 On this faith in providence, see Worden (2012) 13–16, 33–62. The introduction to Woodhouse (1986) established a context. Woodhouse's standard modern-spelling edition of the Clarke manuscript was first published in 1938.
66 Fairfax (1647).
67 Woodhouse (1986) 38.
68 Dramatic possibilities were realised in extracts incorporated in Caryl Churchill's play of 1976 *Light Shining in Buckinghamshire*, revived in England's National Theatre in 2015. Text in Churchill (1985) 208–18.
69 Cowling (1647). For the other figures, see the relevant entries in the *Dictionary of National Biography*, with Rainborough under 'Rainborow'. On Ireton see also Taft (2001); Farr (2006).
70 On its fragmentation see e.g. Bayer (2011) 6–12.
71 Woodhouse (1986) 429–36; Morrill and Baker (2001). On Englishness, see Foxley (2004). Kumar (2003) seems blind to the emotional power of 'Englishness' in popular culture in this period.
72 Woodhouse (1986) 356, 443–5; Gentles (2001); Baker and Vernon (2012).
73 Woodhouse (1986) 26–8. Isaiah Berlin's classic account of this dichotomy is contextualised in Miller (2006).
74 Woodhouse (1986) 8–9. My italic.
75 Woodhouse (1986) 84.
76 George Digby, cited in Fraser (1973) 64.
77 Philip Warwick, cited in Fraser (1973) 62. Other sources on Cromwell's appearance in Marshall (2004) 15–17.
78 John Reresby, cited in Knoppers (1998) 1295.
79 Woodhouse (1986) 19.
80 Woodhouse (1986) 29, 25, 27.
81 Woodhouse (1986) 35–6.

82 Wildman (1647a); abbreviated text in Woodhouse (1986) 439–43.
83 Aristotle *Poetics* 11.1.
84 Woolrych (1987) 243–5 analyses the evidence. Woolrych's commentary on the three days of debate is invaluable; also Mendle (2001).
85 Woodhouse (1986) 53.
86 Woodhouse (1986) 69–70, 73–4.
87 Woodhouse (1986) 102–8.
88 Woolrych (1987) 260.
89 Woodhouse (1986) 122–4.
90 Woolrych (1987) 264–7. *Deus ex machina* – in Greek tragedy the arrival of a god on a crane to resolve the plot.
91 First set out in Rawls (1958).
92 For Cromwell's self-justification, Woolrych (1987) 3. See also Farr (2006) 91–2.
93 Woolrych (1987) 227.
94 *Dictionary of National Biography* 'Sexby, Edward' – entry by Alan Marshall (2010).
95 'Wildman, Sir John' – entry by Richard L. Greaves (2004).
96 Wiles (2020) 176–7. On personation, Weimann (2008) 143–6. The Stanislavskian term 'through-line' is relabelled 'throughaction' in Stanislavski (2008) 312–9.
97 Shklar (1984) 51.
98 Wildman (1647b) 6–7.
99 'Wildman, Sir John' – entry by Richard L. Greaves (2004).

Chapter 4

1 De Tocqueville (1998) 208–9.
2 Goodden (1984); Brasart (1988); France (1990).
3 On Rousseau, see Starobinski (1971); Wiles (2011) 110–46.
4 On Cicero's *De Oratore*, see Wiles (2020) 54–9. On the influence of the ancient world, Parker (1937). Studies of revolutionary rhetoric that have helped me include: Aulard (1882); Gay (1961); Bonnet (1988); France (1992); Principato (1999); Négrel and Sermain, eds. (2002); Linton (2013).
5 Campbell (2006). Linton's essay in this collection is particularly helpful.
6 De Tocqueville (1998) 197, etc.
7 Martin and Marks (2019).
8 For a discussion of this speech, see Wiles (2011) 151–3.
9 Chartier (1991) 33–6; Friedland (2002) 81–90. On the suppression of standing, see Valpy in Howarth (1997) 491–2.
10 On the 'public sphere', see Balme (2014).
11 Brown (2005) 385–6. The standard biography remains Alméras (1905), supplemented by Jacob (1946).
12 Jacob (1946) 16–17.

13 Buchez (1837) 83.
14 Rousseau (2003) 83–95, with footnote on 92. On the debate about Alceste, see Maslan (2005) 90–5. On the letter, Primavesi (1997).
15 Reviews in Proud (1995) 161, 162, 165, 169, 172. Molé played the original role 'admirably' in 1789: Young (1929) 161.
16 Alméras (1905) 142.
17 Beffroy de Reigny (1791) 151.
18 Leon (2009) 74. Maslan (2005) 79 overstates the case for Fabre's radicalism.
19 *'Le Sot orgeuilleux, ou, l'Ecole des élections*': Alméras (1905) 151.
20 Roland (1821) ii.17
21 Proud (1995) 125–6. For Fabre as Alceste in 1779: Alméras (1905) 43.
22 Proud (1995) 124.
23 *Les Précepteurs*: Fabre d'Eglantine (1799) 47–8.
24 Robespierre (1840) 438
25 Jacob (1946) 229.
26 Fabre d'Eglantine (1793).
27 Biography: Dard (1907); Bernier (1995).
28 On *actio*: Principato (2002); Wiles (2020) 42–4. On revolutionary oratory: Bonnet (1988); Sermain (2002).
29 *Réflexions sur la déclamation* in Hérault (1801) 73–103, at 73–4.
30 Hérault (1801) 94–5.
31 Hérault (1801) 82. On the methods of Clairon, see Wiles (2020) 159–69.
32 Brasart (1988) 23–4; the purpose built hall which replaced it in 1793 was little better: Brasart (1988) 129.
33 See Wiles (2011) 185; Wiles (2020) 159–69. On theatre and the cult of feeling: Feilla (2013).
34 Hérault (1801) 92: attributed to 'a friend of d'Alembert'.
35 La Salle (1789) ii. 114–16; cf. Hérault (1801) 89. On the relationship with Hérault: Thuillier (1956), Bernier (1995) 28–9, 32–3.
36 La Salle (1788).
37 La Salle (1789) ii.119.
38 Bernier (1995) 187–8, 191.
39 Maury (1804) – first edition: 1777. On Maury, see Aulard (1882) 213–63.
40 Maury (1804) 75.
41 Hérault (1801) 115–19; Dard (1907) 159–60; Bernier (1995) 66.
42 Hérault (1801) 19.
43 Hérault (1793), Bernier (1995) 87–90, Bourgoing (2016). For an overview of revolutionary festivals: Ozouf (1988).
44 Hérault (1793) *Receuil* 1.
45 Matonti (1998). On the heroic body: Outram (1989) 86–8.
46 Biographies: Badinter and Badinter (1988); Williams (2004).
47 Badinter and Badinter (1988) 19–20.
48 Dubois (2004) 178–82.
49 Condorcet (1795) 338. English translation in Condorcet (2012).
50 On de Grouchy, see Bergès' introduction to: de Grouchy Condorcet (2019).

51 Williams (2004) 272. On the scheme, see Urbinati (2004).
52 *Sur l'instruction publique* [1791]: Condorcet (1847–1849) 7.473–4.
53 *Réponse à l'adresse aux provinces* [1790]: Condorcet (1847–1849) 9. 504.
54 Condorcet (1847–1849) 7.364–7.
55 Condorcet (1847–1849) 7.211–2.
56 La Harpe (1825) 397. On La Harpe, see Todd (1972); Sermain (2002).
57 Pinker (2018) 381.
58 Biography: Valin (2014).
59 Lequinio (1793) 13.
60 Lequinio (1793) 39–40.
61 Lequinio (1793) 41–7.
62 Lequinio (1793) 295–301.
63 Brasart (1988) 110–11.
64 Lequinio (1793) 309–12; Lequinio (1790) 5–6.
65 Lequinio (1793) 301–3. On the audience in the 'tribunes', see Brasart (1988) 69–78.
66 Lequinio (1793) 306–7, 304.
67 See also Ballard (2010) 88–92, 98–108.
68 Valin (2014) 248.
69 Biographies: Tallentyre (1908) ; Luttrell (1990) ; Zorgbibe (2008).
70 Comte de la Marck, cited in de Bacourt (1851) i.86–7.
71 Gastineau and Janin (1860) 258–9.
72 Zorgbibe (2008) 68–70.
73 Mirabeau (1888) 528. See related texts in Baczco (2000).
74 Vergniaud 'Éloge funèbre de Mirabeau' (1791) cited in Chauvot (1856) 523.
75 France (2002).
76 Société d'histoire et d'archéologie de Genève (1962) 361–75; Bonnet (1988) 210–11.
77 Lilti (2017) 180–1. On this theme, see also Friedland (2002) 182–4.
78 Dumont (1832) 192–3.
79 Lafitte (1844) ii.53; first published in 1836. The speech is analysed in Carter (1966) 606–14.
80 Dumont (1832) 211.
81 On the shift: Thompson (1935) 1.116. For an engraving of a debate in the library, see Schama (1989) 528 = fig.135. On Robespierre and the club: Jordan (1985) 68–74. On Jacobin ideology: Linton (2013) 79.
82 On the tensions in the club at this time, see Kennedy (1988) 133–9. Key biographies of Robespierre: Hampson (1974), Jordan (1985), McPhee (2012). On historic perceptions of Robespierre: Jacob (1938); and modern perceptions: Haydon and Doyle (1999) 3–34.
83 Desmoulins (1790) 111–17. Commentaries on the confrontation include Kuhlmann (1911), Zorgbibe (2008) 404–6, Linton (2013) 91. The *Declaration of the Rights of Man and of the Citizen* applied to 'active' citizens, and excluded servants, men under 25, and non-taxpayers.
84 Luttrell (1990) 237. The tradition goes back to Victor Hugo: Hugo (1834).

85 Friedland (2002) 283–4, 290.
86 Robespierre (1790) ; Desmoulins (1790) 108–9.
87 Robespierre (1790) 26–7.
88 Delacroix (1792) 13–14. The French term *comédien* can refer both to an actor and a playwright, Molière famously being both.
89 On the cult of sensibility, see e.g. Schama (1989) 147–61; Feilla (2013).
90 Maslan (2005) esp. 25–30 with n.6 on 222, 139–40; Friedland (2002) 3, 30, 296 and throughout. On rhetoric and representation: Hunt (2004) 19–51.
91 Schama (1989) 579; Jordan (1985) 67, 76; Le Bas in Stéfane-Pol (1901) 107.
92 Alméras (1905) 325.
93 Cole and Chinoy (1970) 14–15.
94 On Brutus, see Andrew (2017); on role models: Schama (1989) 169–72.
95 Speech to the National Convention on 5 February 1794: Robespierre (1841) 405–6.

Chapter 5

1 Schleifer (1980) 78–80, 326–8.
2 Weber (2011). The book first appeared in 1904/5. On individualism, see Schleifer (1980) 306–9; on religion, Lambert (2008).
3 De Tocqueville (2003) 569. I have used the 1848 edition of *De la démocratie en Amérique*, vol. 4. to adapt the Penguin translation and make it more literal. On early American anti-theatricalism, see Bank (2015).
4 See, for example, Arthur Miller's canonical essay of 1949 'Tragedy and the Common Man': Clark and Popkin (1956) 537–9.
5 De Tocqueville (2003) 568; on *Gladiator*, see Reed (2009) 151–74. De Tocqueville's only recorded visits to the theatre were to performances in Philadelphia and New Orleans: Litto (1979) 115.
6 Letter of 4 March 1786 in *Adams Family Correspondence* Vol. 7. *Founders Online*, National Archives, https://founders.archives.gov/documents/Adams/04-07-02-0021.
7 Letters of 20 January 1785 and 20 February 1785 in *Adams Family Correspondence* Vol. 6. *Founders Online*, National Archives, https://founders.archives.gov/documents/Adams/04-06-02-0021, and Adams/04-06-02-0022.
8 Letter of 9 October 1774 in *Adams Family Correspondence* Vol. 1. Spelling and capitalization modernised, here and later. *Founders Online*, National Archives, https://founders.archives.gov/documents/Adams/04-01-02-0111.
9 Letter to François Adriaan Van der Kemp, 9 August 1813. *Founders Online*, National Archives, https://founders.archives.gov/documents/Adams/99-02-02-6125.
10 'A Summary View of the Rights of British America': Jefferson (1963) 70.
11 Shklar 1984 – see my discussion in Chapter 1.
12 See Diggins (2003); Isenberg and Burstein (2019).
13 Jefferson discussed the French Revolution in a letter to William Short, 3 January 1793: *Founders Online*, National Archives, https://founders

Notes to pages 120–124

    .archives.gov/documents/Jefferson/01-25-02-0016. On slavery, see Rothman (2010).
14 Jefferson (1963) 70.
15 Letter to Charles Cushing of 3 April 1756: *Papers of John Adams* Vol. 1. He misquotes Addison's translation of Horace *Odes* 3.3. *Founders Online*, National Archives, https://founders.archives.gov/documents/Adams/06-01-02-0006.
16 Letter of 30 September 1805: *Founders Online*, National Archives, https://founders.archives.gov/documents/Adams/99-02-02-5103.
17 Letter of 21 June 1811: *Founders Online*, National Archives, https://founders.archives.gov/documents/Adams/99-02-02-5649. The adage about Louis XIV is attributed to Viscount Bolingbroke.
18 *Discourses on Davila* [1790] in Adams (1851) 243–5.
19 On Jefferson, see Golden and Golden (2002) 97–9.
20 See e.g. Ferling (1992) 304, 319; Freeman (2001) 42–7; Bernstein (2020) 161–3.
21 Letter to John Taylor, 17 December 1814. *Founders Online*, National Archives, https://founders.archives.gov/documents/Adams/99-02-02-6371.
22 On Adams' republicanism, see Wood (1998) 48ff.
23 Letter to Benjamin Rush, 4 December 1805. *Founders Online*, National Archives, https://founders.archives.gov/documents/Adams/99-02-02-5110.
24 Adams (1810) i.30–1.
25 Adams (1810) i.68–9.
26 Constant (1988) 308–26.
27 See Fliegelman (1993) 28–35, 93–4.
28 Barthes (1977) 182.
29 For a philosophical perspective, see Cavarero (2005). On presidential speech, Hart (1987) 1–21.
30 Diary, 21 December 1758. *Adams Papers. Founders Online*, National Archives, https://founders.archives.gov/documents/Adams/02-01-02-0010-0001-0003.
31 I am grateful for the opportunity to observe an advocacy training course in Keble College Oxford, September 2015.
32 Draft of a letter to an unidentified correspondent. 1758. *Founders Online*, National Archives, https://founders.archives.gov/documents/Adams/02-01-02-0010-0001-0003.
33 See Wiles (2020) 54–9.
34 Diary for 22 January 1807: Adams (1874) 444–5.
35 Letter to François Adriaan Van der Kemp. 9 August 1813. *Founders Online*, National Archives, https://founders.archives.gov/documents/Adams/99-02-02-6125. The critics of Machiavelli include Voltaire and Frederick the Great.
36 Letter to Benjamin Rush. 28 August 1811. *Founders Online*, National Archives, https://founders.archives.gov/documents/Adams/99-02-02-5678.
37 Eastman (2009), esp. 18. Other useful studies of American rhetoric include Cmiel (1990); Warren (1999); Gustafson (2000); Golden and Golden (2002).

38 Parker (1857) 11–12.
39 Blair (1784) 240. On Blair, see Cmiel (1990) 40; Fliegelman (1993) 35; Ulman (1994) 117–46; Golden and Golden (2002) 12; Walzer (2007).
40 Blair (1784) 236.
41 Letter to the President of Congress, 5 September 1780. *Founders Online*, National Archives, https://founders.archives.gov/documents/Adams/06-10-02-0067.
42 My analysis follows Ulman (1994). See also Cmiel (1990); Fliegelman (1993) 28–35.
43 On Sheridan, see Goring (2005) 91–113; on Burgh, Wiles (2020) 203–5.
44 De Tocqueville (2003) 552–9.
45 Letter to James Sullivan, 26 May 1776. *Founders Online*, National Archives, https://founders.archives.gov/documents/Adams/06-04-02-0091; Glenn and Kreider (2020) 1ff; Israel (2017) 174–90.
46 Documentation Hershkowitz (2006); Cliff (2007); O'Malley (2018). McConachie (1992) supplies the context.
47 De Tocqueville (2003) 568. Translation modified.
48 Bloom (2019) 84.
49 Wilentz (1984) 332. On Walsh, see Adams (2005) 25–46.
50 'Speech at Castle Garden' [1842]: Walsh 19.
51 Buckley (1984) 25. Punctuation modernised.
52 On the rioters see Shannon (1963) esp. 40–55; Butsch (2000) 44–65; Adams (2005); Williamson (2013); Bloom (2019) 87–97. On the political context: Ryan (1997) esp. 94–182. On working-class identity: Hirsch (1978).
53 Gerstner (2006) 1–19; Rebhorn (2006–7); Reed (2009) 151–74; Kippola (2012) 89–116.
54 Alger (1877) i.98–9. Alger slightly misquotes the title of Walker's 1791 dictionary designed for speakers of non-standard English.
55 See Mielke (2019) 25–54.
56 On Forrest playing himself, see Alger (1877) i.177–8; McConachie (1992) 77–84.
57 Alger (1877) i.194.
58 Wilson (1950) 490; McConachie (1989) 12.
59 Downer (1966) 257; Bloom (2019) 87.
60 Macready (1875) ii.695. On Macready's art, see Downer (1966) 69–80.
61 Bloom (2019) 66.
62 Diary for 12 December 1848: Macready (1875) ii.607.
63 De Tocqueville (2003) 544.
64 Levine (1988) 68; Teague (2006) 60–1; Kendrick (2021). See also Ryan (1997) 37–8.
65 On the Whig tradition: Howe (1979) 12–68.
66 'Elle le ramène sans cesse vers lui seul, et menace de le renfermer enfin tout entier dans la solitude de son propre cœur.' De Tocqueville (2003) 589 – translation modified. See Schleifer (1980) 306–7.
67 Roach (1998) provides a useful overview.

68 O'Malley (2018) 77.
69 McConachie (1992) 146.
70 Garner (2007) 120–29.
71 *Narrative of the Life of Frederick Douglass, an American Slave* [1845]: Douglass (2016) 41.
72 Douglass (1855) 155, 212.
73 On Bingham, see Ganter (1997); Blight (2018).
74 Blight (1998) 5ff. On action, see Wiles (2020) esp. 42–4.
75 Downer (1966) 38, 76–7.
76 Rankin (1897) 37.
77 Blight (2018) 93. On African-American preaching, see Niles (1984); on its relation to music, Williams-Jones (1975).
78 Douglass (1855) 130.
79 Douglass (1855) 77. I follow Douglass' gendered phrasing.
80 Douglass' prowess as a fighter was established by his victory over the slave-breaker Covey, a tale recounted in Douglass (2016) 62–3; Douglass (1855) 186–90.
81 David N. Johnson [1880] – in Ernest (2014) 7–8.
82 Douglass (1855) 280.
83 Douglass (1855) 282.
84 Douglass (1855) 152–3.
85 Smith (2009) 134.
86 Smith (2009) 144.
87 De Tocqueville (2003) 684–700.
88 De Tocqueville (2003) 699. Translation adapted and more literal.
89 De Tocqueville (2003) 696–7.
90 Wright (2014) 211. On Wright's life, see Baker's introduction to this volume, and Morris (1984). On her lectures, Eastman (2009) 179–210. On the US context: Zagarri (2005).
91 Morris (1984) 27–30; Wright (1819) iv.
92 Eastman (2009) 186–92. Eastman fig.16 reproduces advertisements from the *New-York American*. The performances were juxtaposed on 26/27 January.
93 Beard (2014).
94 On the female Southern voice, see Levander (1998) 77–85.
95 Cited in Lerner (2009) 8, 272.
96 Letter of 1837: Ceplair (1989) 285. On the prophetess, see Campbell (1989) i.30.
97 Woodhouse (1986) 469–71.
98 Ceplair (1989) 283.
99 Letter of 1837 to Angelina: Ceplair (1989) 229. On Quaker dress, see Rumball (2018).
100 Lerner (2009) 10. On rhetoric and deportment, see Cmiel (1990) 67.
101 Letter of 1837 to J. Smith: Lerner (2009) 108.
102 Cromwell (1958) 43.
103 Sermon of 1849: Densmore (2017) 41.

104 Lecture of 1846: Densmore (2017) 25.
105 See McMillen (2008).
106 See the introduction to Thomas (2016).
107 McMillen (2008) 242.
108 On the distinction between liberalism and democracy, see for example Fukuyama (1992) 42–3.
109 McMillen (2008) 250.
110 Putnam (2000) is a modern treatment of the theme.
111 For Stanton's critique of religion, see Davis (2008) 178–95.
112 Biography in Waggenspack (1982) 40–63, with Blair 43.
113 Thomas (2016) 12.
114 Hogan and Taylor (2007).
115 Sennett (1977).
116 Stanton (1898) 188.
117 Mott (1880) 30.
118 See, for example, Gordon (2010). Hornby (1995) is an influential critique.
119 Shklar (1984) 70–8.

Chapter 6

1 Gandhi (2018) 59:11–12. Citations are from the scanned edition of the *Collected Works* issued by the Indian Government (1956–1994), accessible via the Gandhi Heritage Portal. Volume numbers are different in the digitised text published by the Gandhi Sevagram Ashram.
2 Gandhi (2018) 72:60.
3 Sen (2005) 12. Khilnani ([1997] 2012) 15–60 offers a useful introduction.
4 Gandhi (2018) 59:4.
5 Gandhi (2018) 90:216.
6 Sen (1999).
7 Henrich (2020) 410–11.
8 In his 1921 preface to *Hind Swaraj* he accepted the pragmatic necessity of parliamentary politics: Gandhi (1997) 29, n.39.
9 Gandhi (2018) 8:173. The text was first published in episodes in *Indian Opinion*, later issued as a pamphlet.
10 Gandhi (2018) 8:185.
11 On Gandhi's inner voice, see Terchek (1998) 37–40.
12 Tagore (1994–6) iii.846.
13 Gandhi (2018) 29:411. Discussed in Bilgrami (2011) 96.
14 Gandhi (1997) 120.
15 Gandhi (1997) 30–3.
16 Gandhi (1997) 61.
17 Gandhi (1997) 101.
18 Gandhi (1997) 117.
19 Guha (2013) 150.

20 Doke (1909) 28–9.
21 Doke (1909) 41. On the speech defect, Guha (2013) 91. See also Rudolph and Rudolph (1983) 26–9.
22 Gandhi (2018) 48:496–7.
23 Gandhi (2007) 81–2.
24 Gandhi (1997) 102.
25 Gandhi (1997) 102–3, with notes 208, 209.
26 Guha (2018) 340, 343.
27 Guha (208) 381.
28 V. S. Srinivasa Sastri cited in Birkenhead (1965) 281.
29 Letter to his father quoted in Birkenhead (1965) 303. See also Adams (2011).
30 The insight can be traced back to Cicero *De Oratore* 2.185–96.
31 Guha (2018) 869.
32 Churchill ([1950] 1985) 660–1.
33 'The danger of imitation': Gandhi (2018) 54:113–14.
34 Gandhi (1997) 114; Brown (2010) 14, 67.
35 Gandhi (2018) 48:79.
36 Reported by Leonard Elmhirst: Mukherjee (2021) 85.
37 Gandhi (2018) 27:103; Tagore 'The cult of the charkha' [1925] cited in Mukherjee (2021) 107.
38 'The call of truth' [1921] cited in Mukherjee (2021) 91.
39 Gandhi (2018) 23:106.
40 Gandhi (2018) 21:225–6.
41 Tarlo (1996) 67–70, 83–5, etc.; Desai (2009) 81–6.
42 Guha (2018) 409–10.
43 Mahadev Desai in *Young India* 8 October 1931, reprinted in Desai (2019).
44 Chaplin (1964) 335–6.
45 Chaplin (1964) 145, 147.
46 Desai (2009) 32, 90, etc. On Gandhi and costume, see also Gonsalvez (2010) 112–14.
47 Doke (1909) 14–15.
48 Cited in Desai (1995) 202–3.
49 Cited in Lal (1986) 46.
50 'Pathway to Mukti' [1925] printed in Bhushan and Garfield (2011) 157–8, 161. Text corrected from Tagore's typescript in the Online Tagore Variorum available via http://bichitra.jdvu.ac.in/manuscript.
51 Gandhi (2018) 83:293.
52 Gandhi (2018) 90:217–18.
53 'Society and State' [*Swadeshi samaj*]: Tagore (1961) 49–66.
54 Fraser (2019) 111–13.
55 Letter to C. F. Andrews in 1915 cited in Collins (2015) 87.
56 Tagore (1994–6) iii.474–5. Text corrected from the typescript.
57 'City and village', Tagore (1961) 311.
58 Sen (2022) 81.
59 See Wiles (2020).

60 *Natya Sastra* 6.29–30: Ghosh (1967).
61 Haberman (1988) 18–22.
62 Tagore (2001) 237–51.
63 Tagore and Elmhirst (1961) 104–6.
64 Gandhi (2018) 18:240–1.
65 Beg (1986) 179–82; Jinnah (1987) 81. On Jinnah's theatricality, see Devji (2013).
66 Jinnah (1987) 77; Singh (2009) 65; Fraser (2019) 56.
67 Interview with Durga Das cited in Beg (1986) 353. On Nehru's sympathy with his predicament, see Majumdar (1966) 79.
68 See e.g. Ahmed (2020) 116–59.
69 Bharucha (2006) 131–2.
70 Ambedkar (1979) 226–7.
71 Carlyle (1841) 72 cited in Ambedkar (1979) 214. Punctuation as in Carlyle.
72 'The call of truth' [1921], Tagore (1994–6) iii.424.
73 Letter to Myroin H. Phelps [1909], Tagore (2011) 99–104.
74 Sen (2005) 32, 98, 120. The essay on Tagore first appeared in 2001. For the context of the poem, see Acharya (2020).
75 Nussbaum (2006) 394. On differences between Dewey and Tagore, see O'Connell (2002) 235–41.
76 *Sadhana* [1917], Tagore (2011) 169. On the *Upanishads*, see Collins (2015) 40–1, 75.
77 See, for example, Collins (2015) 88–93.
78 Tagore (1994–6) ii.428.
79 'What is Art?' [1917], Tagore (1994–6) ii.357.
80 'The Theatre' [1903], Tagore (2001) 99.
81 Bharucha (2006) 71–2.
82 O'Connell (2002) 160. On Gandhi, see Majumdar (1966) 82–7.
83 Talks in China [1924], http://bichitra.jdvu.ac.in/manuscript.
84 Cited in Kripalani (1962) 191.
85 'An Eastern University' [1922] cited in Ghosh (2020) 37.
86 Tagore and Elmhirst (1961) 106; Kripalani (1962) 190–4; Pritchard (2014); Chakraborty (2017).
87 *Nationalism in the West* [1917], Tagore (1994–6) ii.430, 424.
88 Tagore (2001) 99; Tagore (1994–6) ii.400–1; O'Connell (2002) 129.
89 Henrich (2020) 407–427, 484–9.
90 Tagore (1994–6) ii.420–1.
91 Speech to Japanese passengers on the S-S "Suwa-Maru" [1924], http://bichitra.jdvu.ac.in/manuscript.
92 Mukherjee (2021) 94; 'Talk with socialists' [1947], Gandhi (2018) 17.
93 Banerjee and Duflo (2012) 35–8.
94 Gandhi (1959) 11; Gandhi (2018) 90:307.
95 Chakraborty (2017) 367.
96 Tagore formulated his key principles in 'The Theatre' [1903]: Tagore (2001) 95–9. See Sen (2021) 76–91.

Chapter 7

1. Torri (2022).
2. Knox (1956); Mitchell-Boyask (2008) 56–7.
3. Brook (1968); cf. Debord (1967).
4. McGrath (2002).
5. Castoriadis (1993) 125.
6. Influential ensembles include Théâtre du Soleil, Rimini Protokoll, Théâtre de Complicité, Sojourn Theatre.
7. As founder of 7:84 theatre group. See Michael Billington's obituary in www.theguardian.com/news/2002/jan/24/guardianobituaries.books.
8. Castoriadis (1993) 126–7.
9. See for example Brecht's *Short Organon* 19–22: Brecht (2015) 277–8.
10. Hall (1996) 305, prompting dissent in Heath (2009).
11. Winkler and Zeitlin (1990).
12. Goldhill (2000) 35.
13. Pelling (1997) 235.
14. Williams (1976) 126–30 remains a helpful guide.
15. Cartledge (2016) 129.
16. The essay was co-authored with Barry Strauss. The Pnyx was the Athenian place of assembly. Ober and Strauss (1990) 270.
17. Ober (1989) 152–5. 'Suspension of disbelief' was first postulated by Coleridge in 1817: Coleridge (2014) 270.
18. Pelling (2000) 2.
19. Willis (2005) 24–63. Goff (2009) 78–136 also surveys the modern performance history.
20. The connection to Melos is chronologically hazardous. Goff (2009) 27–35 assesses the 'Melos' theory.
21. Grene and Lattimore (1958) 124. Lattimore's introduction was suppressed in the 2013 edition, but its replacement continues to position the play as a reflection of Melos.
22. Pelling (2005) 100.
23. On display performances by sophists, see Thomas (2003).
24. Gorgias *Encomium of Helen* 11–13. The speech is translated alongside *Palamedes* in Gagarin and Woodruff (1995) 190–5.
25. Thucydides 5.84–116.
26. For the reception of the play, see Macintosh (2009).
27. Arendt (1958) 187.
28. Arendt (1958) 26, 194.
29. Aristotle *Poetics* 6.7. *Dianoia* is sometimes also translated as 'intellect'.
30. Aristotle *Poetics* 19.2.

Notes prior to Chapter 7:

97. Pritchard (2014) 111. On Tagore and outdoor theatre, see Dutt (2020).
98. *Nationalism in the West* [1917], Tagore (1994–6) ii.434.

31 See for example Brecht's *Short Organon*: Brecht (2015) 275.
32 Aristotle *Poetics* 6.16–17.
33 Aristotle *Rhetoric* 3.16.9.
34 Griffith (1999) 278. The passage is still bracketed in Oliver Taplin's recent Oxford translation: Taplin (2020).
35 Text and introduction in Gagarin and MacDowell (1998) 17–47.
36 Gagarin and Macdowell (1998) 92.
37 On the competitive tradition, see Thomas (2003). Sources on judging plays are gathered and analysed in Csapo and Slater (1995) 157–65, alongside other sources about the competition. See also Wilson (2000) 98–102; Roselli (2011) 27–33.
38 See Wilson (2000) esp. 146–55.
39 Plato *Laws* 2.659.
40 Boegehold (1963).
41 On audience expressivity see Roselli (2011) 48–51.
42 Plutarch *Life of Cimon* 8.
43 Aeschines 3.232.
44 Pickard-Cambridge (1968) 98.
45 Aristophanes *Frogs* 1009–10. My translation draws on the interpretation in Dover (1993) 13–14. *Dexiotes* relates etymologically to the 'right' hand; *nouthesia* means literally 'putting in mind'.
46 Aristophanes *Frogs* 1471, citing Euripides *Hippolytus* 612. On the 'competence' of the Athenian audience see Revermann (2006).
47 This can be inferred from the sources in Csapo and Slater (1995) 224–5.
48 On Plato in Sicily see Evangeliou (2019).
49 Plato *Laws* 7.817. Plato's views are articulated by an anonymous Athenian spokesman.
50 Plato *Laws* 3.700.
51 Plato *Laws* 3.700–701.
52 See Balme (2014).
53 Hobbes (1962) 301.
54 Nina Lloyd 'Sir Keir Starmer pledges to smash "class ceiling" with education reforms'. *The Independent* 6 July 2023.
55 The mantra is from *Worstword Ho* (1983). See, for a vivid application to theatre, www.tomphillips.co.uk/works/portraits/item/5434-samuel-beckett.

References

A Briefe Relation of Certain Speciall and most Materiall Passages, and Speeches in the Starre-Chamber: Occasioned and Delivered June the 14th. 1637. at the Censure of those Three Worthy Gentlemen, Dr. Bastwicke, Mr. Burton and Mr. Prynne, as it Hath Beene Truely and Faithfully Gathered from their Owne Mouthes by One Present at the Sayd Censure. 1637. Amsterdam: J. F. Stam.

Abell, Peter. 2014. "Rational Choice Theory and the Analysis of Organizations." In *The Oxford Handbook of Sociology, Social Theory, and Organization Studies*, edited by Paul Adler, Paul du Gay, Glenn Morgan and Michael Reed, 318–345. Oxford: Oxford University Press.

Acharya, Shanta. 2020. "Rabindranath Tagore: Nationalism and Poetry – Message of Universal Humanism." In *Tagore, Nationalism and Cosmopolitanism: Perceptions, Contestations and Contemporary Relevance*, edited by Mohammad A. Quayum, 177–196. New Delhi: Routledge India.

Achen, Christopher H. and Larry M. Bartels. 2017. *Democracy for Realists: Why Elections Do Not Produce Responsive Government: With a New Afterword by the Authors*. Princeton, NJ: Princeton University Press.

Adams, John. 1851. *The Works of John Adams, Second President of the United States. Vol. 6*. Boston, MA: Charles C. Little and James Brown.

Adams, John Quincy. 1810. *Lectures on Rhetoric and Oratory*. Cambridge, MA: Hilliard and Metcalf.

Adams Papers. 2023. Adams Papers Digital Edition. www.masshist.org/publications/adams-papers

Adams, Peter. 2005. *The Bowery Boys: Street Corner Radicals and the Politics of Rebellion*. Westport, CT: Praeger.

Adichie, Chimamanda N. 2022. "Freedom of Speech: Radio 4. 30 Nov 2022." https://downloads.bbc.co.uk/radio4/reith2022/Reith_2022_Lecture1.pdf .2022

Agnew, Lois. 2016. "Demosthenes as Text: Classical Reception and British Rhetorical History." *Advances in the History of Rhetoric* 19 (1): 2–30.

Ahmed, Ishtiaq. 2020. *Jinnah: His Successes, Failures and Role in History*. Gurgaon: Viking.

Alger, William Rounseville. 1877. *Life of Edwin Forrest, the American Tragedian*. Philadelphia, PA: J. B. Lippincott & Co.

Alméras, Henri d'. 1905. *L'Auteur de: Il Pleut, Bergère ... Fabre D'Églantine*. Paris: Société Française d'Imprimerie et de Librairie.
Ambedkar, B. R. 1979. *Writings and Speeches. Vol. 1*. Bombay: Education Department, Government of Maharashtra.
Anand, Paul, Prasanta K. Pattanaik, and Clemens Puppe. 2009. *The Handbook of Rational and Social Choice: An Overview of New Foundations and Applications*. Oxford: Oxford University Press.
Andreski, Stanislav. 1983. *Max Weber on Capitalism, Bureaucracy and Religion: A Selection of Texts*. London: Allen & Unwin.
Andrew, Edward. 2017. "The Role of Brutus in the French Revolution." In *Imperial Republics: Revolution, War and Territorial Expansion from the English Civil War to the French Revolution*, 140–166. Toronto: University of Toronto Press.
Ankersmit, F. R. 2002. *Political Representation*. Stanford, CA: Stanford University Press.
Anthony, Andrew. 2022. "Lend Me Your Ears! The Art of Political Speechwriting." *Guardian*, 11 September. www.theguardian.com/politics/ 2022/sep/11/lend-me-your-ears-the-art-of-political-speechwriting
Applebaum, Anne. 2019. "Boris Johnson's Victory Proves It's Fiction, Not Fact, that Tories Want to Hear." *Washington Post*, 23 July.
Arendt, Hannah. 1958. *The Human Condition*. Charles R. Walgreen Foundation Lectures. Chicago, IL: University of Chicago Press.
   2003. *The Portable Hannah Arendt*, edited by P. R. Baehr. New York and London: Penguin Books.
Arnott, W. G. 1979. *Menander*. Cambridge, MA: Harvard University Press.
Aulard, François Victor Alphonse. 1882. *L'Éloquence parlementaire pendant la Révolution française: les orateurs de l'Assemblée Constituante*. Paris: Hachette.
Bächtiger, André, John S. Dryzek, Jane Mansbridge, and Mark Warren, Eds. 2018. *The Oxford Handbook of Deliberative Democracy*. Oxford: Oxford University Press.
Baczko, Bronisław. 2000. *Une Éducation pour la démocratie: textes et projets de l'époque révolutionnaire*. Geneva: Droz.
Badinter, Élisabeth and Robert Badinter. 1988. *Condorcet (1743–1794): un intellectuel en politique*. Paris: Fayard.
Baker, Philip and Elliot Vernon. 2012. *The Agreements of the People, the Levellers and the Constitutional Crisis of the English Revolution*. Basingstoke: Palgrave Macmillan.
Ballard, Richard. 2010. *The Unseen Terror: The French Revolution in the Provinces*. London: I. B. Tauris.
Balme, Christopher B. 2014. *The Theatrical Public Sphere*. Cambridge: Cambridge University Press.
Bancroft, Richard. 1663. *A Survey of the Pretended Holy Discipline*. London: Richard Hodgkinson.
Banerjee, Abhijit V. and Esther Duflo. 2012. *Poor Economics: Barefoot Hedge-Fund Managers, DIY Doctors and the Surprising Truth about Life on Less than $1 a Day*. London: Penguin.

Bank, Rosemarie K. 2015. "Historiography and Anti-Theatrical Prejudice in Nineteenth-Century America." In *Theatre History and Historiography: Ethics, Evidence and Truth*, edited by Claire Cochrane and Jo Robinson, 48–59. Basingstoke: Palgrave Macmillan.
Barish, Jonas. 1981. *The Anti-theatrical Prejudice*. Berkeley, CA: University of California Press.
Barthes, Roland. 1977. "The Grain of the Voice." In *Image Music Text*, translated by Stephen Heath, 179–189. London: Fontana Press.
Baukol, Bard. 2007. *William Prynne and the Politics of Reaction*. PhD thesis, Arizona State University. Proquest Dissertations Publishing.
Bayer, Mark. 2011. *Theatre, Community, and Civic Engagement in Jacobean London*. Iowa City: University of Iowa Press.
Bayliss, Andrew J. 2011. *After Demosthenes: The Politics of Early Hellenistic Athens*. London: Continuum.
Beard, Mary. 2014. "The Public Voice of Women." *London Review of Books* 36 (6).
Beffroy de Reigny, Louis-Abel. *Almanach général de tous les spectacles de Paris et des provinces, pour l'année 1791*. Paris: Froullé.
Beg, Aziz. 1986. *Jinnah and his Times: A Biography*. Islamabad: Babur & Amer Publications.
Bennett, Susan. 1997. *Theatre Audiences: A Theory of Production and Reception*. 2nd ed. London: Routledge.
Bentley, Eric. 1964. *The Life of the Drama*. New York: Atheneum.
Berger, Peter L. 1963. *Invitation to Sociology: A Humanistic Perspective*. Garden City, NY: Doubleday.
Berlin, Isaiah. 1969. *Four Essays on Liberty*. Oxford: Oxford University Press.
Bernier, Georges. 1995. *Hérault De Séchelles: biographie, suivi de Théorie de l'ambition*. Paris: Julliard.
Bernstein, Richard B. 2020. *The Education of John Adams*. New York: Oxford University Press.
Bers, Victor. 1985. "Dikastic 'Thorubos.'" *History of Political Thought* 6 (1): 1–15.
  2009. *Genos Dikanikon: Amateur and Professional Speech in the Courtrooms of Classical Athens*. Cambridge, MA: Harvard University Press.
  2013. "Performing the Speech in Athenian Courts and Assembly: Adjusting the Act to Fit the Bēma?" In *Profession and Performance*, edited by Christos Kremmydas, Jonathan Powell and Lene Rubinstein, 27–40. London: University of London Press.
Bharucha, Rustom. 2006. *Another Asia: Rabindranath Tagore and Okakura Tenshin*. New Delhi: Oxford University Press.
Bhushan, Nalini and Jay L. Garfield. 2011. *Indian Philosophy in English: From Renaissance to Independence*. Oxford: Oxford University Press.
Bilgrami, Akeel. 2011. "Gandhi's Religion and its Relation to his Politics." In *The Cambridge Companion to Gandhi*, edited by Judith Brown and Anthony Parel, 93–116. Cambridge: Cambridge University Press.
Birkenhead, Earl of (Frederick Winston Furneaux Smith). 1965. *Halifax: The Life of Lord Halifax*. London: Hamish Hamilton.

Blair, Hugh. 1784. *Lectures on Rhetoric and Belles Lettres*. Philadelphia, PA: Robert Aitken.
Blanshard, Alastair J. L. 2014. "The Permeable Spaces of the Athenian Law-Court." In *Space, Place, and Landscape in Ancient Greek Literature and Culture*, edited by Kate Gilhuly and Nancy Worman, 240–276. Cambridge: Cambridge University Press.
  2018. "Afterlife (Modern Era)." In *The Oxford Handbook of Demosthenes*, edited by Martin Gunther, 452–462. Oxford: Oxford University Press.
Blight, David W. 1998. *The Columbian Orator . . . by Caleb Bingham*. New York: New York University Press.
  2018. *Frederick Douglass: Prophet of Freedom*. New York: Simon & Schuster.
Bloom, Arthur W. 2019. *Edwin Forrest: A Biography and Performance History*. Jefferson, NC: McFarland.
Blundell, Mary Whitlock. 1989. *Helping Friends and Harming Enemies: A Study in Sophocles and Greek Ethics*. Cambridge: Cambridge University Press.
Blundell, Sue. 1998. *Women in Classical Athens*. London: Bristol Classical Press.
Boal, Augusto. 1979. *Theater of the Oppressed*, translated by Charles A. McBride, Maria-Odilia Leal McBride. London: Pluto Press.
Boegehold, Alan L. 1963. "Toward a Study of Athenian Voting Procedure." *Hesperia: The Journal of the American School of Classical Studies at Athens* 32 (4): 366–374.
  1995. *The Lawcourts at Athens: Sites, Buildings, Equipment, Procedure, and Testimonia*. Princeton, NJ: American School of Classical Studies at Athens.
Bonnet, Jean-Claude. 1988. "La 'sainte masure', sanctuaire de la parole fondatrice." In *La Carmagnole des muses: l'homme de lettres et l'artiste dans la Révolution*, edited by Jean-Claude Bonnet, 185–222. Paris: A. Colin.
Bosher, Kathryn. 2012. "Hieron's Aeschylus." In *Theater Outside Athens: Drama in Greek Sicily and South Italy*, edited by Kathryn Bosher, 97–111. Cambridge: Cambridge University Press.
  2014. *Epicharmus and Early Sicilian Comedy*. Cambridge: Cambridge University Press.
Bourgoing, Alice de. 2016. *Célébrer la République. Une histoire politique et matérielle de la Fête de l'Unité et de l'Indivisibilité, le 10 août 1793*. Mémoire de Master 2 sous la direction de Jean-Luc Chappey, Université Paris 1 Panthéon-Sorbonne,
Brasart, Patrick. 1988. *Paroles de la Révolution: les assemblées parlementaires, 1789–1794*. Paris: Minerve.
Brecht, Bertolt. 1948. *Parables for the Theatre*, edited by Eric Bentley. Minneapolis: University of Minnesota Press.
  2015. *Brecht on Theatre*, edited by Marc Silberman, Steve Giles and Tom Kuhn. 3rd ed. London: Bloomsbury.
Brook, Peter. 1968. *The Empty Space*. London: MacGibbon & Kee.
Brown, Gregory S. 2005. *A Field of Honor: Writers, Court Culture, and Public Theater in French Literary Life from Racine to the Revolution*. New York: Columbia University Press.

Brown, Rebecca M. 2010. *Gandhi's Spinning Wheel and the Making of India*. London: Routledge.
Buchez, Philippe-Joseph-Benjamin. 1837. *Histoire parlementaire de la Révolution française. Vol. 3*. Paris: Paulin.
Buckler, John. 2000. "Demosthenes and Aeschines." In *Demosthenes: Statesman and Orator*, edited by Ian Worthington, 114–158. London: Routledge.
Buckley, Peter G. 1984. *To the Opera House: Culture and Society in New York City, 1820–1860*. PhD diss., State University of New York at Stony Brook.
Buckley, Terry. 1996. *Aspects of Greek History 750–323 BC: A Source-Based Approach*. London: Routledge.
Butsch, Richard. 2000. *The Making of American Audiences: From Stage to Television, 1750–1990*. Cambridge: Cambridge University Press.
Campbell, Karlyn Kohrs. 1989. *Man Cannot Speak for Her*. New York: Greenwood Press.
Campbell, Peter Robert. 2006. *The Origins of the French Revolution*. Basingstoke: Palgrave Macmillan.
Carey, Christopher. 2000. *Aeschines*. Austin: University of Texas Press.
Carlson, Marvin. 2017. *Performance: A Critical Introduction*. 3rd ed. Abingdon: Routledge.
Carlyle, Thomas. 1841. *On Heroes, Hero-Worship, and the Heroic in History: Six Lectures*. London: J. Fraser.
Carnicke, Sharon Marie. 2009. *Stanislavsky in Focus: An Acting Master for the Twenty-First Century*. 2nd ed. London: Routledge.
Carter, D. M. 2011. "Plato, Drama, and Rhetoric." In *Why Athens?: A Reappraisal of Tragic Politics*, edited by D. M. Carter, 45–67. Oxford: Oxford University Press.
Carter, Rosemary. 1966. *Great Debates of the French Revolution: A Study and Evaluation of the Oratory of the Constituent Assembly (May 1789–September 1791) with Especial Regard to those Speeches Commonly Attributed to Mirabeau*. PhD thesis, University of London, Royal Holloway.
Cartledge, Paul. 2016. *Democracy: A Life*. Oxford: Oxford University Press.
Castoriadis, Cornelius. 1993. "The Greek and the Modern Political Imaginary." *Salmagundi* 100: 102–129.
  1997. "The Greek Polis and the Creation of Democracy." In *The Castoriadis Reader*, edited by David Ames Curtis, 267–289. Oxford: Blackwell.
Cavarero, Adriana. 2005. *For More than One Voice: Toward a Philosophy of Vocal Expression*. Stanford: Stanford University Press.
Ceplair, Larry. 1989. *The Public Years of Sarah and Angelina Grimké: Selected Writings 1835–1839*. New York: Columbia University Press.
Chakraborty, Aishika. 2017. "Dancing Against the Nation? Revisiting Tagore's Politics." In *Tagore and Nationalism*, edited by K. L. Tuteja and Kaustav Chakraborty, 359–379. New Delhi: Springer.
Chambers, Simone. 2003. "Deliberative Democratic Theory." *Annual Review of Political Science* 6: 307–326.
Chaplin, Charlie. 1964. *My Autobiography*. London: Bodley Head.

Chartier, Roger. 1991. *The Cultural Origins of the French Revolution*. Durham, NC: Duke University Press.
Chauvot, Henri. 1856. *Le Barreau de Bordeaux de 1775 à 1815*. Paris: Auguste Durand.
Churchill, Caryl. 1985. *Plays: One*. London: Methuen.
Churchill, Winston. 1985. *The Second World War. Volume IV: The Hinge of Fate*. Boston, MA: Houghton Mifflin Co.
  2016. *Exploring the Official Biography: Churchill's "The Scaffolding of Rhetoric."* The Churchill Project, Hillsdale College. https://winstonchurchill.hillsdale.edu/the-scaffolding-of-rhetoric
Clairon, Hyppolite. 1799. *Mémoires d'Hyppolite Clairon et réflexions sur la déclamation théatrale, publiés par elle-même. Seconde édition*. Paris: F. Buisson.
Clark, Barrett H. and Henry Popkin. 1956. *European Theories of the Drama: With a Supplement on the American Drama; an Anthology of Dramatic Theory and Criticism from Aristotle to the Present Day*. New York: Crown.
Cliff, Nigel. 2007. *The Shakespeare Riots: Revenge, Drama, and Death in Nineteenth-Century America*. New York: Random House.
Clopper, Lawrence M., David Mills, and Elizabeth Baldwin. 2007. *Cheshire including Chester*. London: British Library and University of Toronto Press.
Cmiel, Kenneth. 1990. *Democratic Eloquence: The Fight Over Popular Speech in Nineteenth-Century America*. New York: Morrow.
Cohen, Joshua. 1989. "Deliberative Democracy and Democratic Legitimacy." In *The Good Polity: Normative Analysis of the State*, edited by Alan Hamlin and Phillip Pettit, 17–34. New York: Blackwell.
Cole, Toby and Helen Krich Chinoy. 1970. *Actors on Acting: The Theories, Techniques, and Practices of the Great Actors of all Times as Told in their Own Words*. Rev. ed. New York: Crown.
Coleridge, Samuel Taylor. 2014. *Biographia Literaria*, edited by Adam Roberts. Edinburgh: Edinburgh University Press.
Collins, Michael. 2015. *Empire, Nationalism and the Postcolonial World: Rabindranath Tagore's Writings on History, Politics and Society*. London: Routledge.
Collins, Philip. 2017. *When They Go Low, We Go High: Speeches that Shape the World – and Why We Need Them*. London: 4th Estate.
Condor, Susan, Cristian Tileaga, and Michael Billig. 2013. "Political Rhetoric." In *The Oxford Handbook of Political Psychology*, edited by Leonie Huddy, David O. Sears and Jack S. Levy, 262–300. Oxford: Oxford University Press.
Condorcet, Jean-Antoine-Nicolas de Caritat. 1795. *Esquisse d'un tableau historique des progrès de l'esprit humain: ouvrage posthume de Condorcet*. Paris: Agasse.
  1847–49. *Oeuvres De Condorcet*, edited by Arthur Condorcet O'Connor and François Arago. Paris: Firmin Didot.
  2012. *Political Writings*, edited by Steven Lukes and Nadia Urbinati. Cambridge: Cambridge University Press.

Consigny, Scott. 2001. *Gorgias: Sophist and Artist*. Columbia, SC: University of South Carolina Press.
Constant, Benjamin. 1988. *Political Writings*, edited by Biancamaria Fontana. Cambridge: Cambridge University Press.
Converse, Philip E. 2006. "The Nature of Belief Systems in Mass Publics (1964)." *Critical Review* 18 (1–3): 1–74.
Cooper, Craig. 2000. "Philosophers, Politics, Academics: Demosthenes' Political Reputation in Antiquity." In *Demosthenes: Statesman and Orator*, edited by Ian Worthington, 224–245. London: Routledge.
Cotlar, Seth. 2013. "Languages of Democracy in America from the Revolution to the Election of 1800." In *Re-Imagining Democracy in the Age of Revolutions: America, France, Britain, Ireland 1750–1850*, edited by Joanna Innes and Mark Philp, 13–27. Oxford: Oxford University Press.
Cowling, Nicholas. 1647. *The Saints Perfect in this Life, or Never: Collected and Gathered from Scripture in the Letter thereof, and the Spirituall Sence of the Same. by N. Couling, an Officer in the Army, and a Well-Wisher to the Truth*. London: Giles Calvert.
Craig, Geoffrey. 2016. *Performing Politics: Media Interviews, Debates and Press Conferences*. Cambridge: Polity Press.
Cressy, David. 1999. "The Portraiture of Prynne's Pictures: Performance on the Public Stage." In *Travesties and Transgressions in Tudor and Stuart England: Tales of Discord and Dissension*, edited by David Cressy, 213–233. Oxford: Oxford University Press.
Cromwell, Otelia. 1958. *Lucretia Mott*. Cambridge, MA: Harvard University Press.
Crouch, Colin. 2004. *Post-Democracy*. Cambridge: Polity.
Csapo, Eric. 2004. "The Politics of the New Music." In *Music and the Muses: The Culture of Mousike in the Classical Athenian City*, edited by Penelope Murray and Peter Wilson, 207–248. Oxford: Oxford University Press.
Csapo, Eric and Peter Wilson. 2015. "Drama Outside Athens in the Fifth and Fourth Centuries BC." *Trends in Classics* 7 (2): 316–395.
   2020a. "The Politics of Greece's Theatrical Revolution, ca. 500 – ca. 300 BCE." In *Greek Drama V: Studies in the Theatre of the Fifth and Fourth Centuries BCE*, edited by Hallie Marshall and C. W. Marshall, 1–22. London: Bloomsbury.
   2020b. *A Social and Economic History of the Theatre to 300 BC: Theatre Beyond Athens: Documents with Translation and Commentary. Vol. 2*. Cambridge: Cambridge University Press.
Csapo, Eric and William J. Slater. 1995. *The Context of Ancient Drama*. Ann Arbor: University of Michigan Press.
Dale, A. M. 1954. *Euripides Alcestis*. Oxford: Clarendon Press.
D'Ancona, Matthew. 2021. *Identity, Ignorance, Innovation*. London: Hodder & Stoughton.
Dard, Émile. 1907. *Un Épicurien sous la Terreur: Hérault De Séchelles, 1759–1794*. Paris: Perrin.

Davis, Sue. 2008. *The Political Thought of Elizabeth Cady Stanton: Women's Rights and the American Political Traditions*. New York: New York University Press.

Davis, Tracy C., Ed. 2008. *The Cambridge Companion to Performance Studies*. Cambridge: Cambridge University Press.

de Bacourt, Adolphe Fourier. 1851. *Correspondance entre le Comte de Mirabeau et le Comte de la Marck pendant les années 1789, 1790 et 1791*. Paris: Librairie Ve Le Normant.

de Grouchy Condorcet, Marie-Louise-Sophie. 2019. *Sophie de Grouchy's Letters on Sympathy*, edited by Sandrine Bergès. New York: Oxford University Press.

de Tocqueville, Alexis. 1998. *The Old Regime and the Revolution, Vol. 1*, translated by Alan S. Kahan. Chicago, IL: University of Chicago Press.

2003. *Democracy in America: And Two Essays on America*, translated by Gerald E. Bevan. London: Penguin.

Debord, Guy. 1967. *La Société du spectacle*. Paris: Buchet-Chastel.

Delacroix, Jacques-Vincent. 1792. *L'intrigue dévoilée, ou, Robespierre vengé des outrages & des calomnies des ambitieux*. Paris: Imprimerie de la Vérité.

Densmore, Christopher. 2017. *Lucretia Mott Speaks: The Essential Speeches and Sermons*. Urbana: University of Illinois Press.

Derrida, Jacques. 1978. "The Theater of Cruelty and the Closure of Representation." *Theater* 9 (3): 6–19.

Desai, I. R. B. 2009. *Producing the Mahatma: Communication, Community and Political Theatre behind the Gandhi Phenomenon 1893–1942*. DPhil thesis, University of Oxford.

Desai, Nachiketa. 2019. "Gandhiji Inspired Charlie Chaplin to Make His Classic Movie 'Modern Times'." *The Leaflet*. https://theleaflet.in

Desai, Narayan. 1995. *The Fire and the Rose: Biography of Mahadevbhai*. Ahmedabad: Navajivan.

Desmoulins, Camille. 1790. *Révolutions de France et de Brabant, Vol. 5. no. 55. (Décembre, 1790)*. Paris: Garnery.

1791. *Révolutions de France et de Brabant, Vol. 3. no. 28. (Avril 1791)*. Paris: Garnery.

Devji, Faisal. 2013. "Jinnah and the Theatre of Politics." *Asiatische Studien* 67 (4): 1179–1204.

Diamond, Larry Jay. 2008. *The Spirit of Democracy: The Struggle to Build Free Societies Throughout the World*. New York: Times Books/Henry Holt.

Diderot, Denis. 1995. *Oeuvres complètes, Vol. XX: Paradoxe sur le comédien*. Paris: Hermann.

Diggins, John P. 2003. *John Adams*. New York: Times Books.

Dodds, E. R. 1959. *Plato: Gorgias*. Oxford: Clarendon Press.

Doke, Joseph J. 1909. *M. K. Gandhi: An Indian Patriot in South Africa*. London: The London Indian Chronicle.

Douglass, Frederick. 1855. *My Bondage and My Freedom*. New York: Miller, Orton and Mulligan.

2016. *The Portable Frederick Douglass*, edited by John Stauffer and Henry Louis Gates, Jr. New York: Penguin Books.

Dover, Kenneth. 1993. *Aristophanes: Frogs.* Oxford: Clarendon Press.
Downer, Alan S. 1966. *The Eminent Tragedian William Charles Macready.* Cambridge, MA: Harvard University Press
Dubois, Laurent. 2004. *A Colony of Citizens: Revolution and Slave Emancipation in the French Caribbean, 1787–1804.* Chapel Hill, NC: University of North Carolina Press.
Dumont, Etienne. 1832. *Souvenirs sur Mirabeau et sur les deux premières assemblées législatives.* Paris: C. Gosselin & H. Bossange.
Duncan, Anne. 2006. *Performance and Identity in the Classical World.* Cambridge: Cambridge University Press.
Dunn, John. 2010. "Tracking Democracy." *Political Theory* 38 (1): 106–110.
Dupont, Florence. 2000. *L'Orateur sans visage: essai sur l'acteur romain et son masque.* Paris: Presses Universitaires de France.
Dutt, Dattatreya. 2020. "The Unrealized Theatre of Tagore." In *Rabindranath Tagore's Drama in the Perspective of Indian Theatre*, edited by Mala Renganathan and Arnab Bhattacharya, 109–129. London: Anthem Press.
Easterling, P. E. 1997. "From Repertoire to Canon." In *The Cambridge Companion to Greek Tragedy*, edited by P. E. Easterling, 211–227. Cambridge: Cambridge University Press.
Eastman, Carolyn. 2009. *A Nation of Speechifiers: Making an American Public after the Revolution.* Chicago, IL: University of Chicago Press.
Ernest, John. 2014. *Douglass in His Own Time: A Biographical Chronicle of His Life, Drawn from Recollections, Interviews, and Memoirs by Family, Friends, and Associates.* Iowa City: University of Iowa Press.
Euben, J. Peter. 1993. "Democracy Ancient and Modern." *PS: Political Science & Politics* 26 (3): 478–481.
Evangeliou, Christos C. 2019. "Plato and Sicilian Power Politics: Between Dion and Dionysius II." In *Plato at Syracuse: Essays on Plato in Western Greece*, edited by Heather L. Reid and Mark Ralkowski, 187–200. Sioux City, IA: Parnassos Press.
Everard, Robert. 1652. *An Antidote for Newcastle Priests to Expell their Poyson of Envy which they Vented in a Letter to the L. Generall Cromwell.* London: Printed for the Author.
Fabre d'Eglantine, P. F. N. 1793. *Portrait de Marat.* Paris: Maradan.
  1799. *Les Précepteurs, comédie en 5 actes et en vers.* Paris: Imprimerie de la République.
Fairfax, Thomas. 1647. *A Solemne Engagement of the Army Under the Command of His Excellency Sir Thomas Fairfax; with a Declaration of their Resolutions, as to Disbanding; and a Briefe Vindication of their Principles and Intentions.* London: George Whittington.
Farr, David. 2006. *Henry Ireton and the English Revolution.* Woodbridge: Boydell.
Feilla, Cecilia A. 2013. *The Sentimental Theater of the French Revolution: Performance in the Long Eighteenth Century.* Farnham: Ashgate.
Ferling, John E. 1992. *John Adams: A Life.* Knoxville: University of Tennessee Press.

Finglass, Patrick. 2018. *Sophocles: Oedipus the King*. Cambridge: Cambridge University Press.
Finlayson, Alan. 2007. "From Beliefs to Arguments: Interpretive Methodology and Rhetorical Political Analysis." *The British Journal of Politics and International Relations* 9 (4): 545–563.
　2014a. "The Peculiar Character of Political Speech." In *Back to Earth: Reconnecting People and Politics*, edited by Ed Wallis and Ania Skrzypek-Claassens, 24–34. London: Fabian Society.
　2014b. "Proving, Pleasing and Persuading? Rhetoric in Contemporary British Politics." *Political Quarterly* 85 (4): 428–436
　2021. "Performing Political Ideologies." In *The Oxford Handbook of Politics and Performance*, edited by Shirin Rai, Milija Gluhovic, Silvija Jestrovic, and Michael Saward, 471–483. Oxford: Oxford University Press.
Finlayson, Alan and James Martin. 2014. "Introduction: Rhetoric and the British Way of Politics." In *Rhetoric in British Politics and Society*, edited by J. Atkins, A. Finlayson, J. Martin, and N. Turnbull, 1–13. London: Palgrave Macmillan.
Finley, M.I. 1962. "Athenian Demagogues." *Past and Present* 21 (1): 3–24.
Fischer-Lichte, Erika. 2008. *The Transformative Power of Performance: A New Aesthetics*. London: Routledge.
　2012. "Classical Theatre. In *The Cambridge Companion to Theatre History*, edited by David Wiles and Christine Dymkowski, 73–84. Cambridge: Cambridge University Press.
Fisher, Tony and Eve Katsouraki. 2017. *Performing Antagonism: Theatre, Performance & Radical Democracy*. London: Palgrave Macmillan.
Fliegelman, Jay. 1993. *Declaring Independence: Jefferson, Natural Language & the Culture of Performance*. Stanford, CA: Stanford University Press.
Flinders, Matthew. 2020. "Why Feelings Trump Facts: Anti-Politics, Citizenship and Emotion." *Emotions and Society* 2 (1): 21–40.
Forward, Nicholas. 2012. *The Arrest and Trial of Archbishop William Laud*. MPhil thesis, University of Birmingham. ProQuest Dissertations Publishing.
Foxley, Rachel. 2004. "John Lilburne and the Citizenship of Free-Born Englishmen." *The Historical Journal* 47 (4): 849–874.
France, Peter. 1990. "Speakers and Audience: The First Days of the Convention." In *Language and Rhetoric of the Revolution*, edited by John Renwick, 50–67. Edinburgh: Edinburgh University Press.
　1992. "Beyond Politeness? Speakers and Audience at the Convention Nationale." In *Politeness and its Discontents: Problems in French Classical Culture*, 129–148. Cambridge: Cambridge University Press.
　2002. "A Tale of Two Cities: L'Éloquence à Westminster et à Paris." In *Une Expérience rhétorique: l'éloquence de la Révolution*, edited by Eric Négrel and Jean-Paul Sermain, 35–44. Oxford: Voltaire Foundation.
Fraser, Antonia. 1973. *Cromwell: Our Chief of Men*. London: Weidenfeld and Nicolson.

Fraser, Bashabi. 2019. *Rabindranath Tagore*. London: Reaktion Books.
Freeman, Joanne B. 2001. *Affairs of Honor: National Politics in the New Republic*. New Haven, CT: Yale University Press.
Freeman, Lisa A. 2017. *Antitheatricality and the Body Public*. Philadelphia: University of Pennsylvania Press.
Friedland, Paul. 2002. *Political Actors: Representative Bodies and Theatricality in the Age of the French Revolution*. Ithaca, NY: Cornell University Press.
Fukuyama, Francis. 1989. "The End of History?" *The National Interest* (16): 3–18.
　1992. *The End of History and the Last Man*. London: Penguin.
　2018. *Identity: The Demand for Dignity and the Politics of Resentment*. New York: Farrar, Straus and Giroux.
Gagarin, Michael and Douglas M. MacDowell. 1998. *Antiphon and Andocides*. Austin: University of Texas Press.
Gagarin, Michael and Paul Woodruff. 1995. *Early Greek Political Thought from Homer to the Sophists*. Cambridge: Cambridge University Press.
Gandhi, M. K. 2007. *An Autobiography, Or, the Story of My Experiments with Truth*. London: Penguin.
　1959. *Panchayat Raj*. Ahmedabad: Navajivan Publishing House.
　1997. *Hind Swaraj and Other Writings*, edited by Anthony Parel. Cambridge; New York: Cambridge University Press.
　2018. *Collected Works of Mahatma Gandhi*. Sabarmati Ashram Preservation and Memorial Trust. www.gandhiheritageportal.org
Ganter, Granville. 1997. "The Active Virtue of the Columbian Orator." *The New England Quarterly* 70 (3): 463–476.
Gardiner, Samuel Rawson. 1877. *Documents Relating to the Proceedings against William Prynne, in 1634 and 1637*. London: Camden Society.
Garner, Steve. 2007. *Whiteness: An Introduction*. New York: Routledge.
Garsten, Bryan. 2011. "The Rhetoric Revival in Political Theory." *Annual Review of Political Science* 14 (1): 159–180.
Gastineau, B. and J. Gabriel Janin. 1860. *Les Amours de Mirabeau et de la Marquise de Monnier: suivis des lettres choisies de Mirabeau à la Marquise*. The Hague: Doorman.
Gay, Peter. 1961. "Rhetoric and Politics in the French Revolution." *The American Historical Review* 66 (3): 664–676.
Gentles, Ian. 1997. "The New Model Officer Corps in 1647: A Collective Portrait." *Social History* 22 (2): 127–144.
　2001. "The *Agreements of the People* and their Political Contexts 1647–1649." In *The Putney Debates of 1647: The Army, the Levellers, and the English State*, edited by Michael Mendle, 148–174. Cambridge: Cambridge University Press.
　2012. "The New Model Army and the Constitutional Crisis of the Late 1640s." In *The Agreements of the People, the Levellers and the Constitutional Crisis of the English Revolution*, edited by P. Baker and E. Vernon, 139–162. London: Palgrave Macmillan.

Gerstner, David A. 2006. *Manly Arts: Masculinity and Nation in Early American Cinema*. Durham, NC: Duke University Press.
Ghosh, Deepshikha. 2020. "*Rabindrik-Nritya*, Tagore's New Aesthetic for Indian Dramatic Art: Discourse and Practice." In *Rabindranath Tagore's Drama in the Perspective of Indian Theatre*, edited by Mala Renganathan and Arnab Bhattacharya, 33–43. London: Anthem Press.
Ghosh, Manomohan. 1967. *The Nāṭyaśāstra*. Calcutta: Manisha Granthalaya.
Gladstone, William Ewart. 1968a. *The Gladstone Diaries Vol. 1, 1825–1832*, edited by M. R. D. Foot. Oxford: Oxford University Press.
   1968b. *The Gladstone Diaries. Vol. 2, 1833–1839*, edited by M. R. D. Foot. Oxford: Oxford University Press.
Glenn, Richard A. and Kyle L. Kreider. 2020. *Voting Rights in America: A Reference Handbook*. Santa Barbara, CA: ABC-CLIO.
Glover, Dennis. 2011. *The Art of Great Speeches: And Why We Remember Them*. Cambridge: Cambridge University Press.
Goette, Hans Rupprecht. 2014. "The Archaeology of the 'Rural' Dionysia in Attica." In *Greek Theatre in the Fourth Century BC*, edited by Eric Csapo, Hans Rupprecht Goette, J. R. Green, and Peter Wilson, 77–105. Berlin: De Gruyter.
Goff, Barbara. 2009. *Euripides: Trojan Women*. London: Duckworth.
Goffman, Erving. 1956. *The Presentation of Self in Everyday Life*. Edinburgh: University of Edinburgh Social Sciences Research Centre.
Golden, James L. and Alan L. Golden. 2002. *Thomas Jefferson and the Rhetoric of Virtue*. Lanham, MD: Rowman & Littlefield.
Golden, Mark. 2015. *Children and Childhood in Classical Athens*. Baltimore MD: Johns Hopkins University Press.
Goldhill, Simon. 2000. "Civic Ideology and the Problem of Difference: The Politics of Aeschylean Tragedy, Once Again." *The Journal of Hellenic Studies* 120: 34–56.
Gonsalves, Peter. 2010. *Clothing for Liberation: A Communication Analysis of Gandhi's Swadeshi Revolution*. London: Sage.
Goodall, Jane R. 2008. *Stage Presence*. Abingdon: Routledge.
Goodden, Angelica. 1984. "The Dramatising of Politics: Theatricality and the Revolutionary Assemblies." *Forum for Modern Language Studies* 20 (3): 193–212.
Gordon, Mel. 2010. *Stanislavsky in America: A Workbook for Actors*. New York: Routledge.
Goring, Paul. 2005. *The Rhetoric of Sensibility in Eighteenth-Century Culture*. Cambridge: Cambridge University Press.
Gould, John. 1980. "Law, Custom and Myth: Aspects of the Social Position of Women in Classical Athens." *The Journal of Hellenic Studies* 100: 38–59.
Graeber, David. 2007. "There Never Was a West: Or, Democracy Emerges from the Spaces in Between." In *Possibilities*, edited by David Graeber, 329–374. Oakland, CA: AK Press.
Grant, Ruth W. 1997. *Hypocrisy and Integrity: Machiavelli, Rousseau, and the Ethics of Politics*. Chicago, IL: University of Chicago Press.

Grayling, A. C. 2017. *Democracy and its Crisis*. London: Oneworld.
Grene, David and Richmond Lattimore. 1958. *Euripides III: Four Tragedies*. Chicago, IL: Phoenix.
Grethlein, Jonas. 2011. "The Rise of Greek Historiography and the Invention of Prose." In *The Oxford History of Historical Writing: I. Beginnings to AD 600*, edited by Andrew Feldherr and Grant Hardy, 148–170. Oxford: Oxford University Press.
Griffith, Mark. 1999. *Sophocles: Antigone*. Cambridge: Cambridge University Press.
Grote, George. 1875. *History of Greece. Vol. XII*. New York: Harper.
Guha, Ramachandra. 2013. *Gandhi before India*. London: Allen Lane.
    2018. *Gandhi : The Years that Changed the World, 1914–1948*. London: Allen Lane.
Gustafson, Sandra M. 2000. *Eloquence Is Power: Oratory and Performance in Early America*. Chapel Hill: University of North Carolina Press.
Haberman, David L. 1988. *Acting as a Way of Salvation: A Study of Rāgānugā Bhakti Sādhana*. New York: Oxford University Press.
Haidt, Jonathan. 2012. *The Righteous Mind: Why Good People are Divided by Politics and Religion*. London: Allen Lane.
Hall, Edith. 1995. "Lawcourt Dramas: The Power of Performance in Greek Forensic Oratory." *Bulletin of the Institute of Classical Studies* 40: 39–58.
    1996. "Is there a Polis in Aristotle's *Poetics*?" In *Tragedy and the Tragic*, edited by Michael Silk, 294–309. Oxford: Oxford University Press.
    2002. "The Singing Actors of Antiquity." In *Greek and Roman Actors: Aspects of an Ancient Profession*, edited by P. E. Easterling and Edith Hall, 3–38. Cambridge: Cambridge University Press.
    2006. *The Theatrical Cast of Athens: Interactions between Ancient Greek Drama and Society*. Oxford: Oxford University Press.
    2018. "The Boys from Cydathenaeum: Aristophanes Versus Cleon again." In *How to Do Things with History*, edited by D. Allen, P. Christesen, and P. Millet, 339–363. Oxford: Oxford University Press.
    2019. "Competitive Vocal Performance in Aristophanes' *Knights*." In *Poet and Orator*, edited by Andreas Markantonatos and Eleni Volonaki, 71–82. Berlin: De Gruyter.
Hall, Peter. 2000. *Exposed by the Mask: Form and Language in Drama*. London: Oberon.
Hallward, Peter. 2006. "Staging Equality." *New Left Review* 37: 109–129.
Hampson, Norman. 1974. *The Life and Opinions of Maximilien Robespierre*. London: Duckworth.
Hansen, Mogens Herman. 1999. *The Athenian Democracy in the Age of Demosthenes: Structure, Principles and Ideology*. Norman: University of Oklahoma Press.
Hanvelt, Marc. 2012. *The Politics of Eloquence: David Hume's Polite Rhetoric*. Toronto: University of Toronto Press.
Harding, Phillip. 2000. "Demosthenes in the Underworld: Studies in the *Nachleben* of a Rhetor." In *Demosthenes: Statesman and Orator*, edited by Ian Worthington, 246–271. London: Routledge.

Harris, Edward Monroe. 1995. *Aeschines and Athenian Politics*. New York: Oxford University Press.
Harrison, George. 1987. "Representatives and Delegates: The Soldiers' Politicization and the General Council of the Army, 1647." *Parliaments, Estates & Representation* 7 (2): 115–132.
Harrison, Joseph. 1684. *The Popish Proselyte the Grand Fanatick. Or an Antidote Against the Poyson of Captain Robert Everard's Epistle to the several Congregations of the Non-Conformists*. London: Samuel Tidmarsh.
Harrop, Stephe. 2018. "Greek Tragedy, Agonistic Space, and Contemporary Performance." *New Theatre Quarterly* 34 (2): 99–114.
Hart, Roderick P. 1987. *The Sound of Leadership: Presidential Communication in the Modern Age*. Chicago, IL: University of Chicago Press.
Haydon, Colin and William Doyle. 1999. *Robespierre*. Cambridge: Cambridge University Press.
Heath, Malcolm. 2009. "Should there Have Been a Polis in Aristotle's Poetics?" *The Classical Quarterly* 59 (2): 468–485.
Henderson, Jeffrey. 1990. "The Dêmos and the Comic Competition." In *Nothing to Do with Dionysos?: Athenian Drama in Its Social Context*, edited by John J. Winkler and Froma I. Zeitlin, 261–278. Princeton, NJ: Princeton University Press.
  2007. "Drama and Democracy." In *The Cambridge Companion to the Age of Pericles*, edited by Loren J. Samons II, 179–195. Cambridge: Cambridge University Press.
Henrich, Joseph Patrick. 2020. *The WEIRDest People in the World: How the West Became Psychologically Peculiar and Particularly Prosperous*. London: Allen Lane.
Hérault de Séchelles, Marie-Jean. 1793. *Recueil complet de tout ce qui s'est passé à la Fête de l'Unité et de l'Indivisibilité de la République Française . . . avec les six discours prononcés aux stations par le citoyen Hérault-De-Séchelles, Président de la Convention Nationale*. Paris: Chaudrillié.
  1801. *Voyage à Montbar*. Paris: Solvet.
Hershkowitz, Leo. 2006. "An Anatomy of a Riot: Astor Place Opera House, 1849." *New York History* 87 (3): 277–311.
Hesk, Jon. 1999. "The Rhetoric of Anti-Rhetoric in Athenian Oratory." In *Performance Culture and Athenian Democracy*, edited by Simon Goldhill and Robin Osborne, 201–230. Cambridge: Cambridge University Press.
Hill, Christopher. 1966. "The Many-Headed Monster in Late Tudor and Early Stuart Political Thinking." In *From the Renaissance to the Counter-Reformation: Essays in Honour of Garrett Mattingly*, edited by Charles Howard Carter, 296–324. London: Cape.
  1968. *Puritanism and Revolution: Studies in Interpretation of the English Revolution of the 17th Century*. London: Panther.
  1991. *Change and Continuity in Seventeenth-Century England*. New Haven, CT: Yale University Press.
Hirsch, Susan E. 1978. *Roots of the American Working Class: The Industrialization of Crafts in Newark, 1800–1860*. Philadelphia: University of Pennsylvania Press.

Hobbes, Thomas. 1629. *Eight Bookes of the Peloponnesian Warre Written by Thucydides the Sonne of Olorus.* London: Eliot's Court Press for Henry Seile.
  1962. *Leviathan.* London: Collins.
  1994. *The Elements of Law, Natural and Politic: Part I, Human Nature, Part II, De Corpore Politico; with Three Lives.* Oxford: Oxford University Press.
  2010. *Behemoth, Or, the Long Parliament.* Oxford: Clarendon Press.
Hogan, Margaret A. and C. J. Taylor. 2007. *My Dearest Friend: Letters of Abigail and John Adams.* Cambridge, MA: Belknap Press of Harvard University Press.
Hornby, Richard. 1995. *The End of Acting: A Radical View.* New York: Applause Theatre Books.
Howarth, W. D. 1997. *French Theatre in the Neo-Classical Era, 1550–1789.* Cambridge: Cambridge University Press.
Howe, Daniel Walker. 1979. *The Political Culture of the American Whigs.* Chicago, IL: University of Chicago Press.
Hughes, Alan. 2012. *Performing Greek Comedy.* Cambridge: Cambridge University Press.
Hugo, Victor. 1834. *Étude Sur Mirabeau.* Paris: Guyot-Canel.
Hume, David. 1788. *Essays and Treatises on several Subjects. . . . Essays, Moral, Political, and Literary.* Vol. 2. London: T. Cadell, and Edinburgh: C. Elliot.
  1888. *A Treatise of Human Nature,* edited by L. Selby-Bigge. Oxford: Clarendon Press.
Hunt, Lynn. 2004. *Politics, Culture, and Class in the French Revolution.* Berkeley: University of California Press.
Huntington, Samuel P. 1996. *The Clash of Civilizations and the Remaking of World Order.* New York: Simon & Schuster.
Isenberg, Nancy and Andrew Burstein. 2019. *The Problem of Democracy: The Presidents Adams Confront the Cult of Personality.* New York: Viking.
Israel, Jonathan. 2017. *The Expanding Blaze: How the American Revolution Ignited the World, 1775–1848.* Princeton, NJ: Princeton University Press.
Jackson, Shannon. 2004. *Professing Performance: Theatre in the Academy from Philology to Performativity.* Cambridge: Cambridge University Press.
Jacob, Louis. 1938. *Robespierre vu par ses contemporains.* Paris: A. Colin.
  1946. *Fabre d'Églantine, chef des 'fripons'.* Paris: Hachette.
Jameson, Michael H. 1971. "Sophocles and the Four Hundred." *Historia: Zeitschrift Für Alte Geschichte* 20 (5): 541–568.
Jefferson, Thomas. 1963. *The Thomas Jefferson Papers,* edited by F. R. Donovan. New York: Dodd, Mead & Company.
Jenkins, Hugh. 1998. "Jefferson (Re)Reading Milton." *Milton Quarterly* 32 (1): 32–38.
Jinnah, Fatima. 1987. *My Brother.* Karachi: Quaid-e-Azam Academy.
Jordan, David P. 1985. *The Revolutionary Career of Maximilien Robespierre.* New York: Free Press.
Kallet, Lisa. 2013. "Thucydides, Apollo, the Plague, and the War." *American Journal of Philology* 134 (3): 355–382.

Kendrick, Matthew. 2021. " Shakespeare, Cultural Production, and Class Consciousness in Antebellum New York City: Re-Examining the Astor Place Riot." In *Shakespeare and Civil Unrest in Britain and the United States*, edited by Mark Bayer and Joseph Navitsky, 91–104. Abingdon: Routledge.

Kennedy, Michael L. 1988. *The Jacobin Clubs in the French Revolution: The Middle Years*. Princeton, NJ: Princeton University Press.

Khilnani, Sunil. 2012. *The Idea of India*. London: Penguin.

Kippola, Karl M. 2012. *Acts of Manhood: The Performance of Masculinity on the American Stage, 1828–1865*. New York: Palgrave Macmillan.

Kirby, Ethyn Williams. 1931. *William Prynne: A Study in Puritanism*. Cambridge, MA: Harvard University Press.

Kishlansky, Mark A. 1979. *The Rise of the New Model Army*. Cambridge: Cambridge University Press.

　　1981. "Consensus Politics and the Structure of Debate at Putney." *Journal of British Studies* 20 (2): 50–69.

　　2013. "A Whipper Whipped: The Sedition of William Prynne." *The Historical Journal* 56 (3): 603–627.

　　2014. "Martyrs' Tales." *Journal of British Studies* 53 (2): 334–355.

Knoppers, Laura Lunger. 1998. "The Politics of Portraiture: Oliver Cromwell and the Plain Style." *Renaissance Quarterly* 51 (4): 1283–1319.

Knowles, Ronald. 1999. *Shakespeare: King Henry VI, Part 2*. London: Arden Shakespeare.

Knox, Bernard. 1956. "The Date of the Oedipus Tyrannus of Sophocles." *American Journal of Philology* 77: 133.

Koch, Thomas and Thomas Zerback. 2013. "Helpful Or Harmful? How Frequent Repetition Affects Perceived Statement Credibility." *Journal of Communication* 63 (6): 993–1010.

Krasner, David. 2000. *Method Acting Reconsidered: Theory, Practice, Future*. Basingstoke: Macmillan.

Kripalani, Krishna. 1962. *Rabindranath Tagore: A Biography*. London: Oxford University Press.

Kuhlmann, Charles. 1911. *Robespierre and Mirabeau at the Jacobins, December 6, 1790*. Lincoln: University of Nebraska.

Kumar, Krishan. 2003. *The Making of English National Identity*. Cambridge: Cambridge University Press.

La Harpe, Jean-François de. 1825. *Cours de littérature ancienne et moderne, Tome 4*. Paris: P. Dupont.

La Salle, Antoine de. 1788. *La Balance naturelle: ou essai sur une loi universelle appliquée aux sciences, arts et métiers, et aux moindres détails de la vie commune. Vol. 2*. 'A LONDRES', Paris.

　　1789. *Méchanique morale, ou essai sur l'art de perfectionner et d'employer ses organes, propres, acquis et conquis*. Geneva.

Laera, Margherita. 2013. *Reaching Athens: Community, Democracy and Other Mythologies in Adaptations of Greek Tragedy*. Bern: Peter Lang.

Lafitte, Jean-Baptiste-Pierre. 1844. *Mémoires de Fleury de la Comédie Française*. Paris: Gosselin.
Lai, Amy Tak-Yee. 2019. *The Right to Parody: Comparative Analysis of Copyright and Free Speech*. Cambridge: Cambridge University Press.
Lal, Ananda. 1986.*Three Plays by Rabindranath Tagore: Translated, and with an Introduction*. PhD thesis, University of Illinois at Urbana-Champaign. ProQuest Dissertations Publishing.
Lakoff, George. 2008. *The Political Mind: Why You Can't Understand 21st-Century Politics with an 18th-Century Brain*. New York: Viking.
Lambert, Frank. 2008. *Religion in American Politics: A Short History*. Princeton, NJ: Princeton University Press.
Lamont, William. 2004. "William Prynne." In *Dictionary of National Biography*. Oxford: Oxford University Press.
Lanni, Adriaan. 2008. "The Laws of War in Ancient Greece." *Law and History Review* 26 (3): 469–489.
Leith, Sam. 2011. *You Talkin' to Me?: Rhetoric from Aristotle to Obama*. London: Profile Books.
Leon, Mechele. 2009. *Molière, the French Revolution, and the Theatrical Afterlife*. Iowa City: University of Iowa Press.
Lequinio, J. M. 1790. *École des laboureurs*. Rennes: R.Vatar.
  1793. *Les Préjugés détruits*. 2nd ed. Paris: Imprimerie du Cercle Social.
  1796. *Philosophie du peuple, ou elémens de philosophie politique et morale*. Paris: Pougin.
Lerner, Gerda. 2009. *The Grimké Sisters from South Carolina*. Chapel Hill: University of North Carolina Press.
Levander, Caroline Field. 1998. *Voices of the Nation: Women and Public Speech in Nineteenth-Century American Literature and Culture*. Cambridge: Cambridge University Press.
Levine, Lawrence W. 1988. *Highbrow / Lowbrow : The Emergence of Cultural Hierarchy in America*. Cambridge, MA: Harvard University Press.
Levitsky, Steven and Daniel Ziblatt. 2018. *How Democracies Die: What History Tells Us about Our Future*. London: Viking.
Lilti, Antoine and Lynn Jeffress. 2017. *The Invention of Celebrity: 1750–1850*. Cambridge: Polity.
Lind, Michael. 2020. *The New Class War: Saving Democracy from the Metropolitan Elite*. London: Atlantic Books.
Linton, Marisa. 2013. *Choosing Terror: Virtue, Friendship, and Authenticity in the French Revolution*. Oxford: Oxford University Press.
Litto, Fredric M. 1979. "Democracy and the Drama: Tocqueville and the Theatre in America, 1831–1832." *Língua e Literatura* 8: 105–117.
Lloyd, Michael. 1992. *The Agon in Euripides*. Oxford: Clarendon Press.
Locke, John. 1690. *Two Treatises of Government: In the Former, the False Principles and Foundation of Sir Robert Filmer, and His Followers, are Detected and Overthrown. The Latter is an Essay Concerning the True Original, Extent, and End of Civil Government*. London: Awnsham Churchill.

Loraux, Nicole. 1981. *Les Enfants d'Athéna: idées athéniennes sur la citoyenneté et la division des sexes*. Paris: F. Maspero.
Luttrell, Barbara. 1990. *Mirabeau*. New York: Harvester Wheatsheaf.
Macaulay, Thomas Babington. 1841. *Critical and Miscellaneous Essays*. Vol. 3. Philadelphia, PA: Carey and Hart.
Macintosh, Fiona. 2009. *Sophocles: Oedipus Tyrannus*. Cambridge: Cambridge University Press.
Macready, William Charles. 1875. *Macready's Reminiscences, and Selections from His Diaries and Letters*. New York: Harper.
Maier, Christoph T. 1999. "Mass, the Eucharist and the Cross: Innocent III and the Relocation of the Crusade." In *Pope Innocent III and His World*, edited by John C. Moore and Brenda Bolton, 351–360. Aldershot: Ashgate.
Majumdar, S. K. 1966. *Jinnah and Gandhi: Their Role in India's Quest for Freedom*. Calcutta: K. L. Mukhopadhyay.
Manin, Bernard. 1997. *The Principles of Representative Government*. Cambridge: Cambridge University Press.
Markantonatos, Andreas and Eleni Volonaki. 2019. *Poet and Orator: A Symbiotic Relationship in Democratic Athens*. Berlin: De Gruyter.
Markle, M. M. 1985. "Jury Pay and Assembly Pay at Athens." *History of Political Thought* 6 (1): 265–297.
Markovits, Elizabeth. 2008. *The Politics of Sincerity: Plato, Frank Speech, and Democratic Judgment*. University Park.: Pennsylvania State University Press.
Marshall, Alan. 2004. *Oliver Cromwell, Soldier: The Military Life of a Revolutionary at War*. London: Brassey's.
Martin, Stephen and Joseph Marks. 2019. *Messengers: Who we Listen to, Who We Don't, and Why*. London: Cornerstone Digital.
Maslan, Susan. 2005. *Revolutionary Acts: Theater, Democracy, and the French Revolution*. Baltimore, MD: Johns Hopkins University Press.
Matonti, Frédérique. 1998. "Une Beauté capitale." *Sociétés & Représentations* 6 (1): 309–332.
Maury, Jean-Sifrein. 1804. *Principes d'éloquence pour la chaire et le barreau*. Paris: Théodore Warée.
McConachie, Bruce A. 1989. "The Theatre of Edwin Forrest and Jacksonian Hero Worship." In *When They Weren't Doing Shakespeare: Essays on Nineteenth-Century British and American Theatre*, edited by Judith Law Fisher and Stephen Watt, 3–18. Athens: University of Georgia Press.
    1992. *Melodramatic Formations: American Theatre and Society, 1820–1870*. Iowa City: University of Iowa Press.
McGann, Jerome J. 2002. *Byron and Romanticism*. Cambridge: Cambridge University Press.
McGrath, John. 2002. "Theatre and Democracy." *New Theatre Quarterly* 18 (2): 133–139.
McKenna, Michael and Paul Russell. 2008. *Free Will and Reactive Attitudes: Perspectives on P. F. Strawson's "Freedom and Resentment."* Farnham: Ashgate.

McMillen, Sally G. 2008. *Seneca Falls and the Origins of the Women's Rights Movement*. New York: Oxford University Press.
McPhee, Peter. 2012. *Robespierre: A Revolutionary Life*. New Haven, CT: Yale University Press.
Mendle, Michael. 2001. *The Putney Debates of 1647 : The Army, the Levellers, and the English State*. Cambridge: Cambridge University Press.
Mercier, Hugo and Dan Sperber. 2017. *The Enigma of Reason: A New Theory of Human Understanding*. London: Allen Lane.
Mielke, Laura L. 2019. *Provocative Eloquence: Theater, Violence, and Antislavery Speech in the Antebellum United States*. Ann Arbor: University of Michigan Press.
Miles, James B. 2013. "'Irresponsible and a Disservice': The Integrity of Social Psychology Turns on the Free Will Dilemma." *British Journal of Social Psychology* 52 (2): 205–218.
Miller, David. 2006. *The Liberty Reader*. Edinburgh: Edinburgh University Press.
Mills, David. 1991. "Chester Ceremonial: Re-Creation and Recreation in the English 'Medieval' Town." *Urban History* 18: 1–19.
  1992. *The Chester Mystery Cycle: A New Edition with Modernised Spelling*. East Lansing, MI: Colleagues Press.
Mirabeau, Honoré-Gabriel Riquetti, comte de. 1888. "Discours de M. Mirabeau l'aîné sur l'éducation nationale, en annexe de la séance du 10 septembre 1791." In *Archives parlementaires de 1787 à 1860 – première série (1787–1799) Tome xxx – du 28 août au 17 septembre 1791*, 512–554. Paris: P. Dupont.
Mitchell, Henry H. 1979. *Black Preaching*. San Francisco, CA: Harper and Row.
Mitchell-Boyask, Robin. 2008. *Plague and the Athenian Imagination: Drama, History, and the Cult of Asclepius*. Cambridge: Cambridge University Press.
Mongrédien, Georges. 1965. *Recueil des textes et des documents du XVIIe siècle relatifs à Molière*. Paris: Centre National de la Recherche Scientifique.
Monoson, S. Sara. 2012. "Dionysius I and Sicilian Theatrical Traditions in Plato's Republic." In *Theater Outside Athens: Drama in Greek Sicily and South Italy*, edited by Kathryn Bosher, 156–172. Cambridge: Cambridge University Press.
Moraw, Susanne and Eckehart Nölle. 2002. *Die Geburt Des Theaters in Der Griechischen Antike*. Mainz am Rhein: von Zabern.
Morrill, John and Philip Baker. 2001. "The Case of the Armie Truly Re-Stated." In *The Putney Debates of 1647: The Army, the Levellers, and the English State*, edited by Michael Mendle, 103–124. Cambridge: Cambridge University Press.
Morris, Celia. 1984. *Fanny Wright: Rebel in America*. Cambridge, MA: Harvard University Press.
[Mott, Lucretia]. *Lucretia Mott, 1793–1880*. Pennsylvania: Office of the Journal.
Mouffe, Chantal. 1999. "Deliberative Democracy Or Agonistic Pluralism?" *Social Research* 66 (3): 745–758.
  2000. *The Democratic Paradox*. London: Verso.
  2013. *Agonistics: Thinking the World Politically*. London: Verso.

Mukherjee, Rudrangshu. 2021. *Tagore & Gandhi: Walking Alone, Walking Together*. New Delhi: Aleph.
Müller, Jan-Werner. 2017. *What is Populism?*. London: Penguin Books.
Natali, Carlo. 2013. *Aristotle: His Life and School*. Princeton, NJ: Princeton University Press.
Négrel, Eric and Jean-Paul Sermain, Eds. 2002. *Une Expérience rhétorique: l'éloquence de la Révolution*. Oxford: Voltaire Foundation.
Nelson, Jennifer Ladd. 2000. "Dress Reform and the Bloomer." *Journal of American and Comparative Cultures* 23 (1): 21–25.
Nicholson, Helen. 2014. *Applied Drama: The Gift of Theatre*. 2nd ed. Basingstoke: Palgrave Macmillan.
Niles, Lyndrey A. 1984. "Rhetorical Characteristics of Traditional Black Preaching." *Journal of Black Studies* 15 (1): 41–52.
Norrie, Aidan. 2019. "Kings' Stomachs and Concrete Elephants: Gendering Elizabeth I through the Tilbury Speech." *Royal Studies Journal* 6 (2): 183–203.
Nussbaum, Martha C. 2006. "Education and Democratic Citizenship: Capabilities and Quality Education." *Journal of Human Development* 7 (3): 385–395.
Ober, Josiah. 1989. *Mass and Elite in Democratic Athens: Rhetoric, Ideology, and the Power of the People*. Princeton, NJ: Princeton University Press.
   2000. "Quasi-Rights: Participatory Citizenship and Negative Liberties in Democratic Athens." *Social Philosophy and Policy* 17 (1): 27–61.
   2017. *Demopolis: Democracy before Liberalism in Theory and Practice*. Cambridge: Cambridge University Press.
Ober, Josiah and Barry Strauss. 1990. "Drama, Rhetoric, Discourse." In *Nothing to Do with Dionysos?: Athenian Drama in Its Social Context*, edited by John J. Winkler and Froma I. Zeitlin, 237–270. Princeton, NJ: Princeton University Press.
O'Connell, Kathleen M. 2002. *Rabindranath Tagore: The Poet as Educator*. Calcutta: Visva-Bharati.
O'Connor, Patricia E. 1995. "Discourse of Violence." *Discourse & Society* 6 (3): 309–318.
O'Donnell, Guillermo A. 1998. "Horizontal Accountability in New Democracies." *Journal of Democracy* 9 (3): 112–26.
Olson, Kevin. 2014. "Deliberative Democracy." In *Jürgen Habermas: Key Concepts*, edited by Barbara Fultner, 154–169. London: Routledge.
O'Malley, Brendan P. 2018. "The Astor Place Riots." In *Revolting New York: How 400 Years of Riot, Rebellion, Uprising, and Revolution Shaped a City*, edited by Neil Smith, Don Mitchell, and others, 71–82. Athens: University of Georgia Press.
Osborne, Robin. 1995. "The Economics and Politics of Slavery at Athens." In *The Greek World*, edited by Anton Powell, 27–43. London: Routledge.
Outram, Dorinda. 1989. *The Body and the French Revolution: Sex, Class and Political Culture*. New Haven, CT: Yale University Press.
Owolade, Tomiwa. 2022. "What Chimamanda Ngozi Adichie Gets Wrong about Free Speech." *New Statesman*, 30 November.

Ozouf, Mona. 1988. *Festivals and the French Revolution*. Cambridge, MA: Harvard University Press.
Papastamati–von Moock, Christina. 2015. "The Wooden Theatre of Dionysos Eleuthereus in Athens." In *Architecture of the Ancient Greek Theatre: Acts of an International Conference at the Danish Institute at Athens 27–30 January 2012*, edited by Rune Frederiksen, Elizabeth R. Gebhard, and Alexander Sokolicek, 39–79. Aarhus: Aarhus University Press.
Parker, Edward Griffin. 1857. *The Golden Age of American Oratory*. Boston, MA: Whittemore, Niles, and Hall.
Parker, Harold T. 1937. *The Cult of Antiquity and the French Revolutionaries: A Study in the Development of the Revolutionary Spirit*. Chicago, IL: University of Chicago Press.
Parkinson, John. 2014. "Performing Democracy: Roles, Stages, Scripts." In *The Grammar of Politics and Performance*, edited by Shirin Rai and Janelle G. Reinelt. 19–33. London: Routledge.
Pelling, C. B. R. 1997. *Greek Tragedy and the Historian*. Oxford: Clarendon Press.
  2000. *Literary Texts and the Greek Historian*. London: Routledge.
  2005. "Tragedy, Rhetoric, and Performance Culture." In *A Companion to Greek Tragedy*, edited by Justina Gregory, 83–102. Oxford: Blackwell.
Phillips, David D. 2013. *The Law of Ancient Athens*. Ann Arbor: University of Michigan Press.
Pickard-Cambridge, Arthur. 1968. *The Dramatic Festivals of Athens*, revised by John Gould and David M. Lewis. 2nd ed. Oxford: Clarendon Press.
Pinker, Steven. 2018. *Enlightenment Now: A Manifesto for Science, Reason, Humanism, and Progress*. London: Penguin.
Porter, James. 2009. "Rhetoric, Aesthetics, and the Voice." In *The Cambridge Companion to Ancient Rhetoric*, edited by Erik Gunderson, 92–108. Cambridge: Cambridge University Press.
Potts, John. 2009. *A History of Charisma*. Basingstoke: Palgrave Macmillan.
Powell, Corrin. 2013. "A Philological, Epidemiological, and Clinical Analysis of the Plague of Athens." https://collected.jcu.edu/honorspapers/22
Powell, James M. 2004. *The Deeds of Pope Innocent III*. Washington, DC: Catholic University of America Press.
Pownall, Frances. 2017. "Dionysius I and the Creation of a New-Style Macedonian Monarchy." *The Ancient History Bulletin* 31 (1/2): 21–38.
Primavesi, Patrick. 2017. "The Dramaturgy of Rousseau's Lettre à d'Alembert." In *Rousseau on Stage: Playwright, Musician, Spectator*, edited by Maria Gullstam and Michael O'Dea, 51–75. Oxford: Voltaire Foundation.
Principato, Aurelio. 1999. *L'Éloquence révolutionnaire: idéologie et légende*. Paris: Presses Universitaires de France.
  2002. "Comment restituer l'action oratoire de la Révolution?" In *Une Expérience rhétorique: l'éloquence de la Révolution*, edited by Eric Négrel and Jean-Paul Sermain, 26–33. Oxford: Voltaire Foundation.

Pritchard, Matthew. 2014. "A Poem in a Medium not of Words: Music, Dance and Arts Education in Rabindranath Tagore's Santiniketan." *Arts and Humanities in Higher Education* 13 (1–2): 101–114.

Proud, Judith K. 1995. *P. Fabre D'Eglantine: Le Philinte De Molière*. Exeter: University of Exeter Press.

Prynne, William. 1633. *Histrio-Mastix. the Players Scourge, Or, Actors Tragædie, Divided into Two Parts*. London: Michael Sparke.

——— 1644. *Twelve Considerable Serious Questions Touching Church Government*. London: Michael Sparke.

——— 1649. *Mr VVilliam Prynn His Defence of Stage-Plays, Or, A Retractation of a Former Book of His Called Histrio-Mastix*. London.

Putnam, Robert D. 2000. *Bowling Alone: The Collapse and Revival of American Community*. New York: Simon & Schuster.

Quarmby, Kevin A. 2015. "'Bardwashing' Shakespeare: Food Justice, Enclosure, and the Poaching Poet." *Journal of Social Justice* 5: 1–21.

Radkau, Joachim and 2009. *Max Weber: A Biography*, translated by Patrick Camiller. Cambridge: Polity.

Rai, Shirin, Milija Gluhovic, Silvija Jestrovic, and Michael Saward, Eds. 2021. *The Oxford Handbook of Politics and Performance*. Oxford: Oxford University Press.

Rai, Shirin and Janelle G. Reinelt. 2014, Eds. *The Grammar of Politics and Performance*. London: Routledge.

Rankin, J. E. 1897. "Tribute" In *In Memoriam Frederick Douglass*, 32–38. Philadelphia, PA: John C. Yorston.

Rawls, John. 1958. "Justice as Fairness." *The Philosophical Review* 67 (2): 164–194.

Rebhorn, Matthew. 2006. "Edwin Forrest's Redding Up: Elocution, Theater, and the Performance of the Frontier." *Comparative Drama* 40 (4): 455–481.

Reed, Peter P. 2009. *Rogue Performances: Staging the Underclasses in Early American Theatre Culture*. Basingstoke: Palgrave Macmillan.

Reid, Loren. 1953. "Gladstone's Essay on Public Speaking." *The Quarterly Journal of Speech* 39 (3): 265–272.

Revermann, Martin. 2006. "The Competence of Theatre Audiences in Fifth- and Fourth-Century Athens." *The Journal of Hellenic Studies* 126: 99–124.

Rhodes, P. J. 2003. "Nothing to Do with Democracy: Athenian Drama and the Polis." *The Journal of Hellenic Studies* 123: 104–119.

Ridout, Nicholas. 2008. "Performance and Democracy." In *The Cambridge Companion to Performance Studies*, edited by Tracy C. Davis, 11–22. Cambridge: Cambridge University Press.

Roach, Joseph. 1998. "The Emergence of the American Actor." In *The Cambridge History of American Theatre*, edited by Don B. Wilmeth and C. W. E. Bigsby, 338–372. Cambridge: Cambridge University Press.

Robespierre, Maximilien. 1790. *Discours sur l'organisation des Gardes Nationales*. Paris: Buisson.

——— 1840. *Œuvres de Maximilien Robespierre, avec une notice historique et des notes*. Vol. 3. Paris: Laponneraye.

1841. "Rapport sur les principes de morale politique qui doivent guider la Convention Nationale dans l'administration intérieure de la République, fait au nom du Comité de Salut Public, le 18 pluviôse, l'an 2e de la République." In *Réimpression de l'ancien Moniteur depuis la réunion des Etats-Généraux jusqu'au Consulat. Vol. 18*, 401–408. Paris: Bureau Central.

Robinson, Eric W. 1997. *The First Democracies. Early Popular Government Outside Athens*. Stuttgart: F. Steiner.

——— 2007. "The Sophists and Democracy Beyond Athens." *Rhetorica* 25 (1): 109–122.

Roisman, Joseph. 2004. "Speaker-Audience Interaction in Classical Athens: A Power Struggle." In *Free Speech in Classical Antiquity*, edited by Ineke Sluiter and Ralph Rosen, 261–278. Leiden: Brill.

——— 2005. *The Rhetoric of Manhood: Masculinity in the Attic Orators*. Berkeley: University of California Press.

Roland de La Platière, Jeanne-Marie. 1821. *Mémoires de Mme Roland, avec une notice sur sa vie, des notes et des éclaircissements historiques*. 2nd ed., edited by Albin de Berville and François Barrière. Paris: Baudouin Frères.

Roselli, David Kawalko. 2011. *Theater of the People: Spectators and Society in Ancient Athens*. Austin: University of Texas Press.

Rosenfeld, Sophia A. 2019. *Democracy and Truth: A Short History*. Philadelphia: University of Pennsylvania Press.

Rothman, Adam. 2010. "Jefferson and Slavery." In *Seeing Jefferson Anew: In His Time and Ours*, edited by John B. Boles and Randal L. Hall, 103–125. Charlottesville: University of Virginia Press.

Rousseau, Jean-Jacques. 2003. *Lettre à d'Alembert*, edited by Marc Buffat. Paris: Flammarion.

Roy, Arundhati. 2009. *Listening to Grasshoppers: Field Notes on Democracy*. London: Hamish Hamilton.

Rudolph, Susanne Hoeber and Lloyd I. Rudolph. 1983. *Gandhi: The Traditional Roots of Charisma*. Chicago, IL: University of Chicago Press.

Ruffini, Franco. 2014. *Theatre and Boxing: The Actor Who Flies*. Holstebro: Routledge.

Rumball, Hannah. 2018. "British Quaker Women's Fashionable Adaptation of their Plain Dress, 1860–1914." *Costume* 52 (2): 240–260.

Runciman, David. 2018. *Political Hypocrisy: The Mask of Power, from Hobbes to Orwell and Beyond*. Rev. ed. Princeton, NJ: Princeton University Press.

Rutter, N. K. 2002. "Syracusan Democracy: 'Most Like the Athenian'?" In *Alternatives to Athens: Varieties of Political Organization and Community in Ancient Greece*, edited by Roger Brock and Stephen Hodkinson, 137–151. Oxford: Oxford University Press.

Ryan, Mary P. 1997. *Civic Wars: Democracy and Public Life in the American City during the Nineteenth Century*. Berkeley: University of California Press.

Saint-Just, Louis Antoine Léon de. 1908. "Discours pour la défense de Robespierre." In *Œuvres complètes de Saint-just. Vol. 2*, edited by Charles Vellay, 477–491. Paris: Charpentier & Fasquelle.

Sauter, Willmar. 2000. *The Theatrical Event: Dynamics of Performance and Perception*. Iowa City: University of Iowa Press.
    2021. *Aesthetics of Presence: Philosophical and Practical Reconsiderations*. Newcastle-upon-Tyne: Cambridge Scholars Press.
Saward, Michael. 2010. *The Representative Claim*. Oxford: Oxford University Press.
Saxonhouse, Arlene W. 2005. "The Practice of Parrhêsia." In *Free Speech and Democracy in Ancient Athens*, by Arlene W. Saxonhouse, 85–99. Cambridge: Cambridge University Press.
Schama, Simon. 1989. *Citizens: A Chronicle of the French Revolution*. London: Penguin.
Schechner, Richard. 2019. *Performance Studies: An Introduction*. 4th ed. London: Routledge.
Schleifer, James T. 1980. *The Making of Tocqueville's 'Democracy in America'*. Chapel Hill: University of North Carolina Press.
Schumpeter, Joseph A. 1976. *Capitalism, Socialism, and Democracy*. 5th ed. London: Allen and Unwin.
Scullion, Scott. 2002. "Tragic Dates." *The Classical Quarterly* 52 (1): 81–101.
Seaford, Richard. 1994. *Reciprocity and Ritual in Tragedy: Homer and Tragedy in the Developing City-State*. Oxford: Clarendon Press.
Sen, Abhijit. 2021. *Rabindranath Tagore's Theatre: From Page to Stage*. London: Routledge.
Sen, Amartya. 1999. "Democracy as a Universal Value." *Journal of Democracy* 10 (3): 3–17.
    2005. *The Argumentative Indian: Writings on Indian History, Culture and Identity*. London: Allen Lane.
Senior, Carl, Patrick Stewart, Erik Bucy, and Nick Lee. 2021. "Performance, Politics and Boris Johnson's Brexit." *Frontiers in Psychology* 12: 709–756.
Sennett, Richard. 1977. *The Fall of Public Man*. Cambridge: Cambridge University Press.
Serafim, Andreas. 2017. *Attic Oratory and Performance*. London: Routledge.
Seraphim, Andreas. 2019. "Thespians in the Law-Court." In *Poet and Orator : A Symbiotic Relationship in Democratic Athens*, edited by Andreas Markantonatos and Eleni Volonaki, 347–362. Berlin: De Gruyter.
Sermain, Jean-Paul. 2002. "'Les Formes ont ici une valeur': la position singulière de La Harpe." In *Une Expérience rhétorique l'éloquence de la Révolution*, edited by Éric Négrel and Jean-Paul Sermain, 245–256. Oxford: Voltaire Foundation.
Shannon, William V. 1963. *The American Irish*. New York: Macmillan.
Sharot, Tali. 2017. *The Influential Mind: What the Brain Reveals about our Power to Change Others*. London: Little, Brown.
Shepherd, Simon and Mick Wallis. 2004. *Drama/Theatre/Performance*. London: Routledge.
Shklar, Judith N. 1984. *Ordinary Vices*. Cambridge, MA: Belknap Press of Harvard University Press.

Simmons, A. John. 2013. "John Locke's *Two Treatises of Government.*" In *The Oxford Handbook of British Philosophy in the Seventeenth Century*, edited by Peter R. Anstey, 542–562. Oxford: Oxford University Press.
Sinclair, Robert. 1988. *Democracy and Participation in Athens*. Cambridge: Cambridge University Press.
Singh, Jaswant. 2009. *Jinnah: India, Partition, Independence*. New Delhi: Rupa & Co.
Smilansky, Saul. 2011. "Free Will, Fundamental Dualism, and the Centrality Of Illusion." In *The Oxford Handbook of Free Will*, 2nd ed., edited by Robert Kane, 425–441. Oxford: Oxford University Press.
 2012. "Free Will and Moral Responsibility: The Trap, the Appreciation of Agency, and the Bubble." *The Journal of Ethics* 16 (2): 211–239.
Smith, Zadie. 2009. *Changing My Mind: Occasional Essays*. London: Hamish Hamilton.
Sokolon, Marlene K. 2019. "It's All in the Argument: Euripides' Agōnes and Deliberative Democracy." *The European Legacy* 24 (7–8): 724–737.
Sommerstein, Alan. 2004. "Harassing the Satirist: The Alleged Attempts to Prosecute Aristophanes." In *Free Speech in Classical Antiquity*, edited by I. Sluiter and Ralph Mark Rosen, 145–174. Leiden: Brill.
Sorabji, Richard. 2012. *Gandhi and the Stoics: Modern Experiments on Ancient Values*. Oxford: Oxford University Press.
Stanislavski, Constantin. 1967. *An Actor Prepares*, translated by Elizabeth Reynolds Hapgood. Harmondsworth: Penguin Books.
Stanislavski, Konstantin. 2008. *An Actor's Work: A Student's Diary*, translated by Jean Benedetti. London: Routledge.
Stanley, Luke, Will Tanner, Jenevieve Treadwell, and James Blagden. (2022). *The Kids Aren't Alright: Why Young People Are Detaching from Democratic and Social Norms – and What to Do About It*. www.ukonward.com/wp-content/uploads/2022/09/kids-arent-alright-democracy.pdf
Stanton, Elizabeth Cady. 1898. *Eighty Years and More (1815–1897): Reminiscences of Elizabeth Cady Stanton*. New York: European Publishing Company.
Starobinski, Jean. 1971. *Jean-Jacques Rousseau: la transparence et l'obstacle; suivi de sept essais sur Rousseau*. Paris: Gallimard.
Stéfane-Pol. 1901. *Autour de Robespierre: le Conventionnel Le Bas: d'après des documents inédits et les mémoires de sa veuve*. Paris: Flammarion.
Stephens, Nathaniel. 1658. *Vindiciæ Fundamenti: Or, A Threefold Defence of the Doctrine of Original Sin*. London: Edmund Paxton.
Stewart, Edmund. 2017. *Greek Tragedy on the Move: The Birth of a Panhellenic Art Form c. 500–300 BC*. Oxford: Oxford University Press.
Stock, Kathleen. 2021. "Statement Read in Absentia, 'Hate, Heresy and the Fight for Free Speech', Battle of Ideas Saturday 9th October." https://kathleenstock.com/statement-read-in-absentia-h; this site was later removed from the public domain.
Suiten, Ineke and Ralph Mark Rosen, Eds. 2004. *Free Speech in Classical Antiquity*. Leiden: Brill.

Taft, Barbara. 2001. "From Reading to Whitehall: Richard Ireton's Journey." In *The Putney Debates of 1647: The Army, the Levellers, and the English State*, edited by Michael Mendle, 175–193. Cambridge: Cambridge University Press.
Tagore, Rabindranath. 1961. *Towards Universal Man*. London: Asia Publishing House.
    1994–1996. *The English Writings of Rabindranath Tagore*, edited by Sisir Kumar Das. New Delhi: Sahitya Akademi.
    2001. *Selected Writings on Literature and Language*. New Delhi: Oxford University Press.
    2011. *The Essential Tagore*. Cambridge, MA: Belknap Press of Harvard University Press.
Tagore, Rabindranath and L. K. Elmhirst. 1961. *Rabindranath Tagore, Pioneer in Education*. London: Murray.
Tallentyre, S. G. 1908. *The Life of Mirabeau*. London: John Murray.
Tanner, John S. and Justin Collings. 2006. "How Adams and Jefferson Read Milton and Milton Read Them." *Milton Quarterly* 40 (3): 207–219.
Taplin, Oliver. 2020. *Sophocles: Antigone and Other Tragedies*. Oxford: Oxford University Press.
Tarlo, Emma. 1996. *Clothing Matters: Dress and Identity in India*. London: Hurst.
Teague, Frances N. 2006. *Shakespeare and the American Popular Stage*. Cambridge: Cambridge University Press.
Terchek, Ronald. 1998. *Gandhi: Struggling for Autonomy*. Lanham, MD: Rowman & Littlefield.
Thomas, Rosalind. 2003. "Prose Performance Texts: Epideixis and Written Publication in the Late Fifth and Early Fourth Centuries." In *Written Texts and the Rise of Literate Culture in Ancient Greece*, edited by Harvey Yunis, 162–188. Cambridge: Cambridge University Press.
Thomas, Tracy A. 2016. *Elizabeth Cady Stanton and the Feminist Foundations of Family Law*. New York: New York University Press.
Thompson, J. M. 1935. *Robespierre*. Oxford: Blackwell.
Thuillier, Guy. 1956. "Hérault de Séchelles et La Théorie de l'ambition." *La Revue Administrative* (50): 133–139.
Tileagă, Cristian. 2013. "Political Rhetoric." In *Political Psychology: Critical Perspectives*, by Cristian Tileagă, 144–164. Cambridge: Cambridge University Press.
Todd, Christopher. 1972. *Voltaire's Disciple: Jean-François de La Harpe*. London: Modern Humanities Research Association.
Todd, S. C. 2005. "Law, Theatre, Rhetoric and Democracy in Classical Athens." *European Review of History* 12 (1): 63–79.
Torri, Michelguglielmo. 2022. "The Mahatma and the Muslims. Gandhi's Role in Making India's Partition Inevitable." In *Gandhi After Gandhi: The Relevance of the Mahatma's Legacy in Today's World*, edited by M. Casolari, 57–73. Abingdon: Routledge.
Tydeman, William. 2001. *The Medieval European Stage*. Cambridge: Cambridge University Press.

Ulman, H. L. 1994. *Things, Thoughts, Words, and Actions: The Problem of Language in Late Eighteenth-Century British Rhetorical Theory*. Carbondale: Southern Illinois University Press.

Urbinati, Nadia. 2004. "Condorcet's Democratic Theory of Representative Government." *European Journal of Political Theory* 3 (1): 53–75.

2014. *Democracy Disfigured: Opinion, Truth, and the People*. Cambridge, MA: Harvard University Press.

Valin, Claudy. 2014. *Lequinio: la loi et le salut public*. Rennes: Presses Universitaires de Rennes.

Waggenspack, Beth Marie. 1982. *Elizabeth Cady Stanton's Reform Rhetoric 1848–1854 : A Perelman Analysis of Practical Reasoning*. PhD thesis, Ohio State University. OhioLINK.

Wallace, Robert W. 2004. "The Power to Speak – and Not to Listen – in Ancient Athens." In *Free Speech in Classical Antiquity*, edited by I. Sluiter and Ralph Mark Rosen, 221–232. Leiden: Brill.

Wallis, Ed and Ania Skrzypek-Claasens, Eds. 2014 *Back to Earth*. London: Fabian Society.

Walsh, Michael. 1843. *Sketches of the Speeches and Writings of Michael Walsh. . . Compiled by a Committee of the Spartan Association*. New York: Thomas McSpedon.

Walzer, Arthur E. 2007. "Blair's Ideal Orator: Civic Rhetoric and Christian Politeness in Lectures 25–34." *Rhetorica* 25 (3): 269–295.

Warren, James Perrin. 1999. *Culture of Eloquence: Oratory and Reform in Antebellum America*. University Park: Pennsylvania State University Press.

Waskiewicz, Andrzej. 2020. *The Idea of Political Representation and Its Paradoxes*. Berlin: Peter Lang.

Weber, Max. 1948. *The Protestant Ethic and the Spirit of Capitalism*. London: Unwin.

1958. *The City*. New York: Free Press.

1968. *Economy and Society: An Outline of Interpretive Sociology*. New York: Bedminster Press.

2008. *Max Weber's Complete Writings on Academic and Political Vocations*. New York: Algora.

2011. *The Protestant Ethic and the Spirit of Capitalism*. New York: Oxford University Press.

Weimann, Robert. 2008. *Shakespeare and the Power of Performance: Stage and Page in the Elizabethan Theatre*. Cambridge: Cambridge University Press.

Wiedemann, Thomas E. J. 1981. *Greek and Roman Slavery*. London: Croom Helm.

Wikander, Matthew H. 1986. *The Play of Truth and State: Historical Drama from Shakespeare to Brecht*. Baltimore, MD: Johns Hopkins University Press.

Wildman, John. 1647a. *A Cal to all the Souldiers of the Armie, by the Free People of England*. London.

1647b. *Putney Projects. Or the Old Serpent in a New Forme: Presenting to the View of all the Well Affected in England, the Serpentine Deceit of their Pretended Friends in the Armie* . . . . London.

Wilentz, Sean. 1984. *Chants Democratic: New York City and the Rise of the American Working Class, 1788–1850*. New York: Oxford University Press.
Wiles, David. 1991. *The Masks of Menander: Sign and Meaning in Greek and Roman Performance*. Cambridge: Cambridge University Press.
　1997. *Tragedy in Athens: Performance Space and Theatrical Meaning*. Cambridge: Cambridge University Press.
　2003. *A Short History of Western Performance Space*. Cambridge: Cambridge University Press.
　2007. *Mask and Performance in Greek Tragedy: From Ancient Festival to Modern Experimentation*. Cambridge: Cambridge University Press.
　2011. *Theatre and Citizenship: The History of a Practice*. Cambridge: Cambridge University Press.
　2014. *Theatre and Time*. Basingstoke: Palgrave Macmillan.
　2017. "The Environment of Theatre: Experiencing Place in the Ancient World." In *A Cultural History of Theatre in Antiquity*, edited by Martin Revermann, 63–82. London: Bloomsbury.
　2020. *The Players' Advice to Hamlet: The Rhetorical Acting Method from the Renaissance to the Enlightenment*. Cambridge: Cambridge University Press.
Willett, John. 1964. *Brecht on Theatre: The Development of an Aesthetic*. London: Eyre Methuen.
Williams, David. 2004. *Condorcet and Modernity*. Cambridge: Cambridge University Press.
Williams, Raymond. 1976. *Keywords: A Vocabulary of Culture and Society*. London: Fontana.
Williams-Jones, Pearl. 1975. "Afro-American Gospel Music: A Crystallization of the Black Aesthetic." *Ethnomusicology* 19 (3): 373–385.
Williamson, Elizabeth. 2013. "Fireboys and Burning Theatres: Performing the Astor Place Riot." *The Journal of American Drama and Theatre* 25 (1): 5–26.
Willis, Avery T. 2005. *Euripides' Trojan Women: A 20th Century War Play in Performance*. DPhil thesis, University of Oxford. Oxford University Research Archive.
Wilson, Garff B. 1950. "The Acting of Edwin Forrest." *The Quarterly Journal of Speech* 36 (4): 483–491.
Wilson, Peter. 2000. *The Athenian Insitution of the Khoregia: The Chorus, the City, and the Stage*. New York: Cambridge University Press.
　2011. "The Glue of Democracy?: Tragedy, Structure, and Finance." In *Why Athens? A Reappraisal of Tragic Politics*, edited by D. M. Carter, 19–43. Oxford: Oxford University Press.
Winkler, John J. and Froma I. Zeitlin, Eds. 1990. *Nothing to Do with Dionysos?: Athenian Drama in its Social Context*. Princeton, NJ: Princeton University Press.
Wohl, Victoria. 2009. "Rhetoric of the Athenian Citizen." In *The Cambridge Companion to Ancient Rhetoric*, edited by Erik Gunderson, 162–177: Cambridge: Cambridge University Press.
Wolfe, D. 1933. "Milton, Lilburne, and the People." *Modern Philology* 31: 253–272.

Wood, Gordon S. 1998. *The Creation of the American Republic, 1776–1787*. Chapel Hill: University of North Carolina Press.
Woodhouse, A. S. P. 1986. *Puritanism and Liberty: Being the Army Debates (1647–9) from the Clarke Manuscripts with Supplementary Documents*. London: Dent.
Woolrych, Austin. 1987. *Soldiers and Statesmen: The General Council of the Army and its Debates 1647–1648*. Oxford: Clarendon Press.
Woolrych, Austin, I. J. Gentles, J. S. Morrill, and Blair Worden. 1998. *Soldiers, Writers and Statesmen of the English Revolution*. Cambridge: Cambridge University Press.
Worden, Blair. 2012. *God's Instruments: Political Conduct in the England of Oliver Cromwell*. Oxford: Oxford University Press.
Worman, Nancy. 2004. "Insult and Oral Excess in the Disputes between Aeschines and Demosthenes." *American Journal of Philology* 125 (1): 1–25.
Worthington, Ian. 2000. *Demosthenes: Statesman and Orator*. London: Routledge.
 2012. *Demosthenes of Athens and the Fall of Classical Greece*. Oxford: Oxford University Press.
Wright, Frances. 1819. *Altorf*. Philadelphia, PA: M. Carey & Son.
 2014. *Views of Society and Manners in America*, edited by Paul R. Baker. Cambridge, MA: Harvard University Press.
Wright, Nancy E. and A. R. Buck. 2007. "Cast Out of Eden: Property and Inheritance in Shakespearean Drama." In *The Law in Shakespeare*, edited by Constance Jordan and Karen Cunningham, 73–90. Basingstoke: Palgrave Macmillan.
Young, Arthur. 1929. *Travels in France during the Years 1787, 1788 & 1789*. Edited by Constantia Maxwell. Cambridge: Cambridge University Press.
Yunis, Harvey. 2001. *Demosthenes: On the Crown*. Cambridge: Cambridge University Press.
Zagarri, Rosemarie. 2005. "American Women's Rights before Seneca Falls." In *Women, Gender and Enlightenment*, edited by S. Knott and B. Taylor, 667–691. London: Palgrave Macmillan.
Zarrilli, Phillip B., Jerri Daboo, and Rebecca Loukes. 2013. *Acting: Psychophysical Phenomenon and Process*. Basingstoke: Palgrave Macmillan.
Zorgbibe, Charles. 2008. *Mirabeau*. Paris: Fallois.

Index

Abhinavagupta, 160
actio, 95
action, 148, 176
Adam and Eve, 65, 73–8, 115, 120
Adams, Abigail, 73–8, 137, 142
Adams, John, 118–24
Adams, John Quincy, 122
Adichie, Chimamanda Ngozi, 5
Aeschines, 39–61, 179
  Against Timarchus, 48
  career, 39
agon, 8, 62, 159
  agonistic language, 24
  agonistic politics, 8
  in Greek comedy, 31
  tragic, 62, 177
Alcidamas, 47
Ambedkar, B.S., 163
American Declaration of Independence, 14, 119, 121
Ankersmit, Frank, 13
Antiphon, 177
Arendt, Hannah, 7, 14, 61, 176
Aristophanes, 19–34
  Frogs, 179
  Knights, 30
  Wasps, 31
Aristotle, 66
  on actors, 58
  on collective wisdom, 47
  on *dianoia*, 176
  Poetics, 154, 171, 176
  Politics, 29
  Rhetoric, 9, 24, 29
Assembly
  Athens, 23, 25
  France, 95–6, 104, 108
  See also. Congress
Astor Place Riot, 126–31
Athens
  Festival of Dionysus, 23, 172, 178
  and modern democracy, 7, 57, 111, 166
  nature of Athenians, 20
  theatrical competition, 32, 38, 43, 178
  tribes, 21–2, 178
  voting, 178
audience. *See* crowd behaviour; public listening; theatre; thorubos

Ball, John, 73
Baptists, 76
Barish, Jonas, 69
Barthes, Roland, 123
Beard, Mary, 138
Beckett, Samuel, 183
Bers, Victor, 24
Bhagavad Gita, 147
Bharucha, Rustom, 165, 167
Bingham, Caleb, 131–3
Blair, Tony, 16
Blair, Hugh, 125–6, 132, 142
Bowery B'hoys, 128
Brecht, Bertolt, 56, 171, 176
Brexit, 3, 59
Brook, Peter, 61
Burke, Edmund, 13

Cade, Jack, 75
Calvinism, 64, 70, 88, 115
Carlyle, Thomas, 147, 154, 163
Cartledge, Paul, 172
caste, 155, 163
Castoriadis, Cornelius, 171
Catholicism, 64, 74, 91, 116, 118
Centre for the Future of Democracy, 4
Chaplin, Charlie, 153
character, 55
  Aristotle on, 8, 24, 176
  and choice, 176
  connected to individualism, 155
  constructed by orators, 27, 49
  dramatic, 129, 153–4, 174, 176

people defined by, 89
western construct, 154
charisma, 65, 83, 92, 100
charkha, 151–2, 165
Charles I, King, 69, 71, 81, 86
Churchill, Winston, 4, 11, 150
Cicero, 66, 122–3, 132
  on belief, 10, 57, 125
  on rhythm, 132
  on the virtuous orator, 91, 114
citizenship, 5, 10, 90, 121, 141, 179
  'non-active', 111
Clairon, Hippolyte, 95–6
class, 29–30, 46, 56, 114, 118, 122, 126–8
Cleisthenes, 22
Cleon, 25–34, 53, 58
Clinton, Bill, 16
Collins, Philip, 12
Condorcet, Marquis de, 100–3
Congress, 146, 156–7, 161
Constant, Benjamin, 123
Constitution of the USA, 137
Cromwell, Oliver, 81–9, 170
crowd behaviour, 46–7, 62, 68, 75, 102
culture wars, 5, 180

Dale, Amy Marjorie, 174
Danton, Georges, 92, 115
De Gouges, Olympe, 138
De Tocqueville, Alexis, 90, 117–18, 126, 131, 137, 141
declamation, 97, 115
Declaration of the Rights of Man and of the Citizen, 105
deliberation, 11, 79, 84, 110
  public reasoning, 146
demagogue, 8, 21, 30, 43, 58, 66, 89, 103, 105
democracy
  definitions of, 20, 22, 61, 63–4, 66, 128, 145, 167
  deliberative, 11
  liberal, 7, 12, 14, 32, 77, 90, 141, 144, 174
  local (in the demes), 23
  and religion, 63–5, 72, 77, 90, 100, 108, 162
  representative v. participatory, 59
  and republicanism, 90
  western, 145, 158
Democratic party, 128
demos, 4, 9
Demosthenes, 39–61
  funeral speech, 55
  influence of, 114, 125, 132
  movement, 51
  physique, 42

reputation of, 59, 98, 101
training, 39, 50, 52, 57
Desmoulins, Camille, 109, 111–12, 116
dharma, 157
dialectic, 11, 35
Dionysius of Halicarnassus, 41, 50
dithyramb, 178, 181
Doke, Joseph, 153
double awareness, 24, 177
Douglass, Frederick, 131–7
dualism, 55
Dumesnil, Marie, 96

education, 90, 94, 100, 102, 165, 183
Elizabeth I, Queen, 41
Elmhirst, Leonard, 160
elocutionary movement, 125, 128, 138, 142
eloquence, 42, 68, 102–3, 107, 114, 122
emotion
  authenticity, 24, 54, 107, 114
  codification, 132
  versus cognition, 9, 29, 42, 138
  contagious, 68, 92
  control of, 109, 119
  in the court-room, 24
  emotional truth, 56
  feel in order to express, 123
  persuasiveness of, 27
  pity and fear, 49
  See also. reason
Englishness, 85
Enlightenment, 10, 28, 103, 125, 138, 163
Euripides, 33, 179
  Andromeda, 68
  Hippolytus, 179
  Trojan Women, 174
Everard, Robert, 76, 88
eyes, 57, 133

Fabre d'Eglantine, 92–5, 115
facial expression, 21, 31
Fairfax, Thomas, 79, 81
Federalism, 13, 122
feedback loop, 48, 170
Festival of Unity, 98, 101
Filmer, John, 73
Finlayson, Alan, 11
Fischer-Lichte, Erika, 48
Flinders, Matthew, 5
Forrest, Edwin, 126–9
free will, 3, 60, 73, 76–7, 88, 102
freedom
  as liberty, 8, 61, 72–3, 123, 182
  positive and negative, 82

freedom (cont.)
  of the soul, 164
  of speech, 5, 32, 102

Gandhi, Mohandas, 145–69
  Autobiography, 149
  costume, 150
  Hind Swaraj, 148–9
  inner voice, 151
  Mahatma, 151, 153, 155, 162
  Story of a Soldier of Truth, 147
gender
  equality, 74, 91, 100, 111, 137, 151
  female attire, 138, 140
  as performance, 137
  See also. sexuality; virility
General Will, 114, 166
gesture, 30, 50–1, 96, 108, 125, 140, 149
Gladstone, William, 59, 65
globalisation, 18
gods, 28, 63, 179
Goethe, Johann Wolfgang von, 176
Goldhill, Simon, 172
Gorgias, 10, 34–5, 116, 174
Great Awakening, 135, 138
Grimke, Angelina, 139–40
Grote, George, 43
guilds, 74

Haidt, Jonathan, 2, 11, 28
Hall, Edith, 25, 171
Hall, Peter, 53
Hampden, John, 83
heckling. *See thorubos*
Henrich, Joseph, 146, 164
Hérault de Séchelles, Marie-Jean, 95–100
Hinduism, 162
historiography, 12
Hobbes, Thomas, 16, 66–9, 116, 158
Horace, 57, 120
House of Commons, 59, 73, 78, 102, 148, 162
human rights, 7, 21, 81, 132, 139
Hume, David, 2, 42
humour, 33, 93, 133
hypocrisy, 8, 14–16, 68, 70, 73, 88, 135, 145, 163
  anti-hypocrisy, 143
  British imperial, 145
  inescapable, 119
  religious, 88–9
  and theatre, 16, 70
  three forms of, 14
hypokrites, 169

identification, 10
identity
  groupish, 11
  politics of, 5–6
  social, 74
ideology, 172, 182
improvisation, 48, 67, 98, 108, 140
individualism, 1, 7, 64, 70, 78, 114, 146, 155, 164
  De Tocqueville on, 131, 141
  roots in Christianity, 164
  selfhood, 156
  and social atomisation, 78
  Stanton on, 141–2
  western, 146, 164
inner world, 140
Innocent III, Pope, 13
Ireton, Henry, 81–7
Irish Americans, 128, 131
Irving, Henry, 154

Jack Cade, 128
Jacobin Club, 92–3, 105, 110–15
Jefferson, Thomas, 76, 117, 119, 138, 169
Jinnah, Muhammad Ali, 161
Johnson, Boris, 2
Johnson, Samuel, 154, 163
Judaism, 143

La Harpe, Jean-François de, 92, 102
Lakoff, George, 3
La Salle, Antoine, 97
Lattimore, Richmond, 173
Laud, Archbishop William, 66
law-court, 25
  American, 123
  Athens, 45–6, 177–8
  British, 148
  Indian, 149
lawyers, 46, 95–6, 123, 142
Lequinio, Joseph-Marie, 103–6
Levellers, 63, 76, 81–2
liberalism, 8, 14, 74, 131, 183
Lilburne, John, 76
Locke, John, 74, 120

Macaulay, Thomas Babington, 43
Machiavelli, Niccolò, 124
Macready, William Charles, 126–31
Marat, Jean-Paul, 95
mask
  in Greek theatre, 31, 40, 54–5, 62
  of patriotism, 116
  and *persona*, 68
  and personation, 89

as psychological metaphor, 24, 89
symbol of uniformity, 159
Maury, Jean-Sifrein, 97
McGrath, John, 171
memory, 95
Menander, 54
Milton, John, 76–7
mind–body connection, 72, 160
Mirabeau, Honoré Gabriel Riqueti, Comte de, 106–16
mob, 75, 137
  mobocracy, 156, 161
Molé, François-René Molé, 93
Molière, 14, 89, 93
More, Hannah, 138
Mott, Lucretia, 140, 143
Mouffe, Chantal, 8, 11, 62
Murray, Gilbert, 173
Mytilene debate, 25–38

nationalism, 157, 164, 166
natural law, 82, 120
natural savage, 129
naturalism, 155, 167
nature, ideal of, 98
Norman yoke, 81
Nussbaum, Martha, 164

Obama, Barack, 136
Ober, Josiah, 23, 172
orality, 20, 41, 76, 161
  oracy, 183

Paine, Thomas, 14, 124
panchayat, 147, 166
patriotism, 51, 108, 114
Peasants' Revolt, 73
Pelling, Christopher, 172–3
Pericles, 12, 20–2, 29, 170
persuasion, 2, 9, 11, 23–4, 35, 91, 97
  basis of democracy, 34, 169
  methods of, 97, 174
  purpose of rhetoric, 11
  purpose of theatre, 53, 118
Phocion, 42, 58–9
Pinker, Steven, 102
Plato, 8, 13, 29, 34, 106, 115
  Apology, 147
  body v. soul, 182
  Gorgias, 34–8
  Laws, 178, 180–2
  Republic, 8, 38, 180
pleasure, 29, 36, 81, 118, 178, 181
Plutarch, 21, 34, 58, 91
  Life of Demosthenes, 43–4, 57

Polos (actor), 115
Poole, Elizabeth, 139
populism, 4, 8, 38, 143, 166
possession, 57, 133, 137
preaching, 67, 76, 97, 133
Presbyterians, 72, 78
presence, 13, 61, 65, 97
press, 105, 112, 123, 159
property, 74–5, 81
  and franchise, 78, 85, 90, 111, 126
Protestant Reformation, 63, 141
Prynne, William, 69–76, 146
psycho-technique, 57
public listening, 3, 26, 47, 123, 170
public sphere, 113, 183
Puritanism, 14, 65, 77, 79, 119, 136, 143
Putney debates, 78–89

Quakerism, 139–40
Quintilian, 160

Rainborough, Thomas, 85, 88
rational choice theory, 11
Rawls, John, 87
reason, 27–8, 60, 79, 102, 138, 164
  clear stream of, 164
  and intuition, 2, 28
  language of, 27
  limits of, 2
  as lust, 81
  rationalism, 64, 102, 138
  tied to emotion, 27, 42, 121, 146
representation, 10, 13–14, 69, 115, 154–6, 167, 180
republicanism, 90
rhetoric, 9
  definition, 11, 103
  female orators, 175
  figures of speech, 37, 50
  at Harvard, 122
  as a learnt art, 100
  oratory versus public speaking, 139
  republican tradition of oratory, 133, 143
  rhetorical education, 58
  rhetorical periods, 28, 50, 55
rhythm, 41, 62, 123, 128, 132–3, 139, 160, 165
Ridout, Nicholas, 7
Robespierre, Maximilien, 14, 94, 111–16, 146
role-playing, 25, 72, 95, 116, 120, 128, 162
Roman Republic, 10, 121
romanticism, 141
Rousseau, Jean-Jacques, 13, 16, 91–4, 102, 107, 112, 114
Roy, Arundhati, 1
rule of law, 48, 74

Runciman, David, 14, 69
Rush, Benjamin, 120

Saint-Just, Louis-Antoine de, 42, 92, 106
samaj, 157, 166
sans-culottes, 92, 112
Schumpeter, Joseph, 64
Sen, Amartya, 146, 148, 164
Seneca Falls, 140
Sennett, Richard, 7, 142
sexuality, 52, 67, 70, 77, 101, 104
Shakespeare, William, 128, 136, 138
  Macbeth, 129–30
  and popular culture, 130
Sheridan, Thomas, 125
Shklar, Judith, 14, 89, 119, 143
Siddons, Sarah, 118
sincerity, 53–7, 83, 124, 135, 163, 169
  Adams on, 124
  Arendt on, 7
  enigma of Gandhi, 149
  heart-sincerity, 163
  performance of, 53, 72
  valued by Puritans, 16, 69
  See also mask; truth
slavery, 19, 100, 120, 131–5, 140
Smith, Zadie, 136
Socrates, 147, *See* Plato
Solon, 2, 48, 51, 60
Sophocles
  Oedipus, 170, 176–7
Sparta, 22
speech
  and the body, 62, 77, 123
  language of the body, 149
speechwriter, 174
Stanislavski, Konstantin, 12, 57, 143
Stanton, Elizabeth Cady, 143, 156
Stock, Kathleen, 5
story-telling, 94
swaraj, 147–8
sympathy, 132
Syracuse, 9, 34, 38

Tagore, Rabindranath, 154–68
  dance-dramas, 159
  Gitanjali (35), 164
  plays, 154
  'Society and the State', 157–8
Tartuffe, 14, 89, 94, 115
theatre
  actor training, 12
  as art, 38
  audiences, 56, 68, 117, 155, 181
  auditorium, 92
  and education, 93–4
  as education, 100
  definitions, 61
  Indian (classical), 159
  Indian (popular), 155, 157
  medieval, 74
  as paradigm of democracy, 126
  riots, 126
  versus 'performance', 13, 71
  western rhetorical acting, 159–60
Theatre of Dionysus, 23
theatricality, 26
theatrocracy, 1, 181–2
thorubos, 31, 46, 181
Thucydides, 19, 25, 66–7, 175
tragedy, 9
  city-state as a, 181
  competition, 177–80
  function of, 21
  as literature, 172
  origins of, 22
  as speechmaking, 37
Trump, Donald, 3, 16
truth
  categories of, 2
  emotional, 88, 115
  experiential, 148
  Gorgias on, 175
  in the theatre, 70, 75
  inner, 12, 57, 86, 129, 148
  and language, 59, 161
  and naturalism, 117
  opposite to rhetoric, 38, 67, 147
  passion for, 108
  philosophical v. political, 8
  post-truth, 175
  theatrical, 160
Truth, book by Antiphon, 177

unconscious, 3, 10, 150
Upanishads, 164
USA and Europe, 122

virility, 52, 129, 133, 160
voice, 21, 30, 50–1, 83, 96, 108, 123, 131, 149
  Adams on, 123
  of Aeschines, 39, 50, 55
  and authenticity, 139
  Barthes on, 123
  of Cromwell, 83
  of Douglass, 132–4

of Gandhi, 149
   and identity, 136
   legal, 140
   of Mirabeau, 108
   separated from words, 52
   Southern, 139
   technique, 96, 132, 143
   training of, 50, 96
Voltaire, 91, 102

Walker, John, 128
Walsh, Mike, 127
Warren, Mercy Otis, 138
Washington, George, 121, 124
Weber, Max, 19, 64–5, 74, 117
Webster, Daniel, 133
whiteness, 131, 136
Wildman, John, 83–9
Wright, Fanny, 137–9, 141